FIREBALL & THE LOTUS

by Ron Miller and
Jim Kenney

BEAR & COMPANY
SANTA FE, NEW MEXICO

Library of Congress Cataloging-in-Publication Data

Fireball & the lotus.

Bibliography: p.
1. Spiritual life. 2. Religion — History — 20th
century. 3. Sects — History — 20th century. 4. Cults —
History — 20th century. 5. United States — Religion —
1960-   . I. Miller, Ron. II. Kenney, Jim,
1947-   . III. Title: Fireball and the lotus.
BL624.F52 1987 291 87-26989

ISBN 0-939680-43-2

Copyright© 1987 Ron Miller & Jim Kenney

BEAR & COMPANY
P.O. Drawer 2860
Santa Fe, NM 87504

Cover Art: "The Marriage of Heaven and Earth"© 1981 by Peter Rogers
Cover Photo: Ken Cobean
Cover Design: Angela C. Werneke
Interior Design: Mina Yamashita Graphic Design
Interior Illustrations: Susan Surprise, adapted from
     "The Marriage of Heaven and Earth" by Peter Rogers
Typography: Copygraphics, Inc.
Printed in the United States of America

TABLE OF CONTENTS

Preface   7
    Ron Miller and Jim Kenney

PART ONE: THE AMERICAN MAINLINE

Introduction to Part One   11
    Ron Miller and Jim Kenney

A Roadmap to Religious America   13
    Ron Miller

A Jewish Perspective on the Religious Right   32
    Yechiel Eckstein

Jews and Judaism in the Catholic Lectionary   56
    Mark S. Smith

Law and Story in Judaism and Christianity   65
    Marc A. Gellman

Report from a Far Meridian: Yahweh, God of the Fireball   73
    Gerald Ringer

PART TWO: ENCOUNTERS WITH ALTERNATIVES

Introduction to Part Two   97
    Ron Miller and Jim Kenney

Jesus as Zaddik   101
    Charlotte Golden Kamin

Faith in Islam   113
    Thomas Michel

The Principle of Complementarity and World Religions   124
    Stephen Infantino

A Western Bodhisattva   135
    Mike Foster

One Day, No Day, Each Day, Zen Day   150
    Madeleine Sophie Cooney

Buddhism, Existence, Technology, and Daily Life   160
    Steven Kozan Beck

PART THREE: NEW AGE MODELS

Introduction to Part Three   185
    Ron Miller and Jim Kenney

Shantivanam: Vision and Model of Contemplative Prayer   187
    Michael Hugo

Falling in Love with the Divine: The Magic of Mysticism   201
    Jane Lukehart

Spiritual Growth, Psychological Growth: An Analogy   212
    Dave Lothrop

Reincarnation as Method for the Divine Quest   228
    Barbara Clow

Particle, Wave, and Paradox   249
    Jim Kenney

Modern Cosmology and the Yoga Tradition   274
    Beatrice B. Briggs

The New Natural Selection   285
    Brian Swimme

About the Authors   301
Suggestions for Further Reading   313

Preface

Twelve years ago, a radically new endeavor began to take shape in the Chicago area. Several graduate students in the field of comparative religious thought undertook the animation of a shared vision. Common Ground was born.

At that time, no forum for interfaith study and dialogue existed outside the confines of the university system, and even there, serious hindrances to genuine encounter loomed on all sides. The need was clear for an adult education center that might bring together participants and resources from a multiplicity of backgrounds in order to address the increasingly complex religious and spiritual issues of the modern age.

Over the years a remarkable collection of scholars, educators, and students has facilitated Common Ground's commitment to inquiry and dialogue. The learning experience that has resulted has given powerful expression to the group's animating theme: "Reality is whole and truth is one, for the person willing to stretch and to be challenged, to be curious and questioning."

This volume is the product of a deeply felt wish on the part of Common Ground to reach out to a larger community. We invited some of those who participated in our workshops, lectures, and symposia during the last twelve years to contribute articles addressing the question of a viable planetary spirituality for the twenty-first century. The essays which follow each represent a dimension of the richness and challenge which has become Common Ground.

Artist Peter Rogers, whose painting, "The Marriage of Heaven and Earth," is on the cover of this volume, writes, "If one accepts the comet as a symbol of the male Godhead then, by painting the tail of the comet encircling the Maiden, I had unwittingly painted an icon of the marriage of Heaven and Earth." (Peter Rogers, *A Painter's Quest* [Santa Fe: Bear & Co., 1987], p. 64). We saw this artwork and its underlying image as eloquently expressive of both the theme and the title of our book, *Fireball and the Lotus*, for each of these essays addresses a *conjugium* (yoking together) of apparently distinct elements.

"The Fireball and the Lotus" was the original title of Bea Briggs' article — one she graciously allowed us to use for this entire collection of essays. *Lotus* refers unambiguously to what we understand as spirituality. *Fireball*, quite to the contrary, conjures up a myriad of images. In one sense, the fireball corresponds to the male Godhead, the heaven-sent comet of the artist's work. But it is no less the Earth, the primordial, creative, matter-energy in Brian Swimme's description of the universe. It symbolizes the science and technology of our Western world, from Bea Briggs' perspective. For Gerald Ringer, it again suggests the male Godhead of the artist's conception, but with a harshness far less compatible with connubial bliss. The ambivalence, of course, is both unavoidable and desirable. What merges, emerges as spirituality: the marriage, in whatever form, of the divine and the human.

We would like to extend our thanks to all those who helped in so many different ways to make this volume possible. In particular to our friends at Common Ground, especially Sr. Mary Ann Shea, who served as administrator from 1979 to 1986. To Lake Forest College and the Michael Posen Foundation for grant monies which helped in the preparation of this volume. To Chris Roby, Jenny Quinn, Jack Horn, Tom Meier, and Brad Cihla, our dedicated student assistants at Lake Forest College. And finally to Sherry and Cetta for their patience, love, and support.

Ron Miller
Jim Kenney

January 1987

THE
AMERICAN
MAINLINE

Introduction to Part One

It is the conviction of the editors of this volume that parochial religion cannot provide a spirituality for the planet in the twenty-first century. Neither Christianity nor Buddhism, Judaism, Hinduism, nor Islam can afford a spiritual home for the entire global community. Worldwide missions, efforts to force all people into one religious fold, are essentially wrong-headed. We believe that diversity is the hallmark of creation. Diverse languages, political systems, and religions can foster a unity which enforced uniformity in these areas can only destroy. The authors here assembled address this thesis from a variety of perspectives.

In the opening article, Ron Miller offers a new model for understanding the dynamics of contemporary American religion. Ron identifies the recent explosive growth of the Religious Right as the single most significant phenomenon in American religion today. It is this development which provides a context for Yechiel Eckstein's discussion of the Jewish community's emerging attempt at dialogue with Christian Evangelicals and Fundamentalists. Obstacles to interfaith dialogue are, of course, of many sorts. In his essay, Mark Smith locates an essential and long-standing source of Christian anti-Jewishness at the very heart of the Catholic experience: in its ritual commemoration of the Last Supper, where texts from the Hebrew Bible are juxtaposed with texts from the New Testament in a manner consistently presenting Judaism as Christianity's foil. Marc Gellman's contribution focuses on the development of the Jewish and Christian traditions in terms of the rabbinic categories of *halacha* and *aggada*, affording new insights into some of the mutual misapprehensions that have characterized the relationship between the two traditions throughout their centuries of shared existence. Gerald Ringer's article launches an attack on the entire Judeo-Christian enterprise for its failure to direct sufficient attention and energy to the Goddess. It is his view that this tragic omission has created a state of affairs in which not only our faith but our continued existence into the twenty- first century is threatened.

Thus, Part One portrays the crisis of isolation, prejudice, and hostility inherent in these forms of contemporary religion. At the same time, the authors call our attention to currents of genuine healing and wholeness, dialogue and shared understanding, cooperation and celebration of diversity. The note here sounded gives rise to hope for the emergence of a planetary faith in the twenty-first century.

A Road Map to Religious America

by Ron Miller

It was all so simple in the mid-fifties when Will Herberg wrote, *Protestant, Catholic, Jew.* This book provided a road map of American religion as complete and predictable as a minister, priest, and rabbi seated together at a Brotherhood dinner. It was a road map as tidy as a military chapel's "lazy Susan" centerpiece, capable of being turned to a cross, a crucifix, or two tablets of the Law, depending upon the religious needs of the congregation.

Everyone knew, of course, that there were exceptions to this tripartite terrain. Greek Orthodox Christians existed in the 1950s, along with Mormons, Seventh Day Adventists, and other members of minority religions. But they were considered insignificant enough to be safely ignored. Mainstream America achieved sociological identity by fitting into Herberg's sacred trinity (see Diagram A). Those who fell outside its parameters often described themselves with some embarrassment as "having no religion." World War II had taught us that "atheists didn't exist in fox-holes" and, if there were any, they constituted the ranks from which the much-discussed "Sunday suicides" emerged.

Diagram A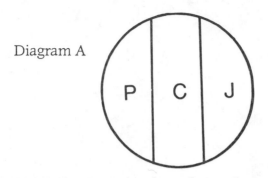

As helpful as this road map was in the mid-fifties, it proves all but useless in the ferment of contemporary American religion. The distinction between Protestants and Catholics, for example, does not represent the most significant division among Christians of the 1980s. The difference between "evangelical" and "liberal" is a much more important key for understanding tensions within the Christian community today. In the 1950s, Christianity was still living in harmony with the patriotic purposes of our nation-state and its military-industrial partners. There were no weapons the U.S.A. could develop that Cardinal Spellman would not hasten to bless. The Protestant establishment was equally ready to run up the red, white, and blue as symbolic synonym for the cross of Jesus. The liberation theology filling libraries today was unheard of then, and clergy of all denominations during the Cold War era would have been as scandalized as the present Polish pope in imagining that theology could use a Marxist economic analysis to define Christian praxis.

The Religious Right was not even a concept in the 1950s, and Fundamentalists were dismissed as backwoods illiterates. What a contrast with 1985, when they are found more frequently in the White House or on prime-time television than in quaint rural churches. When *Good Housekeeping* magazine asked its yearly "Mirror, mirror, on the wall" question not long ago, a Southern Baptist preacher from Lynchburg, Virginia—the Reverend Jerry Falwell—ranked second in the land among the country's "most admired men."[1]

If the change is so dramatic within the Christian community, it is even more spectacular beyond its pale. Swamis were side-show attractions in the 1950s, but now this ancient Hindu monastic title has acquired a new respect, and one can read fascinating books by swamis with Ph.D.'s in psychology.[2] The Dalai Lama, one of the monastic leaders of Tibetan Buddhism, holds meetings with high ranking churchmen in St. Patrick's cathedral. Mosques, ashrams, and meditation centers are springing up across the land, and no amount of effort can make them fit on the Procrustean bed of Herberg's schema.

Somewhere there seems to be a magic line which, when crossed, leads one into the newly developing territories colonized with groups called *cults* by their enemies, and *alternative religions* by their more objective critics. A town in Oregon is renamed after its resident guru; the leader of a major alternative religion is jailed for tax evasions; heated debates continue about the legitimacy of de-programming. The father of a former "cult member" proudly declares in a recent newspaper editorial that his offspring has been successfully rescued from the clutches of a cult, and that evidence for this return to normalcy includes the fact that his son has given up this "nonsense about meditation" and is eating steak again at the backyard barbeque. We sing praises to the Lord that a soul has been saved in suburbia and now offers sacrifices at the family altar.

The real outback of American's religious geography is a territory that the Religious Right declares downright satanic. This is the land of so-called "New Age" thinking. Without much in the way of ritual or formal church, this form of religiosity is disseminated more through conferences and workshops than tent revivals or parish missions. It draws on Christians like Pierre Teilhard de Chardin and Hindus like Sri Aurobindo, but it is just as likely to quote psychics or physicists, astrologers or acupuncturists. Marilyn Ferguson christened it the "Aquarian Conspiracy," since it is a "breathing together" (the root meaning of *conspiracy*) of groups who believe that the planet has moved into a New Age, the Age of Aquarius; Aquarius is the water-bearing sign which brings wholeness and healing to a spiritually thirsty Earth.

A second diagram helps us to see the basic contours of this newly emerging religious terrain (see Diagram B). Herberg's division remains the mainline center of American religion, but four new quadrants now surround the original territory: the Religious Right, the Liberation Left, Alternative Religions, and New Age thinking.

Diagram B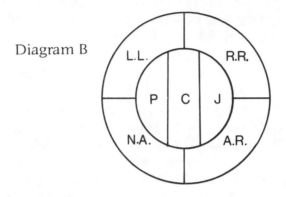

The Religious Right

The leading actor in the ongoing drama of American religion is clearly the Religious Right. It consists of an uneasy alliance of Christians, ranging from extreme Fundamentalists to moderate and theologically sophisticated Evangelicals. The total number of adherents to this segment of Christianity is roughly equivalent to the number of Roman Catholics in the U.S.A. today, about fifty-five million. Conservative Christianity has rightly been called the largest non-denominational denomination in the country.

How far right the Religious Right can swing truly boggles the imagination. There has been recent media attention to some of the racist churches in the radical right, groups which venerate Hitler's *Mein Kampf* as biblical literature and make no pretense of masking an ideology that is viciously anti-Semitic, anti-black, and totalitarian enough to make the Spanish Inquisition look like a Methodist picnic. The Christian Identity movement, with ministers like Richard Butler and Jim Wickstrom broadcasting these basest forms of prejudice, make us realize that the Reverend Jerry Falwell is correct when he claims to be a moderate. So concerned is Falwell not to be identified with some of the extreme views of these groups that he recently sent a book on the subject to every rabbi and Jewish leader in the country.[3]

Since it serves no purpose to caricature these extreme groups and since it is blatantly inaccurate to identify them with all conservative Christians, it seems more fruitful and fair to focus on some of the shared perspectives which unite the otherwise diverse members of the Religious Right, and which distinguish them from the mainline as well as from the liberal Liberation Left. Two characteristics will serve as our focus: their view of salvation and their view of the Bible.

It is difficult for members of the Religious Right to realize that the salvation issue which is so central to their theology simply does not play the same role for many other Christians, let alone for countless non-Christians. This preoccupation with salvation is also tied in with the prominence given to sin. "Conviction of sin" is the foundation of conservative Christian theology, and to understand this throws much light on what might otherwise seem to be theological anomalies. In a recent discussion I had with an evangelical theologian, many members of the audience were horrified when he calmly said that Jews who hear about Jesus Christ and do not believe in him are going to hell. Some months later, I was participating in a forum with another evangelical theologian and was feeling frustrated at my inability to persuade him to see the holiness of other religious traditions. Finally he said to me, with great patience and kindness, "You must understand that all human experience is sinful; so-called Buddhist holiness, Hindu holiness, Jewish holiness, it's all sin."

Conservative Christians do not have the whole developing area of creation theology, so influential in other segments of Christianity, available to them.[4] Creation theology recognizes an "original blessing" which is a dialectical balance to the preoccupation of many Christian theologies with "original sin." It is an affirmation of the goodness of creation, of human beings made in the image and likeness of God, of a human history that continues to manifest God's glory despite human sin. In this context, Christ appears as the reminder of beauty and value in every creature and not merely as the redeemer from sin. One reflects on the children whom Jesus blessed. Who were they? Jewish children. What happened to most of them? Undoubtedly they lived and died as Jews. Did Jesus bless these children knowing that they would burn eternally? And what about the Roman soldiers and officers whom Jesus encountered? Do we have any textual evidence that he tried to convert them from their paganism? Yet he marvelled at their faith and sent them home praising God. Are we again to presume that Jesus blessed them as a prelude to eternal hell? Doesn't this give us some indication that Jesus recognized God's image and work in creation prior to any religious affiliation or identification? An affirmative answer to these questions cannot be entertained within the context of the Religious Right.

Nor does conservative Christianity really understand Amos 9:7, which claims that God has other stories in the world: "Have I not brought up Israel out of the land of Egypt, and the Philistines from Caphtor and Aram from Kir?" God seems to be pleading with Amos to understand that although he works in a covenantal relationship with Israel, he has other children and relationships as well. But conservative Christianity must deny God any dealings with creatures not defined by their language and concepts. The Christian of the Religious Right seems sadly like the small child who cannot understand that his mother and father do love him, although they love his brothers and sisters as well.

One has to recognize the logic and consistency of their conclusions, which rest on particular interpretations of Genesis, Paul, Augustine, and Luther. Their one-sided preoccupation with sin leaves them no alternative but to channel all salvation through the redemptive act of Jesus Christ. I recall a train conversation with a fundamentalist minister who turned to me with a disarming smile and said, "You have to understand that going to hell doesn't have anything to do with how good you are." That statement, from his viewpoint, is not nonsense. Given the central premise of his theology — an unmitigated morass of sin — the minister's remark was as logical as any conclusion in Euclidian geometry. Being good has nothing to do with going to hell.

Since it doesn't seem likely that anyone would invent such an unattractive theology, one must move to the second characteristic underpinning of the conservative Christian position — their view of the Bible. Although there are shades of difference among the Fundamentalists and various brands of Evangelicals, they are all generally committed to a literal reading of Scripture. In other words, when they read John 14:6 ("I am the way, the truth, and the life; no one comes to the Father except through me."), they would all understand these words to have been spoken by the historical Jesus and would understand them to mean that some kind of explicit faith confession, vis-á-vis the person of Jesus Christ, is necessary for salvation. It is very important to see how much unanimity in theological perspective there is here, despite the nuances in style and sophistication found in the Religious Right.

Conservative Christians do not welcome the kind of scholarship suggesting that words attributed to Jesus were probably composed by the author of the Gospel. The mainline Christians' more liberal perspective accepts the evidence of real diversity in the four Gospels, and the fact that they are catechetical documents from four distinct ecclesiastical communities. They understand that the Gospels contain adaptations of sayings or teachings which are attributed to Jesus, but which also involve all the limitations of a transmission from Aramaic to Greek and then into the life-world of a particular Gospel writer and his community. Thus the reliability of the New Testament texts rests on their overall direction, not on the literalness of any particular verse. It is not difficult to see how this variation in interpretation has become a watershed, dividing Christians from Christians in a manner far more significant than denominational differences.

Conservative Christians also tend to lack in-depth knowledge of other world religions. Thus they cannot see parallels in the Hindu devotion to Krishna as an avatar of the divine, or in the Pure Land Buddhists calling upon the name of Buddha for salvation. In other words, they cannot step beyond their particularist perspective enough to entertain the possibility that, just as Jesus is the name for that embodiment of the divine which characterizes Christian experience, Krishna is a name for that same reality among Hindus. If the historical Jesus did say that no one comes to the Father except through him, the "him" in this text more likely refers to his consciousness than to his person. In other words, one can approach God in the intimacy of a parent-child relationship only by sharing in the kind of religious consciousness embodied in Jesus.

Although there are undeniably sincere and prayerful people constituting the vast majority of the Religious Right, I must express alarm in the face of their attempted exorcism of ambiguity. It constitutes an essential resistance to interfaith understanding, and a complete inability to believe that God can have different stories with different peoples. This is an idolatry of the relative, mistakenly identified as an absolute. What results, of course, is an inability to see one's perspective as a perspective. This need not flower into a persecution of "non-believers," but it inevitably bears the seed of prejudice.

Such a viewpoint is inimical not only to dialogue, but to process. Conservative theology tends towards past-tense slogans: "I've found it!" or "Have you been saved?" This has a marketing appeal because an action that has already been completed can better be packaged and dispensed. Liberals are at a disadvantage by being "on the way": reforming rather than reformed, converting rather than converted. Conservative Christianity lends itself easily to mass media salesmanship. This again harbors dangers for a pluralistic society, because a perspective which does not know that it is only a perspective tends to clone itself. To be religious means not only to be Christian, but to be Christian according to a specific definition. This constitutes an essential attack on the diversity of humankind's experience of the divine and, from my viewpoint, constitutes one of the chief dangers threatening the religious future of America.

Alternative Religions

I was convinced she was a Moonie even before she rang the doorbell. My family and I were seated at the dinner table when I saw someone running up the driveway to our front door with an armful of flowers. The enthusiasm and the excessive smile were a tip-off. The young woman said she was Japanese and was collecting money for a youth program. When I asked her if she was affiliated with the Unification Church, she nodded agreement and asked if I was interested in more information about it. I told her that I had studied her church and was not in agreement about its position on "heavenly deception" — that it is permissible to use any "front" in soliciting funds, since it is for a good cause; indeed, the only truly good cause. I told her that there was no "youth program," that the money was really going to the organization itself, and that it was just this kind of misrepresentation which might account for the Reverend Moon's serving a prison term for tax evasion. She pleaded difficulty with my English and ran off to the next house on the block.

The Unification Church is an alternative religion. Some would call it a cult. I tend to avoid the word *cult* and instead point to certain characteristics of groups which render them, in my opinion, dangerous. Deception in fund-raising is one such characteristic. So too is the limitation of contact with the outside world — a cultivation of dependence on the group leader with the consequent devaluation of self-esteem and one's ability to make individual judgments. A totally negative painting of those outside the group is another dangerous sign, as is the belief in black and white answers in a world that is all too often gray.

It is clear from the outset that these traits do not belong exclusively to some of the alternative religions. As in the case of the Religious Right, we find here an excessive clarity about God's plans in human history, and an idolatrous confusion of the finger pointing to the moon with the moon itself . Since this category of alternative religions includes countless groups, it is just as clear that not all of them share this characteristic as it is certain that communities in other segments of the religious geography definitely do.

Once when I was on a panel discussing "cults", I began my presentation by stating that I had joined a cult when I was seventeen. I explained how I had given away all my earthly possessions; lived in a rural setting without newspapers, television, radio, or telephone; received daily instructions from the cult leader; had my incoming mail opened and read; submitted my outgoing mail for reading; had my head shaved; wore a cult uniform identical to that of other cult members; carried not one penny on my person; and had no way of leaving the property owned by the cult. The audience gasped as the details of my cult involvement emerged. There was subsequent embarrassment and an outbreak of relieved laughter when I explained that my cult experience had been in a religious order of the Roman Catholic Church.

This discussion took place at a Catholic college, and there were representatives of anti-cult groups present who were strongly committed to deprogramming methods. I found myself annoyed at their relief. Everything I had narrated was indeed true. Why did my parents not have the right to have their teenage son deprogrammed? Because mine was an established religious institution? That is precisely the point. It means that we are not deprogramming because of the practices but because of the prestige, or lack of it, which the religious group in question enjoys. How can the law of the land be based on a distinction so facile? Today's fad becomes tomorrow's doctrine, and vice versa. If the Catholic Church falls into sufficient disfavor with public opinion, can we start deprogramming Catholic seminarians?

The point seemed obvious to me, though not to the proponents of deprogramming techniques. They accepted certain practices in the seminaries and convents where priests and sisters were trained. It was not the practice which was objectionable but the foreign character of the alternative religion. This led me to understand how some of the groups most violently opposed to the so-called "cults" come to take on the most objectionable characteristics of the organizations they so vehemently oppose. I agree that certain practices — such as financial deceit — should be censured; but that censuring must be across the board. Any laws we make must be ones we are all willing to live by — the old and established religions as well as the alternative ones.

Alternative religions will continue to be part of the American landscape. By and large, I see them as presenting no great danger to American life and liberty. Where they do exhibit objectionable tendencies, let those tendencies be checked by the same legal processes applied to any other organization. However, I believe a great mistake would be made if we rejected all of the emerging alternative religions as dangerous cults. There are literally hundreds of such organizations appearing in the USA today, and I think that our rejection of them en masse would be fired by prejudice much more than by any justifiable concern for the protection of the innocent.

Realizing that not all of the alternative religions are dangerous cults is especially important in the case of Eastern religions. The dialogue between East and West is so desperately needed in our society, and yet is often met with overt or subtle hostility. An example of the former leapt out at me recently from the morning newspaper. A Hindu community from Chicago planned to build a one-million-dollar temple in a Chicago suburb. The city council meeting was inundated with conservative Christians waving their Bibles and protesting that God opposes all idol-worshipping heathens. It is sad that this kind of opportunity for dialogue cannot be greeted with enthusiasm. But as we saw in our consideration of the Religious Right, this particular posture has neither the wisdom nor the security for penetrating relative forms in search of the absolute.

The subtler hostility to the East is less dramatic but no less prevalent. The mere fact that one can earn a Ph.D. in philosophy at any university in this country without having the slightest acquaintance with the long and sophisticated discussion of metaphysical, ethical, and epistemological issues of Buddhism and Hinduism is one of those embarrassments we will be hard pressed to explain in some not-too-distant future. Thomas Merton, though he died in 1968, was still far ahead of his time due to the fact that, as a novice master for Catholic monks in the 1950s, he saw the necessity of exposing them to the monastic wisdom found in Eastern traditions.

Do we ever ask ourselves why so many people turn to the spirituality offered by teachers from the East — exiled Tibetan Buddhists in Berkeley and Boulder, Hindu swamis in our major cities, Zen masters on both coasts and in Minnesota? I ask college students in my religion classes, after I have explained the meaning of a guru, whether there are any gurus in our Western religions. They laugh in disbelief. Would they go to their minister, priest, or rabbi to discuss spiritual growth? Generally they would not. They see these spiritual leaders more as offering practical advice in the areas of weddings, baptisms, first communions, and bar and bat mitzva ceremonies. It is not that our Western religions lack spiritual teachings, but somehow these mainline religions have become more like each other in being American than diverse, by tapping their own traditions of inwardness. Being American primarily means knowing how to run a business.

Many American religious institutions have thrived as businesses. They struggle to stay in the black and to move masses of people on and off the parking lots on schedule. One pastor sent his congregation a small record (the parish was affluent enough that he could presume everyone had a turntable) explaining the church's financial programs. A congregation member mused that it would have been delightful, though totally beyond belief, if the parishioners had received a record discussing prayer. Even Eastern religions seem to adopt the facade of business soon after their arrival on our shores, but vestiges of other interests and concerns seem to cling to them a bit longer. Perhaps just long enough to become contagious to our Western religions.

The Liberation Left

The Liberation Left consists of all those people who do not count in most mainline and conservative churches. Thus there are black theologies of liberation, women's theologies of liberation, gay theologies of liberation, and Third-World theologies of liberation — to name just a few. Liberation theology speaks with the voices of all those who are unheard and unseen in our mainstream society — all the people who do *not* appear on the television shows of the Religious Right, who are *not* invited to participate in Ronald Reagan's parades, and who are *not* invited to Rome by the Pope. Put them all together and you have a fairly good line-up of the Liberation Left. Its organizational unit is the "base community" (*comunidad de base*). This is a group of Christians meeting for prayer and the study of God's Word, who are ready to follow the consequences in their daily lives.

How do these groups differ from the mainline churches or, for that matter, from the Religious Right? Both the mainline churches and the Religious Right tend to be hierarchical — whether in the Roman Catholic form, or in the similar pattern of the white-male-minister dominated conservative groups. Both the mainline churches and the Religious Right tend to be arranged in large organizational structures — dioceses, conferences, districts. Both the mainline churches and the Religious Right have a religion oriented primarily, though certainly not exclusively, on a vertical axis: myself and God. Many participants attend their place of worship to be saved, to get grace, to avoid backsliding, or to safeguard the ticket to heaven they have been promised. A spirituality of "Jesus and me" is prevalent, and the emphasis is on the personal pronoun when the question is asked, "How can I be saved?"

The base community, on the other hand, has a grass-roots structure. Distinctions between clergy and laity lose their meaning as people experience themselves as brothers and sisters equally confronted by the Word of God. Church activity is primarily within the small group — the people who know and interact with each other daily. Sin and salvation are not absent from their vocabulary, but are part of a horizontal framework of meaning where sin more often refers to corrupt social structure than to individual failures in areas of drinking or sex.

Sin and salvation, in other words, take on a more societal and corporate dimension. Sin includes the oppression of exploited people, rendering it all but impossible for them to achieve their dignity and freedom as God's children. Salvation, too, cannot be reduced to the Religious Right's "four spiritual laws" nor to the mainline's requirements for good standing in the church. Salvation involves the liberation of whole societies of people and ultimately of all humanity. "Are you saved?", becomes almost meaningless as a question addressed to individuals, when all of humankind must be saved together.

Liberation theologians are not hesitant to use the economic analyses of Karl Marx or of anyone else who can help them understand the dynamics of their oppression. They see the world through a different lens than that used by the mainline. Violence for the First World is, above all else, an attack on person and private property. For liberation theologians in a Third-World context, violence is the very system which suppresses whole segments of the human community.

This leads to radically different perspectives on the peace that Christians believe Christ came to bring to the world. For conservative Christians, and many in the mainline as well, peace means the maintenance of American supremacy. If possible, one wants to keep the peace without war, though political and economic sanctions and other means of control are allowable. Strong police forces keep the peace by restraining angry, poor people in the inner city. Right-wing dictators keep the peace by containing the rage of oppressed populations in developing nations. Ultimately, nuclear weapons targeted on Soviet civilian population centers keep the peace by deterring our major enemy from any attempt to challenge our national interests anywhere in the world. From this perspective, violence is essentially a disturbance of the status quo at any level — neighborhood, national, or international.

From the perspective of liberation theology, peace is "a dynamic process through which justice is established amid the tensions of history."[5] The Religious Right and many in the mainline say, "*Si vis pacem, para bellum!*" (If you want peace, prepare for war). The Liberation Left and the liberal wing of the mainline say, "If you want peace, pursue justice." The pastoral letter of the American Catholic bishops of May 3, 1983 reflects this orientation when it states: "Peace must be built on the basis of justice in a world where the personal and social consequences of sin are evident."[6] It is no small wonder that many have marked this document as Marxist, for it clearly deviates from mainline identification with the status quo.

The liberation theologians share some of their vision with the creation theologians mentioned earlier. Both see God calling us to a world where we are challenged to live as a family. Not absolute ownership, but stewardship, describes our relation to the things of this world. We are co-creators of this garden world, and we are commissioned to serve and to preserve it (Genesis 2:16).[7] The access all human beings should have to the common fruits of the garden is a basic component of the justice that God seeks in all our doings. It was precisely a lack of this

justice which led to the outcries of Israel's prophets and which reverberates in New Testament teachings. Those who want peace must hunger and thirst for justice and actively pursue it as an intergral part of
Christian praxis.

Do the liberation theologians condone violence in the pursuit of
this justice? Again, the question is ambiguous. What kind of violence
do we mean? The violence of the oppressor or the violence of the vic-
tim? Ironically, I am writing these words as a house guest in a lovely
villa perched on the slope of Las Brisas, an exclusive neighborhood
overlooking the Bay of Acapulco, Mexico. In the city below, I see poor
people picking through garbage cans and malnurtured children clinging to mothers whose eyes reflect the despair of abject poverty.

The entrance to the hillside paradise of Las Brisas is patrolled by
heavily armed guards. For those of us living here, violence would be
the intrusion of someone into this area to inflict harm on our person
or property. In other words, violence would consist of disruption of the
status quo. The guards would have no hesitancy in shooting someone
breaking into this multi-million-dollar enclave. I am embarrassed by
the realization that I am such an apt symbol for the First-World men-
tality. But it is the world of white male privilege in which I have spent
my life, a world where I have never known hunger or lack of access to
the garden's fruits.

What does violence mean, however, to the people outside the gate?
It is so difficult to perceive the world from another perspective. Sometimes when I am talking about this in class, I casually take my brown-
bag lunch out of my attaché case. I ask the class, "Does this sandwich
excite any feelings in you?" The students don't quite get my drift but,
of course, are indifferent to that bit of cheese and bread. I ask us then
to imagine ourselves being so hungry that desperate restraint is needed
not to lunge across the room for that sandwich, so hungry that one
would be tempted to turn one's best friend over to the police for a taste
of it. Few of us really know what that means. Perhaps we never can and
never will. But that world outside the gates of privilege does exist and
we cannot understand liberation theology unless we recognize it, try
to think ourselves outside the gate looking in, outside the gate of white,
male, straight, First-World privilege. Then we must try further to understand that the injustice felt outside the gate is the essential problem
liberation theology tries to address. It is that very injustice that is most

experienced as violence in the Third World.

For many mainline and conservative Christians, liberation theology merely puts a religious label on a politically subversive movement. But for the theologians of liberation, there can be no authentic religiosity which fails to address the total socio-economic and political reality of human beings and their communities. Salvation, total wholeness, and healing cannot be effective in a privatized sphere. A greater awareness of interrelatedness is one of the characteristics that the liberation theologians share with the New Age thinkers we will be considering next. None of these categories, after all, is watertight; because they are not logical entities but dimensions of experience and life, they necessarily leak into one another.

New Age Thinking

Perhaps the most telling insight into New Age thinking is the realization that its conception as an alternative to something called "old age" thinking misses the point. Ecologists remind us that "competitive exclusivity" provides the greatest threat to ecological well-being; that is precisely what New Age thinking hopes to avoid. Turning a samsaric wheel in which today's fad replaces yesterday's orthodoxy only mimics progress. Defining our position as one which is essentially against another position both muddies our own vision and lures us ineluctably to an identification with our professed opponent. Thus New Age thinking tries to appreciate each view and yet bring it into focus through a juxtaposition with all other perspectives. Even "old age" thinking — linear, analytic, left-brained — has its virtues. In short, in the "New Age" everything is preserved, but viewed through a new paradigm, a model of radical interrelatedness.

New Age thinking finds its symbol in the dawning Age of Aquarius. This change of planetary configuration expresses the fundamental New Age conviction that we have indeed reached a new stage of planetary development. In some ways, this New Age seems to be the obverse side of the nuclear age born on August 6, 1945. Einstein claimed that the atom bomb changed everything but our way of thinking. The New Age paradigm may well contain precisely the changed way of thinking that will enable us to meet the planetary threat presented by the current yoking of nuclear weapons to neolithic notions of conflict resolution.

Part of the challenge and apparent confusion of New Age thinking is created by the realization that it can be approached from any point on the spectrum of human experience. My own background was such that my first encounters with it stemmed from my study of religion. In the mid-sixties I participated in a conference on Pierre Teilhard de Chardin, Jesuit priest and paleontologist, poet, man of science, and mystic. It was in his writings that I first glimpsed the spiralling dynamism in which creation both explodes into diversity and converges into unity. Orthodoxy no longer meant statically preserving the past but using it to sight the future. God no longer appeared to me as an old man sitting on a cloud tallying our mistakes but as a youthful presence bounding ahead of us and challenging us to catch up. Teilhard de Chardin portrayed a divinity calling for co-creators in a world not yet finished. It came as no surprise to me some twenty years later to read that Marilyn Ferguson found this man to be the most cited influence among the sample of people she characterized as New Age thinkers.

A second signpost of New Age thinking for me was the man whose influence has skyrocketed since his death in 1968. Thomas Merton's famous 1948 autobiography begins with the words: "On the last day of January 1915, under the sign of the Water Bearer, in a year of a great war, and down in the shadow of some French mountains on the borders of Spain, I came into the world."[8] His latest biographer notes that: "Whether Thomas Merton was aware of it or not, he had become, in both poetry and prose, a poet of the rain, appropriate enough for one born under the sign of the Water Bearer."[9] Merton has proved to be among the most influential of Aquarians.

When Merton became novice master for the Trappist monks at Gethsemane, Kentucky in the 1950s, he grasped with great clarity an intuition eluding most religious people even to this day. He saw that training a monk in the Christian tradition necessitated studying and transmitting a monastic wisdom which far transcended the parameters of Western Christianity. This led him to a life-long pilgrimage of study and meeting across the divisions of world religions. Just as the boundaries of Earth's nations are invisible to the astronaut viewing our planet from space, so too do the mystic's eyes register no real and absolute boundaries between religions.

Dialogue based on an interfaith theology stands out as a hallmark of New Age groups. Real dialogue entails empathetically entering into the viewpoint of another person and appreciating it on its own terms. It means seeing the other not as an adversary but as a true partner in the search for truth. Hinduism throws light on Christianity, and vice versa. Spiritual traditions enrich the concepts and practice of Western psychotherapy. eastern wisdom recognizes a convergence with recent developments in Western science. Dialogue opens countless doors of enrichment in every direction.

Holism has become a cliché, but its central insight is just beginning to reshape our understanding of health, education, politics, and religion. Physicians meet with philosophers and professors of religion to understand why the patient's trust in them is such an important factor in the healing process. Teachers move towards the realization that interdisciplinary learning should be the rule rather than the exception. Religion is examined for the impact it has on "the other six days of the week."

I recall a snowy evening when I was addressing a peace and justice group at a local church. Towards the end of the evening, an elderly woman raised her hand to announce with considerable conviction that it was getting more and more challenging to be a Christian. She said that she used to think her principal duties as a Catholic Christian were to go to church on Sunday, avoid eating meat on Fridays, and say her morning and evening prayers. Now she understood her faith to include being informed on nuclear weapons proliferation in the U.S.A., racism in South Africa, new forms of meditation, and liturgical dance! Here is a woman who understands holism. Without having heard the word, she has already become an active part of the New Age. From the New Age perspective, religion's primary purpose is not belief, but transformation. Truth is not so much found in good answers as in good dialogues and good directions.

The Future

Having briefly examined these four quadrants which surround the older religious geography, we naturally find ourselves speculating about the future. Now that we have our new road map, where will it take us? Like any other map, it does not take us anywhere; only we do that. But it may offer some orientation in our consideration of possible futures. It is my own conviction that the mainline center will hold, that it will carry the weight of America's religious future well into the next century at least. However there are two possible scenarios for the interaction of the mainline with all that is happening around its edges.

The first kind of future (see Diagram C) would be based on a defensive reaction by the mainline, much like the kind of entrenchment opted for by the Catholic Church at the time of the Reformation. This hostility to the outer circle would, in my opinion, leave the mainline impoverished, with little to offer future religious seekers in our country.

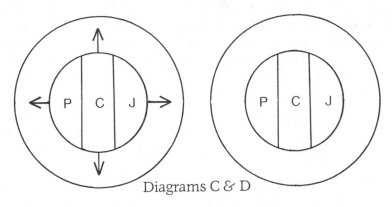

Diagrams C & D

The second kind of future would be created by the mainline's inclusion of certain elements from the outer circle (see Diagram D). Perhaps it would absorb some of the feeling for American grass-roots life reflected in the Religious Right, as well as some of the conservative's appreciation for the power of the media and the necessary relationship between religion and politics. From the Liberation Left it might be weaned from its First-World blindness, its tendency towards a vertical ("Jesus and me") faith, and choose to integrate religion with the demands for planetary justice. From the alternative religions, the mainline may learn zeal, meditation, even the power of non-action. And from the New Age consciousness, the mainline may accept more holistic models of embodying love and embracing transformation.

There are, of course, numerous other possible futures. The Religious Right could succeed in its goal and make this a "Christian nation" in its own image and likeness. Liberation theologies could convert the mainline completely to an agenda of world revolution by marginalized people. The mainline could virtually disappear in a mighty wave of missionary activity by the Moonies or Muslims. Our churches and synagogues could turn into ashrams or zendos overnight, or perhaps the mainline will melt in the birth of the New Age miracle. But these futures seem less likely to me. The defensive scenario, on the other hand, seems possible — and frightening enough to be resisted. The incorporation scenario also looks possible — and hopeful enough to be pursued. In the end, the road map remains only that: a map for journeyers and seekers.

Endnotes

1. *Good Housekeeping*, January, 1985. Number 1, of course, was President Reagan.

2. Read, for example, Swami Ajaya (the former Dr. Alan Weinstock), *Psychotherapy East and West* (Honesdale, PA: Himalayan Press, 1983).

3. The book Falwell sent was: Merrill Simon, *Jerry Falwell and the Jews* (Middle Village, N.Y., Jonathan David Publishers, Inc., 1984).

4. See, for example, any of the books by Matthew Fox, especially *Original Blessing* (Santa Fe: Bear & Company, Inc., 1983).

5. Jose Miguez Bonino, *Doing Theology in a Revolutionary Situation* (Philadelphia, Fortress Press, 1975), p. 116.

6. National Conference of Catholic Bishops, "The Challenge of Peace: God's Promise and Our Response" (Washington, D.C., The United States Catholic Conference, 1983), p.18.

7. For a beautiful exposition of this text and theology, see Helen Kenik, "Towards a Biblical Basis for Creation Theology," *Western Spirituality: Historical Roots, Ecumenical Roots* ([1978] Bear & Company, Inc., 1981), pp.27-75.

8. Thomas Merton, *The Seven Storey Mountain* (New York: Harcourt, Brace, and Company, 1948) p. 3. It is interesting to note that he was born just a few days after Alan Watts, another New Age thinker discussed in Mike Foster's article.

9. Michael Mott, *The Seven Mountains of Thomas Merton* (Boston: Houghton Mifflin Company, 1984), p. 241.

A Jewish Perspective on the Religious Right

by Yechiel Eckstein

Ron Miller's article provides a helpful context for locating my own purpose of exploring the Religious Right from a Jewish perspective. The rise of Evangelicals in recent years has prompted mainstream Christians and Jews alike to respond with a mixture of fascination and fear. Evangelicals are certain to have a major impact on the social fabric of this country; they ought, therefore, to be taken seriously. Understanding — rather than negative or positive stereotyping — would be helpful.

Most people remain ignorant about the Evangelical community. In its 1982 joint program plan, for example, the National Jewish Community Relations Council admitted its lack of knowledge, stating, "There remains a great need for a thorough examination of the Evangelical movement with a view to providing guidance for Jewish groups in establishing and maintaining relationships with suitable elements within that movement. . . .We renew our recommendation of last year that such an examination be undertaken by national members and all agencies that have the resources to do so."

The Jewish community, by and large, has viewed the rise of the Evangelical movement with a special degree of anxiety. While a small minority view them as allies and give them unqualified support, most Jews are guarded and leery about cooperating with them. Still others, deeply alarmed by the Evangelicals' growing political power, refuse to have anything to do with them.

Jewish anxieties with regard to Evangelicals have demographic, sociological, and political roots, as much as theological ones. Jews and Evangelicals have only recently begun to live in the same geographic areas, to meet one another, and to conduct dialogues with one another. It is fair to say that until recently most Jews had never met an Evangelical before, and vice versa. The absence of contact has contributed to the ignorance of each other that the two communities often share.

It would be a mistake to conclude that no dialogue is possible between the two communities. There have been many noteworthy changes in past decades in Jewish-Christian relationships as a whole, and even in the manner in which interreligious programming is conducted. A movement that was marked by an attempt to homogenize the two faith communities on the basis of tolerance, civility, and brotherhood has recently become institutionalized, and is seeking to advance substantive dialogue and genuine understanding and cooperation among Christians and Jews. Change *is* possible.

Before the Jewish community rushes to "dialogue" with the Evangelical community, however, certain questons must be answered. For example, are all Evangelicals right-wing? How do Evangelicals differ, theologically and politically, from Catholics and liberal Protestants, as well as among themselves? We should also be critically discerning as to which Evangelical groups actively support Hebrew-Christian outreach groups like "Jews for Jesus" or seek to transform America into a "Christian nation," and which do not. Which segments of the Evangelical community should the Jewish community cooperate with? Is the prevalent view that all Evangelicals have anti-Semitic attitudes accurate? To put it simply: is the Evangelical movement good for the Jews?

The Evangelical-Jewish relationship is still in its embryonic stages. Certain Jewish groups have sponsored conferences and trips to Israel with Evangelicals. Others oppose such cooperative efforts. Neverthe-less, as the dialogue between the community matures, some of the negative stereotypes we have of one another may be dispelled, as may many — though not necessarily all — of our fears and anxieties.

Constant monitoring of fringe elements will still be necessary. But serious inroads *can* be made toward nurturing a positive relationship between Jews and most segments of Evangelicals through dialogue and mutually cooperative enrichment and concern.

Who Are the Evangelicals?

The word "evangelical" stems from the New Testament Greek word for "good news" or "gospel," with the implication being the *spreading* of that gospel. Evangelicals differ as to the precise meaning of the word, since it can describe a person, a position, or a movement. A more his-torical approach to the term would define it as a movement which evolved as a defense of historic Christian Orthodoxy in response to the Enlightenment. At the core of the concept, both ideologically and ety-mologically, is the Bible itself, especially the New Testament. In that sense, it can be said that the Protestant Reformation was an "evangel-ical" event, in that it stressed the return to the Bible (*sola scriptura*).

Religion can be described as the glasses through which we view the world. Our concepts of reality and ultimate meaning are filtered through faith. For traditional Jews, the Torah serves as "the Jewish glasses," and for this reason the scroll occupies "center stage" in the synagogue (i.e. the Ark). Central to Christian ethos, and particularly to the Evangelical view, is the person of Jesus and the authority of scripture.

At the heart of the Evangelical worldview is the belief that every-thing in life should be shaped by the gospel of the life, death, and resur-rection of Jesus. Whether it be liturgy, social action, politics, or science, all are measured by and viewed through the prism of the Christian Bible, and all are subject to its authority.

There is no typical Evangelical nor is there a consensus as to what constitutes Evangelical belief. There are, however, three ideological characteristics which distinguish the Evangelical from the "mainstream" Catholic or Protestant Christian. The distinction between Evangelical and non-Evangelical Christians frequently lies in the degree to which these three principles are actually stressed, rather than simply in their presence.

1) *Centrality of Scripture.* The world is viewed through the lens of Scripture — the Word of God, rather than the opposite. The centrality of the Bible is the key to all Evangelical affirmations and the Bible serves as the principle source of all religious authority.

2) *A stress on the person of Jesus,* or on God's immanence more than God's transcendence. It is for this reason that Evangelicals often speak of Jesus in very personal terms, as they might talk of a close friend.

3) *Being "born again."* This can best be understood as a personal experience of commitment to Jesus as Lord and Savior and a spiritual rebirth through the regenerating power of the Holy Spirit. The term stems from the New Testament Book of John 3:18 which quotes Jesus as saying, "Truly, truly I say to you, unless one is born of water and Spirit, he cannot enter the Kingdom of God . . .you must be born again." Non-Evangelicals understand this as referring to the act of baptism, which can be performed on a child and which fulfills the concept of "water and Spirit." Baptists and Evangelicals, however, would be inclined to require of the individual not just the physical act of baptism (i.e. water) but the personal decision to accept the lordship of Jesus (i.e. spirit). Rather than being baptized as infants, most Baptists and Evangelicals make a choice to be baptized. In this interpretation, baptism can only be performed when individuals are adults and can consciously accept Jesus as their personal savior.

Despite the lack of consensus regarding the term "evangelical," it is fair to say that an Evangelical is one who upholds *Scripture* (the Word of God) over a humanistic tradition that accommodates the Christian tradition unduly, who relates to the *person of Jesus* rather than to Jesus as a paradigm, and who stresses *regeneration* or being "born again" through the spirit of God. *Undergirding all these principles is the belief in the Christian imperative to disseminate this threefold gospel or good news.* The Jewish community should keep in mind, therefore, that central to the Evangelical Christian's identity is the commission to evangelize all non-Christians. This follows from an "exclusive truth claim" which Ron Miller rightly identifies as a central tenet of the Evangelical Christian.

Evangelicals or Fundamentalists?

In the nineteenth and early-twentieth centuries, Christians who followed these three principles were generally referred to as Fundamentalists, with the connotation being that they had returned to the fundamentals of the Church. The Fundamentalist movement stood in opposition to the Modernist one, comprised of liberal Christians who were viewed as having over-accommodated to modernity at the expense of rigid biblical doctrine. More recently, however, the generic term used to describe such Christians is "Evangelical," while "Fundamentalist" is reserved for the more conservative right-wing portion of the Evangelical community. Today the nomenclature "Fundamentalist" often conveys the pejorative connotation of "backward," unlike its original positive meaning of "those who have returned to the Christian fundamentals."

In other words, there has been significant change in the way we classify Christian believers of the sort described above. While today nearly all Fundamentalists would regard themselves as Evangelical, the opposite is no longer the case. Some Evangelicals, especially those in the center and left-wing, would take offense at being referred to as Fundamentalists. When in doubt, it is wiser to use the term "Christian," which is appropriate for all such people, including Fundamentalists.

As with most religious groups, there is a wide spectrum in the Evangelical community. Evangelicalism crosses all sectarian lines and is not a "denomination" in its own right (although certain denominations tend to be almost entirely Evangelical). Thus, for example, there are Methodist, Presbyterian, Baptist, and even Catholic Evangelicals (although most Catholics with such views characterize themselves as *charismatic*). The largest group of Evangelical Christians in America belongs to the Southern Baptist movement, itself the largest Protestant body in the country. The Assemblies of God and other Pentecostal groups that stress faith, healing, and "speaking in tongues" are among the fastest growing Evangelical groups.

It is estimated that there are between 40 and 50 million Americans in the United States who describe themselves as Evangelical Christians, though they are far from being a cohesive body. While most Evangelicals, particularly the conservative ones, come from the rural South, this concentration is changing as Evangelicals gradually enter more and more into mainstream urban life and society.

The major theological issue currently dividing "liberal" from "conservative" Evangelicals is whether or not Scripture is inerrant and infallible. Conservatives would insist that, in the words of Evangelical theologian Harold Lindsell, the Bible is "without error historically or scientifically." However, attitudinal, cultural, and stylistic factors, perhaps even more than theological ones, are the real dividing lines separating Evangelicals from Fundamentalists.

According to a recent Gallup poll, 20% of Evangelicals regard themselves as "left of the center," 31% as "middle of the road," and 37% as "right of the center," on the Evangelical spectrum. Non-Evangelicals, however, often mistakenly lump all Evangelicals together as a monolith (much to the distress of both liberal and conservative Evangelicals, neither of whom wish to be associated with the other). There are fundamental differences between Jerry Falwell and Billy Graham, *Christianity Today* and *Moody Monthly* magazines, Pat Robertson and Bob Jones, and between Criswell Center and Wheaton College, to name a few examples. These differences are especially pronounced when it comes to Jews, Judaism, and Israel.

For the purposes of this essay, the Evangelical community is divided into the categories of "left," "center," and "right." These categories are necessarily generalized; each can itself be subdivided into a left, center, and right as well.

The Evangelical Left

The left-wing of the Evangelical spectrum is most widely associated with the Sojourners community in Washington, D.C., which has only recently begun to receive media coverage and public attention. Their magazine, *Sojourners*, stresses a variety of ethical and social justice issues such as the exploitation of the Third World, nuclear armaments, abortion, poverty, apartheid, pacifism, and the issue of Palestinian Arab rights. They are a responsible group of devout Christians concerned with world peace and justice, though they often oppose the theology invoked by liberal Protestant groups such as the National Council of Churches, the umbrella organization for thirty-two Protestant groups. The Sojourners community and the Evangelical Left as a whole are a small minority among Evangelicals, in terms of both their numbers and influence. They oppose many of Israel's policies, particularly criticizing its treatment of Palestinian Arabs, and the escalating arms race in the Middle East and throughout the world. Also, *Sojourners'* editorials and articles have at times been extremely critical of Israel, and the magazine has sponsored a number of programs such as the two "La Grange Conferences" (1979, 1981) with the Palestinian Human Rights Campaign, which intended to attract Christians to the Palestinian Arab cause.

The principle non-theological issue separating mainstream Jewish organizations and the left-wing Evangelicals is the Israeli-Arab conflict, though the latter would also tend to be more pacifist than the organized Jewish community. There would be overall agreement on a host of domestic and social justice issues, though the two groups have rarely, if ever, worked together. The Left might be the most inclined of all Evangelicals to accept religious pluralism and the right of Jews to fulfill themselves through their Jewish faith. The Evangelical Left's ideological overlap with most segments of liberal Protestantism is striking. We can look foward to more cooperative efforts on the part of those two Christian groups in the years ahead, especially on the issues of poverty, nuclear policy, and the Middle East.

The Evangelical Center

The Evangelical Center has its own left, center, and right-wings. It is most visibly identified with such seminaries as Wheaton, Fuller, and Trinity, magazines such as *Christianity Today*, and organizations such as "The Evangelical Theological Society" and "National Association of Evangelicals" (NAE) — an umbrella organization of thirty-nine Evangelical denominations and numerous churches and individuals. The NAE publishes a quarterly newsletter, "United Evangelical Action," as well as a monthly magazine, "NAE Washington Insight," which deals with public and political affairs.

One of the lesser-known but highly beloved "centrist" Evangelicals in the eyes of the Jews was the late Dr. G. Douglas Young, former dean of Trinity Seminary, who moved to Israel in the early 1950's to express solidarity with the Jewish people. Young founded "The Holy Land Institute" and "Bridges for Peace" organizations to increase the Evangelical understanding and support for Israel. Dr. Young, a resident of Israel for almost thirty years, was given an award by Jerusalem Mayor Teddy Kolleck, and was respected by the Jewish community in Israel and the United States. Like most Centrists, he did not actively attempt to proselytize the Jews and, as a result, was widely trusted by them.

Christianity Today is the major magazine published by this segment of the Evangelical community and is a religious publication highly regarded even by non-Evangelicals. Some of the greatest Evangelical scholars of our time have served as its editors, including Carl Henry, Harold Lindsell, and Kenneth Kantzer. The publication generally takes a balanced, middle-of-the-road approach and tends to be in agreement with mainstream Jewish sensibilities. While many Fundamentalists view *Christianity Today* (and the Centrist movement as a whole) as having "gone soft" on evangelicism, most still have great respect for it.

Centrists are inclined to support Jews and Israel, though not uncritically, and not for the same theological, prophetic reasons often motivating the Right. Their solidarity stems more from a sense of justice for the Jewish people, and for geopolitical, moral, and strategic reasons, than it does from eschatological considerations — although these motives are not entirely absent.

A number of dialogue conferences have been held in recent years between Jews and this segment of Evangelicals. As a result, they now have a greater awareness and appreciation for the Jewish condition than do either the Right or Left. Following one such conference, *Christianity Today* published a four-page article entitled "Concerning Evangelicals and Jews" (April 24, 1981) stating that it "sorrowfully acknowledged anti-Semitic statements and actions on the part of some Evangelicals," and calling for "repentance, restitution, and action which will ferret out, expose and actively oppose incipient and overt anti-Semitism that creeps into society."

"To attack Jews," the editorial continued, "is to attack Evangelicals, and such attacks will be resisted by Evangelicals as attacks against themselves." While the centrist group will in all likelihood never issue a formal call for an end to the evangelism of Jews, rarely if ever do its members participate in aggressive proselytizing which singles out Jews for missionary activity. Moreover, such Evangelicals would be inclined to repudiate proselytizing efforts which apply "unworthy pressure," "manipulation," "bribery," or "deception." The same *Christianity Today* editorial, for example, states that "a small number of Jewish Christians disguise their Christianity to attract unsuspecting Jews to Christianity. This is deceitful, contrary to New Testament teaching, and unworthy of Evangelical Christians. We must insist on ethical integrity as the first law of any Christian witness."

While the Evangelical Center can be counted on to play an active role in defending Jews and even Judaism, its attitude towards Israel is not unqualifiedly positive. Moreover, on those occasions when Centrist support for Israel is forthcoming, it is generally not in the politically aggressive form taken by the Evangelical Right. Petitions, telegram campaigns, and other forms of lobbying on political issues which affect Israel, for example, are more likely to emanate from the Evangelical Right than from the Center.

The Evangelical Right

There are few purely theological issues that distinguish the Evangelical Right from the Center, except perhaps the biblical inerrancy question cited earlier. On the socio-cultural, demographic, and political levels, however, there are major differences. While the Centrists have been quietly involved in political affairs for decades, the Evangelical Right has in recent years begun employing aggressive tactics on behalf of their right-wing causes. They have mastered a variety of political techniques which they hope will bring America back to what they often refer to as the "Judeo-Christian" moral foundations on which the United States was built. Their means of achieving this goal include political action training seminars, voter registration drives, "hit lists" of political candidates, legislative alerts, telephone networks to mobilize the public, full use of television airwaves, newsletters and fundraising letters which posit the scriptural framework for the desired action, rallies, and more.

Let us use the Moral Majority (recently renamed "the Liberty Federation") as a primary example of the Evangelical Right. The Moral Majority, reportedly the largest of the Christian far-right political groups and certainly the most well known, was founded in 1979 by Reverend Jerry Falwell, a Lynchburg, Virginia pastor and host of the "Old Time

Gospel Hour" TV show. The Moral Majority aims to "bring America back to God" by mobilizing support at local, state, and national levels for favorable candidates and legislation. Moral Majority membership is about four million. It has a sophisticated network reaching all fifty states, and claims to have registered millions of new voters. While its impact on the outcome of various political races has been widely debated, it certainly plays an influential role in some Congressional races where Moral Majority members are a significant number of the delegates to the state Republican convention.

There is widespread confusion regarding this group, to the point that many people mistakenly view all Evangelicals as members of the Moral Majority, or at least ideologically and politically compatible with it. One of the most common complaints raised by Evangelicals at dialogue meetings is the public's tendency to confuse them with the Moral Majority.

The following is a partial list of Reverend Falwell's organized ministry: President, Moral Majority, Inc.; Chancellor, Liberty Baptist College; Pastor, Thomas Road Baptist Church; President, Elim, Inc.; President, Lynchburg Christian Academy; President, Treasure Island Youth Camp; President, Liberty Home Bible Institute; Chancellor, Liberty Baptist Seminary; and President, The Old Time Gospel Hour, Inc. This institutional empire reflects Falwell's long-time commitment to "saturation evangelism," his term for "preaching the gospel to every available person at every available time by every available means."

The Moral Majority is anathema to many Christians, the majority of Evangelicals probably view it with mixed feelings. On the one hand, many of them are fed up with policies which they believe have led to a deterioration in the moral fabric of our society, and with the laws which have relegated religion solely to the confines of church, synagogue, or family. On the other hand, they also wish to preserve certain constitutional freedoms, especially those of finding the proper role of religion in public policy. In addition, they are concerned with the Evangelical Right's views and policies towards Jews, Israel, and matters of constitutional rights.

Jerry Falwell has said, "I support the Jews, first for biblical reasons; I take the Abrahamic covenant literally, God has blessed America, because we have blessed the Jews. . .God has raised up America in these last days for the cause of world evangelization *and* for protection of His people, the Jews. I don't think America has any other right or reason for existence than these two purposes." (Interview, *Christianity Today*, September 4, 1981) One of the most commonly invoked biblical passages used by conservative Christians to undergird their support for Jews and Israel is, "And I (God) will bless those who bless you (Israel) and curse those who curse you" (Genesis 12:3). In other words, many Evangelicals genuinely believe that the reason America has been blessed as it has, is because of its favorable treatment of Jews and Israel.

But regional Moral Majority representatives have made statements which are anti-Semitic, or—to be charitable—which unwittingly exhibit prejudices. Reverend Daniel Fore, once chairman of New York's Moral Majority, has said that "Jews have a God-given, almost supernatural ability to make money," and that "Jews control the media in this city (New York)." Falwell repudiated Fore and later apologized for his remarks, characterizing them as "naive and uninformed." Fore no longer serves on the staff of the Moral Majority.

Falwell has repeatedly denied that he or any part of the Moral Majority is anti-Semitic, citing his support for Israel and the fact that Jews and even rabbis are among the Moral Majority's membership. He himself has been known to let slip an anti-Semitic remark or two, although, I believe, naively and unintentionally. Speaking at an "I Love America" rally on the steps of the state capital in Richmond, Virginia, Falwell said, "I know a few of you here today don't like Jews. And I know why. He can make more money accidentally than you can on purpose." In that very talk, however, Falwell added, "I want to stand with the Jews. If that's where God blesses, I want to stand close."

The Moral Majority has placed full-page newspaper ads across the country asserting that "one cannot belong to Moral Majority, Inc. without making the commitment to support the state of Israel and to support the human and civil rights of Jewish people everywhere. No anti-Semitic influence is allowed in Moral Majority, Inc."

There are those, myself included, who view many of the hostile statements which express negative stereotypical attitudes towards Jews as inadvertant, and reflective of the Right's cultural naivete. The Right has a lack of awareness of the historical abuse of such canards and of Jewish sensitivities to them. Others view them as expressions of the duplicitious and/or anti-Semitic character of the Evangelical Right.

At a time when many liberal Christian groups have been unduly critical of Israel, Evangelicals remain among its staunchest, most ardent, and vocal Christian supporters. Much of the theological underpinning for this support is derived from the biblical promise that God would bless those who bless Israel and curse those who curse her. Another theological rationale is that the rise of the state of Israel, as well as other events transpiring in the Middle East, are viewed as the fulfillment of biblical prophecies. Sometimes even trivial events in the Middle East are interpreted as signs of the imminent return of Jesus, the battle of Armageddon, rapture, the period of tribulation, and the ultimate conversion of the Jews. (Evangelicals differ on the precise order in which these events are to take place.)

Many Evangelical Right supporters of Israel insist that their commitment to Israel and the Jewish people is also based on humanitarian considerations. Thus, the previously cited newspaper ad spelling out the Moral Majority's basic conviction also states, "Many Moral Majority, Inc. members, because of their theological convictions, are committed to the Jewish people. Others stand upon the human and civil rights of all persons as a premise for the support of the State of Israel. Others support Israel because of historical and legal arguments. Regardless, one cannot belong to Moral Majority, Inc. without making the commitment to support the State of Israel in its battle for survival . . ." Similarly, in his interview with *Christianity Today* (September 4, 1981) Falwell said, "I also support the Jews because I think, historically, the evidence is on their side that Palestine belongs to them. Legally, they have had the right to be in the land since 1948. I also support the Jews because from the humanitarian perspective, they have the right to exist, and there are a hundred million neighbors who are committed to their extinction. I also support the Jews because they are the only friends America has in the Middle East."

Today the Evangelical Right includes the most politically active of pro-Israel Evangelical groups. It shows its support through Holy Land tourism, promotion of Israel's cause on television, and through letter writing and telegram campaigns. The potential for building even more pro-Israel humanitarian, moral, and political involvement among this segment of Evangelicals is extremely great.

However, in the AWACS campaign, arguably one of the most significant battles the Jewish community has had with the Reagan administration, the Evangelical representatives and senators all voted with the president, against the interests of Israel. While the Congressman insisted that their votes were cast in support of the president, not against Israel, the fact remains that in this crucial instance the traditional Democratic alliance of labor, liberals, and blacks proved to be the more reliable. Individuals such as Falwell lobbied against the sale — but how hard they lobbied is arguable. Such incidents set back those Jews who argued for pursuing a new alliance with the Christian Right, even at the expense of the old Jewish-liberal coalitions.

Despite the fact that the Moral Majority and some other segments of the Christian Right have no formal "hit list," the causes they espouse and the allies they attract have, at times, adversely affected congressional support of Israel. In 1980, for example, the New Right played a significant role in turning out of office Senators Frank Church (former chairman of Senate Foreign Relations Committee), Dick Clark, and Birch Bayh. Church, Clark, and Bayh had strong pro-Israel records.

It appears that while the Evangelical Right may in fact be genuinely pro-Israel, when it comes to electoral politics the Right tends to apply its muscle to social, family, and religion-oriented issues almost to the exclusion of Israel-related ones.

Along with many Americans, Jews are deeply concerned with the Evangelical Right's attempt to "Christianize America." Until recently, a leading representative of the Moral Majority spoke on a number of occasions of the desire to establish a "Christian Republic" and a "Christian Bill of Rights." When challenged, however, they generally claim that they do not seek to establish a theocracy, to erode personal liberties, or to promote "Christian-only" government officials or political candidates. Rather, they wish to redress what they consider to be the moral decline in America. The Moral Majority, in its own words, seeks "to serve as a special interest group providing a voice for a return to moral sanity in these United States of America." It is anti-drugs, anti-pornography, anti-abortion, anti-ERA and certain homosexual rights, and it strongly supports voluntary school prayer and greater defense budgets. It insists that those sharing these and other common concerns — be they Catholic, Jewish, Protestant, or Mormon — are welcome in the movement.

Furthermore, the Moral Majority claims that it does not have a "hit list" of candidates disagreeing with its policies; that it is committed to pluralism; that it desires to influence, not control, government; that it does not wish to deprive women or homosexuals of their civil rights; that it does "not believe that individuals or organizations which disagree with the Moral Majority, Inc. belong to an immoral minority." However, these summaries of Moral Majority positions sometimes contradict other statements emanating from Moral Majority representatives. The spokesmen often attempt to hold on to both sides of an issue without alienating people on either side and without violating the organization's tax exempt status. At times this has been most difficult.

There are other vocal Fundamentalist groups to the right of the Moral Majority which actively try to censor certain school and library books, deprive homosexuals of their constitutional rights, alter the constitution, or bypass the Supreme Court in light of their positions on various social and political issues. The Moral Majority, on the other hand, gives assurances that it does not seek to abrogate or curtail constitutional rights, nor to ban nor censor books, but that its members are well within their own constitutional rights to use all legal means to press through causes they believe in.

The Electronic Church

In recent years there has been a boom in religious broadcasting, which is a key ingredient of the Evangelical Right's program. The "electronic church," a term coined by Reverend Ben Armstrong, director of the National Religious Broadcasters, comprises some 1700 religious radio stations, 50 television channels devoted to religious programming, and over 1000 programs distributed to secular stations. Richard Hirsch, secretary of communications for the U.S. Catholic Conference, described the electronic church as "primarily Evangelical Christian in orientation, personality-centered and self-supported by contributions from listeners and viewers."

For years, most of the networks restricted their free-time programming allotment to mainline Jewish and Christian organizations, leaving Evangelicals with the sole option of purchasing air time — which many did. As a result of their early recognition of television's value as a communications tool, Evangelicals now dominate the "electronic church." Estimates of the percentage of Americans who watch or listen to at least one religious program a week run as high as 50%, but the actual number of regular viewers is approximately 13.6 million, or 6.2% of those households with televisions. Indeed, a 1985 Nielson study found that 40.3% of American households with TVs regularly watched at least one Christian TV show, rivalling the audience for the popular TV series "Dynasty".

Dr. William Martin of Rice University, a recognized authority on the electronic church, reports on surveys (*The Atlantic*, June 1981) indicating that audience estimates for major Christian shows are highly inflated. Martin, along with Jeffrey Hadden and Charles Swann, wrote in "Prime Time Preachers: The Rising Power of Televangelism," that not only is the viewing audience much smaller than previously assumed, but it is declining and the funds are drying up. Electronic church personalities would dispute these figures and claims.

Who are the most important electronic evangelists?

1) *Jimmy Swaggart*, based in Louisiana, has perhaps the largest viewership of all TV preachers. He is intensely charismatic, stressing faith healing. He has also been known to make some rather derogatory remarks about Catholics at times.

2) *Pat Robertson* is the host of the "700 Club" based in Virginia, and is the force behind the Christian Broadcasting Network (CBN), a twenty-four hour service which offers religious programming to cable systems. Robertson is credited with bringing the electronic church to prime-time, and anticipating the potential of TV's new technologies. He is widely regarded as one of the most culturally sophisticated of the electronic church preachers, having received his law degree at Yale and been greatly influenced by his father, who was a U.S. senator. Like most other TV evangelists, Robertson is an ardent supporter of Israel. At the time of this writing, he is strongly considering running for the office of president of the United States, a feat that, while remote, is not nearly as implausible as most people believe.

3) *Robert Schuller*, California based, is famous for his Crystal Cathedral, which has two 90-foot, electronically controlled doors which open to allow drive-in churchgoers. His basic message of positive thinking and his overall moderate stance have brought him a large following in the mainline Christian community as well.

4) *Rex Humbard*, based in Akron, Ohio. One of the few with a northern base, Humbard's is the earliest established television ministry.

5) *Oral Roberts*, based in Tulsa, Oklahoma, where he has built his

own university and hospital.

6) *Jerry Falwell*, of Virginia, is host of the "Old Time Gospel Hour," and is the evangelical most identified with conservative political activities.

Evangelicals and the Political Process

Evangelical attitudes towards politics and other public policy issues are influenced by the fundamental question of the proper role of the Church in this country. There are two commonly held opinions on this matter.

1) The Church is *in* but not *of* this world. Therefore, it is appropriate for Christians to criticize, support, and even lobby governmental institutions and authorities on behalf of Christian values and ideals, but they should avoid becoming part of the political establishment. For this same reason, Pope John Paul ordered Father Drinan and others to leave their political posts, since they were too closely identified with the powers-that-be.

Those sharing this first outlook are inclined to oppose such groups as the Moral Majority, which they view as being too closely related to power structures of this world. They also oppose liberal groups such as the National Council of Churches, for the same reasons.

2) The Church is *in and of* this world. The Christian is therefore obliged to become part of the system, if necessary, in order to change it for the better. He must be prepared to choose specific worldly means, instruments, and philosophies in order to achieve specific Christian goals. Liberation theology, a popular worldview especially in the Third World, suggests that Christianity must actively pursue the liberation of the oppressed, as the biblical Exodus motif has taught.

This question of the role of the Church vis-á-vis politics and the governing authorities is especially important for Catholics in Latin America. The pope has taken a moderate, balanced position by lending conditional support to liberation theology, provided that it not become too closely aligned with the existing powers, or "Caesar's world."

It would be hard to find a consensus among Evangelicals on the question of what the proper relationship between the Church and society should be. Sectors of the Evangelical Right come very close to

identifying capitalism as "God's way," while many on the Evangelical
Left seem to promote some form of socialism as the divine will.

Whatever the theological framework of their political involvements,
Evangelicals have clearly become more deeply involved in lobbying
and political action for candidates and values expressing their religious
positions. While they have a significant impact on public policy,
however, Evangelical political clout can be exaggerated. In the March
1981 issue of *Commentary*, Seymour Martin Lipset and Earl Raab assert
that "the electoral swing towards conservatism and the emergence of
the political Evangelical movement were *parallel* developments which
may have been mutually reinforcing rather than related to one another
as cause and effect...The political Evangelical groups...did not
create the Republican landslide (of 1980). Rather, it reflected the country's conservative political swing, which occurred among all groups—
and more, as we have seen, among non-Evangelicals than among
born-agains." In other words, resurgence of conservatism in America
and the rise of the *political* right, may have very little or nothing at all
to do with the rise of the Evangelical movement, notwithstanding the
Moral Majority.

The Gallup Poll found no differences between Evangelicals and
non-Evangelicals on key issues such as nuclear power, capital punishment, and domestic government spending, though Gallup did find that
Evangelicals were nearly five times as likely as non-Evangelicals to
regard "decline in morals" as one of the most important problems facing our nation. The differences between Evangelicals and non-Evangelicals lie primarily in areas relating to personal behavior such as
homosexuality, abortion, prayer in public schools, and the like—but
Evangelicals are not unanimous even on these issues.

Jewish Responses to Evangelicals

There remains a good deal of confusion among Jews about
Evangelicals. Of course, lack of understanding is not limited to the
Jewish community. Due to demographic, sociological, and theological
factors, and because of deep-seated fears harbored especially by
European-born Jews toward the more devout Christians, Evangelicals
remain largely misunderstood by Jews, and Evangelical motives for

supporting Israel are perceived as unclear and suspect. And while friendly, frank, and meaningful dialogue conferences, as well as other cooperative programs, have recently developed between Jews and Evangelicals, the relationship must still be described as in its incipient stages. One thing remains abundantly clear — Jews are anything but dispassionate on the subject of Evangelicals, and on the Moral Majority and "Evangelical Right" in particular.

Many Jews oppose cooperating with Evangelicals, particularly the Evangelical Right, which they view as a threat to Jewish interests. Rabbi Alexander Schindler, president of the Union of the American Hebrew Congregations (Reform) and past president of the Conference of Presidents of Major American Jewish organizations, has written, for example, that "the Moral Majority and those other religious and political organizations with which they are in coalition reveal themselves to be a threat to American democracy, to America's Jews and therefore, also to Israel."

While Schindler did not accuse Falwell outright of being anti-Semitic, he insisted that Falwell's "exclusivist emphasis on a Christian America and the tools he chooses to build it . . .create a climate of opinion which is hostile to religious tolerance. . . Such a climate is bad for civil liberties, human rights, social justice, interfaith understanding and mutual respect among Americans. Therefore, it is bad for Jews."

Echoing Schindler's feelings, Albert Vorspan, director of the Commission on Social Action of Reform Judaism, castigated "those Jews willing to embrace the Moral Majority because it is strong on Israel" when, in fact, it "cannibalizes American politics, fosters division and exclusivity and promotes reactionary causes."

The American Jewish Congress denounced the Moral Majority outright in a policy statement. While acknowledging the Moral Majority's support for Israel, the AJC statement condemned it for "using religion as an instrument for political coercion" and pledged "to oppose the movement on many of its domestic policies and practices."

On the other hand, Jewish advocates of the alliance with the Evangelical Right can be found among the Orthodox, who are similarly concerned with what they perceive to be the moral deterioration of society. Some right-wing Orthodox Jews likewise seek to redress this climate by supporting legislation promoting school prayer, and opposing ERA, drugs, and abortions.

For example, right-wing Orthodox Rabbi Abraham Hecht, president of the Rabbinic Alliance, is an advocate of much of the Moral Majority agenda. He once characterized the leaders of the Moral Majority as "men of integrity, sharing many traditional beliefs of the Jewish people. . .values which have long ago been rejected out of hand by Schindler and his ilk." Hecht denounced as "false and absolutely without foundation" Schindler's accusations that the Moral Majority fosters anti-Semitism. He also stated that, "As one who has met and cooperated with the Moral Majority, I can safely state the ominous threats created by Schindler's fantasy are totally unfounded and without proof."

Zionist organizations and leaders have also treated the Moral Majority, and other groups on the Evangelical Right, quite favorably. Some Zionist organizations tend to put aside Evangelicals' theological motives for supporting Israel and their positions on civil liberties, and instead confine their relationship solely to practical matters benefitting Israel. In a widely publicized and controversial gesture, former Prime Minister Begin bestowed the Jabotinsky award on Jerry Falwell. While this act shocked many liberal Jews, it must be acknowledged that Falwell and others on the Evangelical Right have been outspoken in their support for Israel. At times, the Christian Right sounds more hawkish than even many Jews, as when they insist that Jerusalem, the Golan Heights, and all of Judea and Samaria should be annexed to Israel. Zionist groups have by and large committed themselves to working closely with this segment of the Christian community, which they perceive as Israel's best friend in the Christian community today.

Conclusion

The Evangelical Right's aggressive involvement in political affairs on behalf of ultra-conservative causes has been deeply disquieting for most Jews. While appreciating the Evangelical support for Israel, many Jews are uneasy about being intimately involved in another community's worldview and divine eschatalogical plan for salvation. They also suspect that the Evangelical support for Israel may be part of a ploy to convert the Jews. Moreover, they fear that the eventual failure of the Jews to convert en masse could be viewed as the principle factor delaying Jesus' Second Coming, causing Jews to be seen as obstructing the final redemption of the world. In short, a large number of Jews fear that the relationship could backfire, and that Evangelicals could come to resent Jews when they find that their love for the Jewish people and strong support for Israel has not converted the Jews to Christianity. Many scholars believe that this dynamic also prompted Martin Luther and Mohammed to initially love, and subsequently despise, the Jews.

Still other Jews are convinced that at a certain point Evangelicals will "call their chips in" and ask Jews to support various ultra-conservative social and political causes as a quid pro quo for their support of Israel. If and when they find this support not forthcoming, the likelihood of a falling-out between the two communities will be increased. There are also many Jews who believe that the Evangelicals treat Israel as an expendable instrument of God, and would be inclined to passively accept Israel's destruction and the Jew's suffering, reinterpreting them as part of God's will and divine plan, rather than actively defending Israel in what may be Armageddon.

Jewish dialogue with mainstream Evangelicals, however, has already produced some gratifying results. As the dialogue with the Evangelical Right matures, it is hoped that they, too, will become more sensitive to Jewish concerns for pluralism and civil liberties. With increased contact, many Jewish apprehensions about Evangelicals can be alleviated. As the relationship between these two great faith communities evolves, and they pursue a course of dialogue with one another, they will learn that many of their shared anxieties were either unfounded in the first place or can be addressed without rancor or fear.

In the long term, the key to a healthy relationship is realism of expectations. Evangelicals and Jews will perforce come to the recognition that while they may share much in common, in fact their central convictions clash. The principal conviction shaping the backbone of Evangelical identity is world evangelism, to proclaim the gospel of Jesus Christ to all people, including Jews. The central force guiding Jewish life today, especially in the aftermath of the holocaust, is to survive as Jews. This clash does not necessarily mean, however, that Evangelical-Jewish relations are ultimately doomed to failure. It is possible to build a modus vivendi despite the conflict between the two communities' core self-definitions.

To sustain any kind of positive relationship, both will have to engage in a "give and take" process, affirming their central commissions, albeit in the way that is least objectional to the other. Jews will acknowledge that in a democratic country such as America, people have the right to preach as they believe, while others have the right to ignore them and disregard their remarks. Jews must also become more aware of the centrality of mission for many Christians, and more sensitive to the fact that they regard it as their duty to fulfill that mandate. On the other hand, various Christian thinkers have argued that Christianity is an additional divine covenant, or an opening-up— not a suppression, of the Jewish covenant. It follows that Jews are not in *need* of adopting Christianity to achieve fulfillment and salvation. Jews will, undoubtedly, bid Evangelicals adopt some form of this double-covenant theory with them as many liberal Protestants and Catholics have. Jews will ask Christians to refrain from missionary efforts towards them "until the full number of Gentiles enter in" (Romans 11:25). Should this prove to be too theologically difficult, Jews will request that Evangelicals regard dialogue as the proper forum in which to "preach the gospel" to them, and abandon the zealous and even cult-like techniques often employed in attempts to convert them.

In truth, it is the Christian's commission *to testify* through words and deeds to the truth of the Christian message, while it is God's prerogative *to act* upon the individual through the Holy Spirit and possibly bring about his conversion. It is reasonable, therefore, for Jews to demand that Evangelicals fulfill their missionary commission decently and courteously, through dialogue, by model, teaching, and joint cooperation, without the insistence on converting them. Certainly, Jews will ask responsible Evangelicals to be especially alert to evangelizing efforts that involve any sort of manipulation, deception, or excessively aggressive tactics, and to refrain from giving moral and financial support to the many Hebrew-Christian para-church groups that target Jews for conversion.

Despite the many ambivalences and anxieties Jews harbor towards Evangelicals, the relationship is an important one to both communities. The dialogue that has evolved is in the process of maturing and is already beginning to bear fruit. While there remain many areas in need of further joint exploration, and others upon which there is irreconcilable disagreement, there is certainly a greater spirit of cooperation, understanding, appreciation, and respect evident among members of both communities toward each other today than there was just a few years ago.

On a More Personal Note

Over the past nine years, I have been fortunate to have had the opportunity to work with and befriend Evangelical religious leaders and lay people from various parts of the ideological spectrum. I also had occasion to spend two weeks in Israel with a number of leading conservative Southern Baptist ministers, including Reverend Bailey Smith, then president of the Southern Baptist Convention. His widely publicized remark that God does not hear the prayer of Jews brought the entire issue of Evangelical-Jewish dialogue into question and overall disrepute.

To my pleasant surprise, I found that while I have remained unalterably opposed to the theological intolerance of much of the Evangelical Far Right, many of my other preconceptions were totally unfounded. Bailey Smith, for example, is a warm and sensitive individual who was deeply hurt by the entire episode and who, in my estimation, is a genuine friend of Israel *and* of the Jewish people. While he may still maintain that God does not answer the prayers of those who do not call out to him through Jesus, including the Jews, I believe him when he says he would "go to the death for the right of the Jews to pray as they wish." While he and most Evangelicals no doubt hope for ultimate Jewish acceptance of Christianity, their frequent portrayal in the Jewish community as anti-Semites is, in my estimation, inaccurate and unfair. The same is true of the many Centrist Evangelicals who often are asociated with the Fundamentalists on the Right. There are enough *real* anti-Semites around for Jews to fight. The Holy Land Fellowship of Christians and Jews, which I head, is actually designed to address this issue. Included among its central objectives is the goal of bringing about better Christian understanding and support of Jews, Judaism, and Israel. The Jewish community should also seek to facilitate a better Jewish understanding of the Christian community, particularly its conservative wing, and a deeper awareness of its diversity and poten-

tial for cooperation with Jews on a variety of mutually beneficial concerns, especially Israel. Jews need not create false enemies by lump-
ing all Evangelicals together in one mass stereotype of evil intent.

While many Jews are troubled by the emergence of the
Evangelical Right, and in certain instances legitimately so, it must be
acknowledged that Christians have successfully highlighted some of
the key moral issues facing American society today. At the root of their
"success" lies the deep disenchantment many Americans feel toward
governmental, religious, and cultural institutions.

Some Christians and Jews in the (liberal) mainstream are suffering from a crisis of faith, having rejected fundamentalism and ex-
tremism of all kinds, but still lacking a spiritual center to their lives.
Many of those who call themselves believers in God have effectually
become secular and materialistic; their religious mores have become
civil, urbane, compartmentalized, and personalized, while their
tolerance for other viewpoints has often led to apathy and relativism
for their own.

The Moral Majority, and other Fundamentalist groups, are clearly
addressing the concerns of many Americans. They have brought into
focus issues which the mainline groups have either neglected or not
been able to fully resolve. They have credibly diagnosed aspects of the
American condition and tried to capitalize on the widespread mood of
insecurity and frustration over society's moral decay. We have, in fact,
become dangerously vulnerable to demagogues and platforms profess-
ing return to the nostalgic past. Addressing the issues and learning
from the responsible Evangelicals could protect against excesses. Some
of the vehemence of Jewish reaction reflects a certain discomfort at
the discovery of a values crisis within.

Church historian Martin Marty has noted that the religious problem of our age is that the tolerant often lack commitment and the committed often lack tolerance. This is true. I sometimes wonder, however,
whether much of the vociferous Jewish opposition to Evangelicals
stems not only from the fear of the unknown but from feelings of insecurity within Jewishness, not only from the anxiety over the imposition
of Christianity in society but from fear lest society be undergirded
with religious values of any kind. Some Jews camouflage their disdain
for transcendence and religion in absolutist interpretations of the First
Amendment, which calls for the separation of church and state.

The issue of rethinking Jewish attitudes on the church-state issues would take a monograph unto itself—and much more. All Jews have a legitimate concern that a good purpose, i.e., inserting religious values into American life, not end up as asserting Christian values, thus excluding the views and violating the conscience of non-believers. But absolutist approaches to the separation issue can mask aggressive secularism. Triumphalist secular values—as in the Soviet Union—have often been just as inimical to Jewish rights as has the aggressive imposition of religious values. One might conclude that a balance of power between secularism and religion creates the best setting for Jewish safety and creative survival. Hopefully, the Religious Right of Christianity will respect this balance as much as we Jews.

Jews and Judaism in the Catholic Lectionary

by Mark S. Smith

The understanding of Jews by non-Jews is a problem that extends to many Christian denominations. In the previous article, Rabbi Yechiel Eckstein describes the complex issues involved in building understanding between American Judaism and the Evangelical Right within American Protestantism. Similarly, American Catholicism has been engaged in constructive dialogue with Judaism over the last twenty years. One area within Roman Catholicism that deserves further examination in its attitudes towards Jews and Judaism is the Roman Catholic Sunday lectionary, the book prescribing the scriptual texts to be read in the Sunday liturgy.

Dr. Eugene Fisher[1] recently asked me to examine how the Roman Catholic lectionary's juxtapositions of Old Testament passages with New Testament readings affect Roman Catholic perceptions of Jews and Judaism. The task was not to critique isolated texts from the New Testament. Rather it was to observe how juxtapositions of Old and New Testament passages may function in developing Catholics' understanding of Jews and Judaism. What messages do the lectionary's readings convey about the relationship of Christianity and Judaism? This essay is a report on the Sunday readings for the three-year cycle of the Roman Catholic lectionary.

By and large the lectionary exhibits the discretion of its authors, the Consilium for the Implementation of the Constitution on the Sacred

Liturgy.[2] It contains selections from all major portions of Scripture. For this the Consilium is to be thanked, and the following analysis is in no way intended to detract from the achievement which the lectionary represents. It does nonetheless contain particular juxtapositions of Old and New Testament readings which reflect poorly on Catholic understanding of Jews and Judaism.

I.   The Jews

The first category in need of analysis consists of those juxtapositions which implicitly make negative statements about Jews as a group. More specifically, particular Sunday selections, merely by uniting Old and New Testament passages, unnecessarily depict Jews as a class of persons utterly lacking in spiritual vitality. These particular examples suggest that "the Jews" in general are "stiff-necked sinners" who rejected God's plan of salvation in Old and New Testament times (and by implication, in the present time as well). Five cases from the lectionary illustrate how this message is conveyed.

The worst depiction of Jews as a class of sinners and prophet-killers comes from the fourth Sunday of Lent of Year B. The Old Testament reading is 2 Chronicles 36:15-17, 19-23. The passage reviews the history of Israel: "All the princes of Judah, the priests and the people added infidelity to infidelity, practicing all the abominations of the nations and polluting the Lord's temple which he had consecrated in Jerusalem." The passage also tells how the people of the Lord mocked God's messengers until God's wrath was inflamed beyond remedy. John 3:14-21, the gospel of the day, tells its audience that "Whoever believes in him avoids condemnation, but whoever does not believe is already condemned for not believing in the name of God's only Son." Together these two texts suggest that Jews as a group lack faith, while Christians generally and generously respond to God's ways, thanks to the efficacious work of Jesus. This particular juxtaposition of passages is unnecessary. The first text reflects a self-criticism of Jews by Jews, and should only be presented in this context. Unfortunately, the lectionary as a Christian document distorts the value of this passage as a sign of repentance by Jews. Originally an indication of Jews turning to the Lord, the passage in the lectionary instead functions to condemn the Jews for not turning to Jesus.

The readings for the third Sunday of Lent in Year A include Exodus 17:3-7, Romans 5:1-2, 5-8, and John 4:5-42 (optionally John 4:5-15, 19-26, 39, and 40-42). The passage from Exodus depicts the Jews quarreling with Moses in their sojourn through the wilderness. The Jews "grumbled against Moses" and "tested the Lord." The reading from Romans stresses that those who accept Jesus gain access to God. The gospel reading in both its shorter and longer forms states that Jesus is the Messiah. The overall messages of these three passages are (1) Jesus is the Messiah and the single means to everlasting life (John); (2) those who fail to believe in Jesus do not gain access to God (John and Romans); and (3) the Jews tested God in the wilderness. What emerges from this juxtaposition is the implication that, just as Jews as a group rejected God in the wilderness, they rejected God's only Son and therefore lack access to salvation. As a result of this set of readings, Roman Catholics could infer that Jews and Judaism as a whole are spiritually bankrupt.

More explicit in suggesting how the Jews always rejected God's purposes are the readings of the twenty-seventh Sunday of Ordinary Time in Year A. The Old Testament text is the parable of the vineyard in Isaiah 5:1-7. This parable explains how the vineyard (Israel and Judah) yielded poorly despite the strenuous efforts of its keeper (God). The gospel is Matthew 21:33-43, in which Jesus engages the chief priests and the elders of the people with another parable of a vineyard. Jesus tells his audience how Israel has rejected its God and refused God's purposes. He asks his audience if they have ever read: "The stone which the builders rejected had become the keystone of the structure." In both the Old and New Testaments, the Jews as a class seem to reject God's plan. The unfortunate but possible message is that all Jews reject God in all ages. This stereotype is cemented by the contrasting positive picture of Christian life in the day's reading from Philippians 4:6-9.

The last two Sunday readings which depict Jews in an overly negative fashion are Trinity Sunday of Year A and the twenty-fourth Sunday of Ordinary Time of Year C. Trinity Sunday of Year A contrasts the infidel Jews in the wilderness (Exodus 34:4-6, 8-9) with the salvation afforded only through Jesus (John 3:16-18). The gospel, overlapping exactly with that of the fourth Sunday of Lent of Year B (described above), condemns those who do not believe in Jesus. This, of course, indicts all Jews wholesale. The twenty-fourth Sunday of Ordinary Time of Year C likewise declares how "stiff-necked" the Jews were in Sinai. They were "depraved." The epistle, 1 Timothy 1:12-17, describes how Christians may come to eternal life. The gospel contrasts the mercy of Jesus with the very lack of mercy on the part of the Pharisees and scribes.

These five depictions of Jews as a class of God-rejectors deserve no place in the lectionary.[3] They help to form stereotypes about the Jews that are first and most importantly false. They are also damaging to Christians' understanding of their own origins. In its ongoing quest for self-understanding, the Church continually returns to its Lord and therefore Jesus' own Jewish heritage. The Old Testament contains many fine examples of the Jews' love and faithfulness to God. Besides the significant scholarly quest for Jesus and his Judaism,[4] the Church is slowly coming to grips with its own intrinsic bond to Judaism.

The Church's examination of its Jewish roots and its concomitant dialogue with Judaism requires the elimination of these five Sunday sets of readings from the lectionary. These readings not only impugn Jews and Judaism, they also impugn Christianity's spiritual heritage. Since they are only five in number, this remedy is all the more imperative.

The lectionary itself provides a positive model for correcting this flaw. The readings from Corpus Christi of Year B show the Israelites agreeing with one voice to do all the Lord has told them, and forming a covenant with the Lord (Exodus 24:3-8). This reading stands in healthy continuity to the gospel reading of the Last Supper (Mark 14:12-16, 22-26). The willing participation of the Israelites in the book of Exodus is echoed by the role of the disciples in the gospel. The covenant of the Exodus reading stands in relationship, albeit undefined,[5] to that of the Last Supper.[6] This selection of readings sends to its audience a spiritually valuable message: Christians' inclination toward God's covenant is learned from their Jewish forbears. This selection from the lectionary proves how inappropriate are the five selections which paint Jews so negatively as a group.

II. Universal Peace in Jesus' First Coming?

Another group of Sunday readings deserves comment since it affects the relationship of Judaism to Christianity, and also distorts the sense of the Old Testament passages themselves. The readings from the lectionary sometimes juxtapose an Old Testament reading which describes universal peace or the transformation of nature, with a gospel text which proclaims Jesus in a number of ways. The conveyed message is that Jesus and Christianity represent the fulfillment of universal peace or the transformation of nature. The problem, put simply, is that the first coming of Jesus did not produce a transformation of nature or a universal reign of peace, and as a result these juxtapositions of the lectionary perpetuate a falsehood.

For example, universal peace is foretold in the first reading (Isaiah 2:1-5) for the first Sunday of Advent in Year A. A reference to the Lord Jesus Christ in the epistle of the day, Romans 13:11-14, implies that Jesus is the agent of this universal peace. The second Sunday of Advent in Year A extends the message. The Old Testament reading, Isaiah 11:1-10, proclaims universal peace via the "shoot" from the "stump of Jesse." John the Baptist, in the gospel Matthew 3:1-12, heralds the coming of a figure "more powerful than I." The figure who fulfills both readings is, of course, Jesus — at least for Christian ears. The third Sunday of Advent in Year A adds the feature of transformation to the coming of God in the Old Testament selection.[7] The trend reaches its highpoint in the Christmas Vigil Mass, Christmas Midnight Mass, Christmas Mass at Dawn, Christmas Mass During the Day, and Epiphany. (The readings for these masses are the same for all three years of the lectionary.) The Christmas Vigil Mass juxtaposes the new and universal glory of Zion[8] with an account of Jesus' birth.[9] The Christmas Midnight Mass mentions a universal and eternally peaceful reign and attributes it to the messianic figure[10] in another account of Jesus' birth.[11] The Christmas Masses at Dawn and During the Day make comparable selections.[12] The readings for Epiphany likewise attribute to Jesus' first coming the universal glory of the Lord.[13]

Combining such Old Testament passages, which proclaim universal peace and transformation of nature, with readings about Jesus' first coming, conveys the message that it was Jesus who ushered in these conditions. In Advent and Christmas, Christians all understand that Jesus fulfills and brings to pass universal peace. In a qualified sense, a Christian may discern the peace of the Christian life, and assert its universality by virtue of Christianity's presence throughout the world. This, however, quite belies the Old Testament passages themselves. The Old Testament texts portend an era of externally manifest peace. All persons shall see this come to pass. Jesus' first coming, however, has not brought this condition into being; war and hatred of all stripes are still very much unredeemed. Jesus and Christianity have not in fact produced the messianic age. (This, of course, is a very old Jewish objection to Christian claims about Jesus.)

The fundamental problem lies in the disparity between the Old Testament passages regarding the Messiah and the messianic age versus the early Church's new understanding of them, thanks to its experience of Jesus. The Christian interpretation of Jesus relies on two types of Old Testament passages: those about the Messiah and the messianic age, and those regarding the Suffering Servant. While the early Church applied both types to Jesus' first coming, the early Church also understood that the full manifestation of Jesus' identity and the transformation of the world would not transpire until his manifestation in glory (called the *parousia* in the New Testament). The Jewish tradition has not included in its understanding of the Messiah and the messianic age any reference to the Suffering Servant. The Jewish and Christian traditions, therefore, hold different views of the Messiah. More importantly, the Old Testament does not know this Christian interpretation (and reinterpretation). Similarly, no single Old Testament passage includes the basis for the Christian interpretation, since by definition the Christian interpretation requires more than one Old Testament text.

Therefore the interpretation of Jesus according to the second category of readings misinterprets Jesus insofar as his first coming did not produce universal peace. This category asserts what is historically false. Moreover, it robs the Church today of one of the attitudes prominent in the early Church, namely a posture of eager waiting for the Lord. Finally, it steals from Jews and Christians as a single group one of the shared elements of faith. Both Judaism and Christianity await the coming of the Messiah. Therefore the modern Church should be glad to imitate the early Church, which longed eagerly for the historical return of the Lord. By so doing, it would restore its historical credibility and remove an undesirable and unnecessary barrier to healthier relations with Judaism.

The Church might follow suit by re-examining and perhas modifying the Sunday readings which attribute the achievement of universal peace or the transformation of nature to the first coming of Jesus. Here again the lectionary provides a positive model for consideration. The readings for the first Sunday of Advent in Year C show the continuity of Jewish longing for the "just shoot" of David in Jeremiah 33: 14-16 with the early Church's yearning for the coming of the son of man in Luke 21:25-28, 34-36.[14]

III.   Prophecies About Jesus?

Just as the second category of selections equates Jesus with the Davidic Messiah, so the third category of readings connects Jesus with other figures or prominent aspects of Old Testament "prophecies." Strictly speaking, these attributions are a matter of Christian interpretation, not subject to rejection on historical grounds. The lectionary, for example, interprets Jesus as the Suffering Servant.[15] The lectionary by implication designates Jesus as the prophet promised by Moses [16] and the prophet predicted in Malachi.[17] Jesus is the son of man (the thirty-fourth Sunday of Ordinary Time in Year B). The traditional proto-evangelium of Genesis 3:9-15 also finds its way into the lectionary.[18] The covenant of Jeremiah 31:31-34 is fulfilled in Jesus,[19] and Jesus and the early Church represent the return of the Spirit.[20] The Church treasures these readings. Some of them rightly instruct Catholics to follow the example of Jesus as the humble Suffering Servant, while others offer Catholics a glimpse of God's intimate love for them.

Nonetheless a hidden danger lies in these readings. In conjunction with the lectionary selections of the first and second categories, those of the third category convey the message that Jesus' first coming and the early Church have brought to fulfillment all things promised in the Old Testament. The difficulty is the implication that Christianity completely fulfills Old Testament religion and that Judaism is exhausted by Christianity. While these juxtapositions will not necessarily be misinterpreted in this way (and indeed Christians should hope that they would not be), the fact that they could be so misconstrued is enough reason to re-examine them. Furthermore, the lectionary does not sufficiently counterbalance the impression that Jesus' first coming and the Church constitute the end-all of the Old Testament. On the contrary, Judaism has a wealthy spirituality and liturgical life which Christians would do well to explore.

It is necessary, therefore, to eradicate the juxtapositions of the first category. The selections of the second and third categories should also be reconsidered. A reduction in their number is a potential solution, since it would lessen the impact on Catholics without evacuating the Church's core faith in Jesus as the Messiah. This reexamination is necessary for a deeper understanding of early Christian tradition, historical credibility, healthier links with Judaism and our Jewish sisters and brothers, and, most importantly, our faithfulness to our God.

Endnotes

1. Dr. Fisher is the Executive Director of the Secretariat for Catholic-Jewish Relations of the National Catholic Conference of Bishops in the United States. I wish to thank him and Professors Gerald J. Sloyan and Mary Charles Bryce for reading this text and offering helpful comments.

2. *The Roman Missal, Lectionary for Mass* (New York: Catholic Book Publishing Co., 1970).

3. One might add to these five examples a sixth one, namely the fourteenth Sunday of Ordinary Time in Year B (Exodus 2:2-5 and Mark 6:1-6).

4. For a helpful treatment, see John T. Pawlikowski, *Christ in the Light of the Christian-Jewish Dialogue* (New York: Paulist Press, 1982), 76-135.

5. The epistle for the day, Hebrews 9:11-15, weakens the value of this example, for it does intend that Jesus is the fulfillment and transformer of Jewish priestly practices.

6. A Christian audience might be inclined to interpret that the Christian covenant fulfills and replaces the Jewish covenant.

7. Isaiah 35:1-6, 10.

8. Isaiah 62:1-5.

9. Matthew 1:1-35 or 1:18-25.

10. Isaiah 9:1-6.

11. Luke 2:1-14.

12. Isaiah 62:11-12 with Luke 2:15-20 and Isaiah 52:7-10 with John 1:1-18 (optionally John 1:1-5, 9-14).

13. Isaiah 60:1-16.

14. Passages that should therefore be reconsidered are: Year A: the fourth Sunday of Advent, the fourteenth and twenty-eighth Sundays of Ordinary Time; Year B: the second, third, fourth Sundays of Advent, the eleventh, twenty-third and thirty-fourth Sundays of Ordinary Time; and Year C: the second and fourth Sundays of Advent, the fifth Sunday of Lent, the second, fourteenth, twenty-first and thirty-fourth Sundays of Ordinary Time.

15. Years A, B, and C: Baptism of the Lord and Passion Sunday; Year A: the second Sunday of Ordinary Time; Year B: the twenty-fourth Sunday of Ordinary Time.

16. Year B: fourth Sunday of Ordinary Time.

17. Year C: the thirty-third Sunday of Ordinary Time.

18. Year B: the tenth Sunday of Ordinary Time.

19. Year B: the fifth Sunday of Lent.

20. Years A, B, and C: Mass of the Lord's Supper on Holy Thursday.

Law and Story in Judaism and Christianity

by Marc A. Gellman

Mark Smith has provided us with an excellent account of how the stories of the Hebrew Bible can be used to endorse theological concepts quite foreign to their origins. This process of using biblical texts for homiletical purposes is called *midrash* in Hebrew, and it is a rabbinic invention which created constantly new meanings for ancient texts. I would now like to pursue this tradition of midrash so as to shed light on the universal challenge of any living tradition, to wit, the use and development of laws and stories as a central dynamic force for creativity and innovation in the holy community.

I bring for recognition and elucidation two categories of Jewish life and literature which are, I believe, categories in the life and literature of all peoples. As to our present concern, they are uniquely important categories for the understanding of the state of Jewish-Christian dialogue in our time.

In Jewish tradition, these two categories are called by the Jewish tradition, *halacha* and *aggada*. *Halacha* means law. *Aggada* means story. The dialectic of law and story, of *halacha* and *aggada*, is arguably the most definitive and dynamic dialectic in the entire Jewish experience. All Jewish literature is identified as either halachic or aggadic in nature. Indeed, the most practical definition of *aggada* is, "anything which is not *halacha*".[1] *Halacha* is derived from the Hebrew verb *halach* meaning, "to walk," and *aggada* is derived from the Hebrew verb *hagid* meaning, "to tell". *Halacha* — the way one walks — is the path, the way, the code of proper conduct. *Aggada* — the way one talks — is a story which connotes, inspires, explains, amuses, or chastizes, but never commands. As a collective noun, *halacha* refers to the corpus of Jewish legal literature as preserved in the Hebrew Bible and Talmud, and the rabbinic commentarial tradition up to our own time. The *aggada* is the corpus of Jewish stories preserved in that very same literary tradition, beginning with the Hebrew Bible and continuing in an unbroken chain until today. In such a literary religious tradition in which the sacred scriptures yield both halachic and aggadic materials, it is no surprise that the Jewish masters of *halacha* and the Jewish masters of *aggada* were often the same people. Yet the categories of law and story, though often mastered by the same rabbis, were never confused or conflated. Thus the rabbinic dictum: "one must never derive a law from a story".[2] Indeed *halachot* were derived by very strict juridical hermeneutics while *aggadot* did not require such scrupulous adherence to authoritative exegetical rules.

Thus Jewish laws were very carefully codified, topically indexed, and well preserved from Maimonides' first code in the twelfth century to Joseph Karo's last approved code in the sixteenth.[3] Jewish stories, however, were never systematically collected or organized until the *Wissenschaft des Judentum* movement of liberal German Jews such as Leopold Zunz, H. Albeck, and Teodor and Wilhelm Bacher. Their battle with the halachic orientation of Orthodox Judaism was the cause for their often exaggerated emphasis on the aggadic elements in the Jewish tradition, which had been so long deprecated in comparison to the legal elements. The birth of Reform Judaism in Europe was in large measure a movement of aggadic reclamation. The inspirational, aphoristic sweep of aggada was better suited to the secular bourgeois spirit of the times than were the starkly particularistic and categorical commandments of the halacha. As we shall observe later, this conflict between a halachic and an aggadic *Tendenz* by no means originated in the nineteenth century. The dialect of law and story is central for an understanding of every nodal point in Jewish life and literature.

A man of enormous religious and literary sensitivity and scope was at the center of the halacha / aggada conflict precipitated by the rediscovery of aggada by nineteenth-century German Reform Jews. His name was Hayim Nahman Bialik. His essay — *Halacha V'aggada* — is the single most insightful elucidation of the law and story dialectic in Jewish experience.[4] Indeed the essay forms the basis for understanding the general phenomenology of law and story in any living religious tradition.

Bialik maintains that halacha and aggada are two indissolubly linked aspects of the life and literature of Judaism. They are complementary, symbiotic, and antagonistic in different respects. He is far from minimizing the truly opposite characteristics of law and story, as is evidenced by his opening words:

> Halacha wears an angry frown; Aggada a broad smile. The one is the embodiment of the Attribute of Justice, iron-handed, rigorous and severe; the other is the embodiment of the Quality of Mercy, essentially lenient and indulgent, as mild as a dove. The one promulgated coercive decrees and knows no compromise; the other, presumes only to suggest and is sympathetically aware of man's shortcomings; she is indecisive and weak willed. Halacha represents the body, the actual deed; Aggada represents the soul, the content, the fervent motive. Halacha enjoins a dogged adherence and imposes upon us stern obligations; Aggada, on the other hand, holds out the prospect of continual rejuvenescence, liberty and freedom.

Despite the fundamental differences between halacha and aggada, Bialik constantly stressed their irrefrangible unity:

> They are to each other what the word is to the thought; what the deed is to the concept. Halacha is the crystallization, the necessary and ultimate consummation of the Aggada; Aggada is the real content, as well as the soul of Halacha . . . A living Halacha is the embodiment of an Aggada of the past and the seed of the future, and so conversely; for the beginning and the end of these two are indissolubly joined and linked with each other.[5]

Thus for Bialik, law and story, though informed by different realms of human consciousness, are both essential elements in the dialectical unity which is the Jewish tradition. Halacha represents the rational, pragmatic impulse in the Jewish tradition; the impulse for a clear and binding code of life which is fixed and enduring, revealing God's steadfastness and rectitude. The categorical voice of halacha speaks through commandments, *mitzvot*, and points to God the Commander, the *metzaveh*, who endows the most mundane acts of daily life with divine nobility and holiness.[6] Halacha meets the realist's preference for life as it is, and for the preserving, stabilizing, and protective elements in tradition. *Halacha is the realm of the fixed.*

Aggada represents the poetic, imaginative impulse in the Jewish tradition; the impulse for embellishment, innovation, and improvisation, revealing God's immediacy and personal engagement. The inspirational voice of aggada speaks through parable, maxim, allegory and legend, and points to the Creator who has knit together the destiny of the world and the destiny of his chosen people. Aggada meets the idealist's preference for life as it should be or could be or might be, and thus seeks out the inspirational, exhortative, and narrative elements in the tradition.[7] *Aggada is the realm of the fluid.*

The aggadic retelling of what was originally told and the halachic relegislating of what was originally legislated are the two foci around which the religious-literary tradition of Judaism has grown. Aggada is the populist, democratic focus of the tradition. Since the inner logic of a story allows an open-ended, free, playful approach in which no authoritative rule is to be derived, aggada is the property of the common man. Each person is free to develop aggada according to their own inclinations and methods.[8] Not so the halacha, which requires a fixed resolution, an authoritative pronouncement on legal disputes. Like all law, authority is central to the very enterprise of jurisprudence, and thus halacha is the domain of the trained jurist — the domain of rabbinic authority.

Yet it was precisely this rabbinic authority, central to a vital halachic Jewish life, which was disintegrating in the secular post-Emancipation Europe of Bialik. The long history of the Jewish community's self-control in Europe through the rabbinic authority in the *kehilot* was over by the mid-seventeenth century and Bialik's essay was a hopeless protest against the consequent dessication of halacha which followed. He understood that both a vital halacha and a vital aggada were necessary for a vital Jewish life and literature.

> Aggada without Halacha is as one bereaved, ending in utter futility
> and destroying the energetic vigor of its devotees. He who says, 'I honor
> nothing but Aggada' — go now and see whether his Aggada is not a poor
> and fruitless flower. He is very much like the man who plucks the
> blossom but is heedless of the fruit. In the end he shall not find any
> blossoms any more. No fruit, no seed; whence then the blossom?[9]

Bialik's target was the "emancipated" modern Jew who could not
abandon halacha fast enough in order to bask in the great secular cultures
of Western Europe. Bialik nurtured a deep passion for both halacha and
aggada and was prophetic in his concern over the future of a Judaism
in which the subtle dialectic of law and story was broken.

> A people that is unpracticed in the combining of Aggada with
> Halacha exposes itself to everlasting perplexities and is in danger of
> forgetting the one direct way which leads from will to accomplishment,
> from yearning to realization. Halacha that is joined with Aggada in
> a co-partnership, gives ample testimony of a people's health and
> maturity. A widowed Aggada, however, is always an evidence of a peo-
> ple's decrepitude and shows that it is in need of invigoration.[10]

Bialik was a Jew who wrote for Jews, and yet his essay speaks to a
universal dialectic of law and story in religious life and literature. All
living traditions have their own halacha and aggada. The Buddhist tradition calls law, *vinaya* and story, *sutta*. In Hinduism the name for law is
dharma, story is *sutra*. Islam preserves these two categories under the
names *shari'a*, law, and *hadith*, story. Actually *shari'a* means path or way,
which is exactly the meaning of *halacha*, and *hadith* comes from the root
meaning, "to tell or narrate", exactly as does *aggada*. The categories of
law and story exist in Christianity, the focus of our present concern, but
their relationship is more complex than in the previously mentioned
religious traditions.

Essentially, the dialectic of law and story has been deeply broken
in the Christian tradition, so that what has been produced is, in Bialik's
words, a "widowed aggada". Christianity has a rich aggadic tradition
and a rich halachic tradition but, from the beginning, the two have not
formed the dialectical "copartnership" of which Bialik spoke. One can

point to several instrumental causes for the breakdown of the law / story nexus in Christendom.

First is Christian clericalism. Halacha cannot be confined in scope to the clergy if it is to have a dynamic power for the entire religious tradition of a people. The development of Christianity as a clerical religion forced the creation of a twofold law, one for the clergy and one for the laity. The status of the clergy's law is inevitably higher than that which applies to the laity. The Jewish halacha, though legislated by an elite, applied to every Jew equally and thus forced a degree of legal sophistication upon the non-rabbi which was not created for the non-priest. The danger facing all clerical religions is the abandonment of aggada for the clerics and the abandonment of halacha for the laity. This has remained a persistant threat to vital Christian life even after the Reformation.

By far the most important cause for the breakdown of the law and story dialectic in Christianity, however, is Judaism itself. Christianity was born as a critique of Judaism, as a response to the innermost concerns of Judaism. As the dialectic of law and story was central to Jewish tradition, the division between law and story was a central Christian reaction to Jewish tradition. Of course, the central figure was Paul, whose anti-halachic bias formed a core element in New Testament writings. "The law taught me sin" is a declaration of independence from law, and from the indissoluable unity of law and story which Paul rightly saw as characteristic of the "traditions of the fathers". As Bialik pointed out, "Halacha is the Attribute of Justice. . . Aggada the Attribute of Mercy." The Pauline bias split these two attributes, conceived of in Judaism as two unified attributes of God, into two opposed attributes. The "old Israel" lived in error, not recognizing that the law had been negated and transformed by a merciful act of divine grace—the death of Christ. Law and story were no longer complementary foci of the religious life. In Christianity after Paul, they became diametrically and antithetically opposed alternatives.

The credit for the definitive proof of this thesis belongs to a Christian patristics scholar and theologian, Rosemary Ruether. Ms. Ruether's book, *Faith and Fratricide*, is an exposition of the anti-Jewish elements in Christian scriptures and Christian tradition. Anti-Jewishness, called by Ruether the "left hand of Christianity," emerges from the inner logic of the Christian claim.[11] The cause is the "antithetical theology" produced by early Christianity in response to the "dialectical theology" of Judaism.

> The Jewish Bible and the midrashic literature generated by it ex-
> hibit the dialectical tensions *between* law and grace, letter and spirit,
> the particular and the universal, sin and repentance, error and truth,
> abandonment and redemption. The New Testament replaces these
> structures with a *series of antitheses*, in which the 'new' Israel can find
> itself (undialectically) affirmed only by means of an (undialectical)
> negation of the "old"[12]

Law is the domain of the fixed, the stable, the enduring elements in a tradition; story is the domain of the fluid. For Paul, expecting the immediate *parousia*, the abandonment of *halacha* was of no concern. The final sublation of all categories — of all existence — was imminent. For the long tradition of Christianity, however, the domain of the fluid could not endure. Apocalyptic tension cannot be supported indefinitely. Even within the New Testament, the emerging exigencies of the fixed domain present themselves as problematics of the new church foundation. The meeting of Peter and Paul is the early church meeting of the new halacha and the old ecstatic aggada of expectation and immediate hope.

The Christian tradition continued to grow beyond Paul to the gospels and then to the church fathers, the anti-Nicene fathers, the post-Nicene fathers, and on and on to our own day. Similarly, the Jewish tradition grew on beyond the Hebrew Bible to the Mishna, the Gemara, the Midrash, the Targumim, the Saboraim and the Gaonim and on and on to our own day. Yet the Christian church carried within it the antithetical theology of its genesis, a theology in which halacha and aggada — law and story — were made to live separate lives.

The chastisements of Bialik concerning the dangers of a "widowed aggada" were directed at pre-Holocaust European Jewry. The chastisements of Rosemary Ruether are directed at post-Holocaust Christendom. Both saw the terrible specter of a tradition divided against itself. Bialik spoke to the victims. Ruether speaks to the victimizers. Bialik's words are for a tradition which seeks survival, Ruether's for a tradition which must seek repentance.

Endnotes

1. *Encyclopedia Judaica*, Vol. II (Jerusalem: Keter Publishing House, 1972), p. 354. *Aggada* is the Aramaic form, *Haggada* is the Hebrew form. We have chosen to use *aggada* so as not to create confusion, since The Haggada is the Passover narrative.

2. Talmud Yerushalmi *Pe'ah* 2:6, 17a.

3. Actually the first code was by Rav Isaac of Fez (Alfazi), but the incomparable *Mishna Torah* of Maimonides was the first code to use the systematic order of the law. The *Shulhan Aruch* of Joseph Karo with the notes of Moses Isserles is the consummation of Jewish codes.

4. H.N. Bialik, *Halacha and Aggada*, unpublished Siegal translation, p. 3. An edited version of this work appears in *Modern Jewish Thought*, ed. N.N. Glatzer (New York: Schochen, 1977), pp. 55-64.

5. Ibid, p. 4.

6. Ibid. pp. 3, 22.

7. Ibid.

8. Hai Gaon, in: B.M. Levin, ed., "The Collection of the Great Teachers," Tractate Hagigah. Quoted in the *Encyclopedia Judaica*, p. 354; see note 1.

9. Bialik, *Halacha and Aggada*, p. 27.

10. Ibid.

11. Rosemary Ruether, Faith and Fratricide *(New York: Seabury, 1974)*. Of special importance for this discussion is Chapter Five, pp. 228-245, esp. pp. 239-245.

12. Quoted from an important review article of post-Holocaust Christian history and theology by Emil L. Fackenheim, "The Nazi Holocaust as a Persisting Trauma for the Non-Jewish Mind," *Journal of the History of Ideas*, Vol. XXXVI, No. 2., April-June, 1975. p. 375. A concise summary of the thesis presented at length in *Faith and Fratricide* can be found in Rosemary Ruether, "Anti-Judaism is the Left Hand of Christology," in Robert Heyer, ed. *Jewish-Christian Relations*, (New York: Paulist Press, 1974). pp. 1-9.

Report from a Far Meridian: Yahweh, God of the Fireball

by Gerald Ringer

Rabbi Gellman quotes the Talmudic prohibition against deriving a law from a story. In some ways, my article may contradict that, urging the adoption of a new way of walking (the root meaning of *halacha*) or of a new law from the repressed story of the Goddess in Judaism and Christianity.

America and Russia, the atomic-age superpowers, may be likened to trees rooted in the soil of the Judeo-Christian spiritual heritage. Jesus' teaching, "Each tree is known by its own fruit" (Luke 6:44), is taken seriously here: the titanic arming for nuclear war might be seen as the fruit of two great oaks. Hindu India does not threaten humanity with extinction; nor does Confucian China. The threat is from Judeo-Christian America and Russia, with their cherubic coteries of Judeo-Christian allies. Following Jesus' injunction — "First take the log out of your own eye" (Luke 6:42b) — we are not immediately concerned with the speck in our alter-ego's eye.

Our method may be called "psychocultural interpretation." Its foundation is Swiss psychologist Carl Gustav Jung's theory of myth and symbol. It is "cultural" in that it interprets the myth, health, and destiny of a culture rather than of an individual patient. Whereas Jungian analytical psychology interprets dreams, we interpret the contents of a great cultural treasury of our civilization's collective vision: the *Holy Bible*.[1] The aim of the systematic study parenting this report is to use the Bible as a work of unconscious confession, bringing to light the content relevant to religious pathogenesis of nuclear war.

The Structure of the Problem: An Overview

Judeo-Christian culture suffers an arbitrary patrization (masculinization) at the expense of matrist (feminine) values.[2] If the Goddess preceded the God, then any primal "sin," represented in the Eden myth as a sin against a masculine Creator, actually would have been sin against a feminine deity. The world of experience ruled by the Goddess is largely instinctual, in contrast to that ruled by God, which is characteristically thought-conscious. As consciousness develops, the thinking function progressively displaces the matrist reliance on instinct. However, it is not thinking, but intuition, through which an individual obtains a sense of wholeness and meaning. God's warning, "In the day that you eat of it [the fruit of the tree of knowledge] you shall die" (Genesis 2:17), points to the fact that when primitive man and woman put thinking in place of instinctual intuitiveness, they became aware of death; in the West, the fear of death has become a major psychocultural disease.

A useful interpretive theme is serpent symbolism, mythologically representative of the Goddess and her values. The Great Mother has the serpent as her prime attribute; an eagle- or sky-God like Yahweh is necessarily in a state of war with the serpent if he is to preserve his authority and dominion. Yet the serpent-way may be the most important avenue to creativity and healing.[3]

The issue becomes critical at the foot of Mt. Sinai, in Ch. 32 of Exodus. Even as the shock waves from Eden come down to us as psychocultural reality, so too do the shock waves from Mt. Sinai. Experience and time prove, however, that Yahweh and his followers are dependent on the chthonic resources of the unconscious. Without them, the spirit's urge to be "up, up, and away" — to realms beyond the peak's forbidding brow — can end in a life-rending crash. In Chapter 21 of Numbers, Yahweh authorizes the people to break the prohibition against graven images. However in countless other instances, the Bible tells how the people are thrown back onto their own resources, forced surreptitiously to seek the serpent power for healing: *idolatry*!

The prohibition against "making images" proves to be a pervasive mandate of the Judeo-Christian psyche: it lives with us interminably as a force of Fate. This prohibition is part of the repression of matrist values by patrist forces — a decisive factor in the Judeo-Christian onto-genesis of transgression, and a powerful moving force in the religious pathogenesis of nuclear war.

The parent exploration revealed strong evidence that the central religious symbol of the atomic age is the fireball of the nuclear bomb. In the halcyon years of atmospheric testing, it occupied our skies much as the cross once shone in the sky for Emperor Constantine: "In this sign you shall conquer." Symbolic correlatives of the fireball appear frequently in the Bible, where they may be recognized as manifestations of righteous wrath. The motif haunts the pages of the Bible, conducting the Judeo-Christian heritage along its fated way from the Garden to its prophesied grave at Armageddon.

The Fallacy of a Patrist Eden, and Its Implications

As late as 1939, while writing *Moses and Monotheism,* Sigmund Freud could rest comfortably on the presupposition shared by the vast majority of his contemporaries: that life in the prehistoric primal horde was governed by males, and was under a value system of masculine provenance. This presupposition is reflected (and in part generated) by the Book of Genesis — with grave historical consequences.

The presuppositon of an inherent, God-given patrist supremacy has been subtly but powerfully influential in the process shaping Western culture, character, and destiny. Two maxims deserve to be kept in mind: 1) an individual's God tends to function psychosocially as their ego-ideal (model for attitude and behavior), and correlatively 2) relationships between God and individual or culture tend to be laden with mutual contamination between the parties. This formulation expresses the negative (shadow) side of the following correlation by Jung: ". . . transformations of the God-image. . . run parallel with changes in human consciousness, though one would be at a loss to say which is the cause of the other."[4]

The philosopher Alfred North Whitehead complains,

> . . .the doctrine of an aboriginal, eminently real, transcendent creator, at whose fiat the world came into being, and whose imposed will it obeys, is the fallacy which has infused tragedy into the histories of Christianity and of Mahometanism.[5]

He identifies three cultural streams that have fed the Judeo-Christian tradition — all three patristic in character: "the ruling Caesar [as tyrant]. . ., the ruthless moralist [Yahweh's prophets], [and] the unmoved mover [the abstracted Aristotelian deity]." But he notes that a fourth stream joins these — "the Galilean origin of Christianity" which

> dwells upon the tender elements in the world, which slowly and in quietness operates by love; and it finds purpose in the present immediacy of a kingdom not of this world. Love neither rules, nor is it unmoved; also it is a little oblivious as to morals. It does not look to the future, for it finds its own reward in the immediate present.[6]

Himself no mystic, Whitehead here supports the matrist ingredients of mystic vision attainment and the maintenance of the heart's ease. These are values that have come to be regarded as exotic and are grudgingly envied by *dis-eased* Westerners.[7]

In the present work, psychocultural interpretation looks, as it were, through the lens of the nuclear bomb's fireball. The patrist values may then be seen to favor the pathogenesis of nuclear war; the matrist, to foster creative alternatives. From this perspective, Western culture is seen to have historically instilled and rewarded patrist virtues, e.g., strength, voraciousness, domination, rationalized intellection, judgmentalism, parochialism, intolerance — and held them as inherent, natural, and godlike. This has occurred at the expense of complemenary feminine virtues, e.g., yieldingness, nurturance, receptiveness, emotional sensitivity, mercifulness, wholeness, accommodation — held generally to be threatening, subversive, and inferior.

It is noteworthy that, in spite of all the lip service paid "God's love," the matrist values promulgated by Jesus are honored mainly in the breach. Whitehead's first three streams — ruling, ruthless, and abstract-ifying — exemplify pilot values; the values of the Galilean stream tend to get repressed by them. This points to a general principle that has held practically throughout the three millennia of this heritage: avatars of patrist values never cease attacking and repressing matrist values, but avatars of matrist values, by their nature, do not strike back with equivalent ruthlessness. Like the Taoist's water which humbly seeks low places, they act by means of gentle persuasion. Ultimately, however, the matrist is vindicated. The Goddess Nemesis ("Wisdom" in Proverbs) inexorably punishes folly — her trump card being nuclear war. Thus Judeo-Christian civilization is inherently devoted to the invocation of its own Nemesis, symbolized as the Armageddon envisioned by St. John of Patmos.

Serpent Power: The Primordial Rule of the Great Mother

Modern research has uncovered a wealth of evidence supporting the inaccuracy of the impression, conveyed by Genesis and accepted as divine writ for almost three millennia — that prehistory is strictly a patrist show. The poet-mythologist Robert Graves writes:

> The language of poetic myth anciently current in the Mediterra-nean [region] and Northern Europe was a magical language bound up with popular religious ceremonies in honor of the Moon-goddess, or Muse, some of them dating from the Old Stone Age. . . . The language was tampered with in the late Minoan times when invaders from Central Asia began to substitute patrilineal for matrilineal institu-tions and remodel or falsify the myths to justify the social changes.[8]

Jean Shinoda Bolen, M.D., a Jungian analyst, points to the power-ful symbolism of the serpent in literature to explain Goddess-rule:

Snakes had been symbols of the pre-Greek Great Goddess of old Europe, and serve as symbolic reminders (or remnants) of the powers once held by the female deity. (Crete 2000-1800 B.C.) One famous early representation of the deity was a female Goddess with breasts bared, arms outstretched, and a snake in each hand. . . .

I think of women who gain a sense of their own power and authority as "reclaiming the power of the snake," which was lost by feminine deities and human women when the patriarchal religions stripped the Goddesses of their power and influence, cast the snake as the evil element in the Garden of Eden, and made women the lesser sex.[9]

The Garden:
Restoration of a Fractured Myth

In the Garden of Eden myth, the Garden itself symbolizes the ouroboric, unconscious wholeness of the psychic state prior to the dawn of consciousness. The eating of the forbidden fruit symbolizes an archaic coming-to-consciousness — a radical break from the primitive state of harmony with Mother Nature's instinctual embrace. From his distinguished cultural perspective, Graves speculates on the empirical situation:

> Ancient Europe had no gods. The Great Goddess was regarded as immortal, changeless, and omnipotent. . . . Men feared, adored, and obeyed the matriarch; the hearth which she tended in a cave or hut being their earliest social centre, and motherhood their prime mystery. . . .[10]

The religious concept of free choice between good and evil, which is common to Pythagorean philosophy and prophetic Judaism, developed from a manipulation of the tree-alphabet. In the primitive cult of the Universal Goddess to which the tree-alphabet is the guide there was no room for choice: her devotees accepted the events, pleasurable and painful in turn, which she imposed on them as their destiny in the natural order of things. The change resulted from the Goddess' replacement by the Universal God.[11]

The significant implication is that any primal offense committed by Adam would have been an offense against the values and authority of a Goddess — not a God. Writers of the Bible presupposed that their God had ruled Paradise, but everywhere they portray him as characterologically unfit to do so. Utilizing more recent insights, we might attempt to reconstruct a different view of humankind's childhood:

The Mother ruled in a manner reminiscent of the ancient Hindu concept of karma, i.e., with unmediated justice and compensation based on harmony with nature. She was Nemesis of the apple bough, wisely controlling all the apples, and seeing that everybody ate of the sweet and digestible tree of life. Death, while not absent, nevertheless was not a cause of fear and anxiety, and all lived in a condition of heart's ease. What came along to change things?

The Eden myth makes it clear that the Hebrew people are quintessentially creatures of oppressive moral consciousness. How could they be otherwise? Their God keeps interjecting himself as a moral and avenging intermediary in history, beginning with Genesis. Yahweh's ubiquitous and effervescent morality is contagious among the biblical *dramatis personae*: the patriarchs, the prophets, the priests, and of course the people, who are the ultimate repository of the collective unconscious. It comes as no surprise that the fateful tree is that of the knowledge of *good and evil*, i.e., of dualism taking the distinctive form of moral conflict. But why "knowledge?" Why is the twig in Eden bent toward *knowledge* of good and evil?

The Birth of the Fireball of Righteous Wrath

In trying to answer the question, "Why *knowledge*?," the sceptic might argue that the serpent's explanation ought not to be relied upon, considering its slippery source. But we might gain some understanding by reviewing the dramatic consequences of eating this forbidden fruit. Freud's terminology suits here; we might conclude that these consequences represent the reality principle as it ripens into a repressed death instinct. Adam and Eve become conscious of pain, the burden of labor, the danger posed by the snake, female submissiveness, male dominance — and "... [they] were taken from dust, and to dust [they]

shall return" (Genesis 3:19). Enter the fear of death and its cohort, anxiety over the sufferings the future might hold. Immediately (and this is
of utmost significance), in most intimate association with all of this
knowledge, Yahweh injects the fireball of his righteous wrath: "a flaming sword which turned every way, to guard the way to the tree of life"
(Genesis 3:24).

The Symbolism of Serpent Power

We have seen that in the unconscious, ouroboric embrace of the
Garden, the serpent leads Adam into the unconscious depths of his being. From this is called the latent power to know good and evil—i.e., to
become conscious. As the phallus inseminates the womb, so the serpent symbolizes the power to enter the womb and call forth life. These
are symbolic ways of saying that energies and forms of experience may
be introjected into the unconscious, which is womb-like in that it carries forms for the experiencing—nay, the birthing!—of life. Thus the
Goddess' control of the serpent is symbolic of her control over life.
When a small child is hurt, mother kisses away the pain; when a person's
creativity is blocked (*dis-eased*), the serpent within can exercise unblock-
ing and healing power. The *caduceus*, given to Hermes by the Sky-god
Zeus, features two intertwined serpents—startlingly reminiscent of Dr.
Bolen's bare-breasted Goddess with a snake in each hand. Hermes
bears the caduceus as emblem of his office, herald of Hades, the chthonic
place of the healing python. The caduceus, minus messenger's wings,
is the emblem of Aesclepius, god of healing and Apollo's son, who was
delivered through the midwifery of many-talented Hermes.[12]

Yahweh's words in Eden, "And I will put enmity between you and
the woman" (Genesis 3:15), are tantamount to a notice that God is dis-
membering Eve—tearing her from the part of herself that is her power
over life; it is comparable to the castration of a male. Yahweh in effect
devours the Goddess who inherently, and ineradicably constitutes a
fateful threat to his autonomy, power, authority—and his vaunted
credibility.

Mt. Sinai in the Pathogenesis of Nuclear War

The serpent symbol instinctively seeks that archetype whose images include the womb, Hades (e.g., Plato's *Er* myth), the sea (oceanic womb of life), the fire of divination, and the unconscious. Eve (like Wisdom, Gaea, and Mary), in her anima role, succors and guides the serpent to "The Place." Thus the prohibition against making graven (and molten) images takes on a deepened meaning. It appears as one of the Ten Commandments, where its terminology is suggestive of in-depth psychology: "You shall not make for yourself a graven image, or any likeness of anything that is in heaven above, or that is in the earth beneath, or that is in the water under the earth" (Exodus 20:4). We recognize here a veiled reference to the archetypes. Yahweh is warning the people not to be distracted from true worship, even when numinous archetypal images try to force their way into consciousness. Specifically, the taboo is on those archetypes of religious-spiritual significance that would tend to deflect the flow of energy away from Yahweh and the work of his Chosen People: "You shall not bow down to them or serve them."

The book of Exodus contains the familiar story of Moses' forty days and nights "with the Lord" (Exodus 24:18). Leaving the people to wait in the valley, Moses communes with a God who is virtually in the process of a nuclear explosion: glorified spirit flies into the sky, analogous to the photons of a nuclear bomb blast; remaining below is the mundane, sodden world, analogous to the ash of the spent bomb.[13] Such explosions are often experienced by patients who undergo dissociations in madness. With that experience reverberating throughout his being, Moses descends to the valley, where he finds the people reveling in wine and dancing naked around a golden likeness of a bull (Exodus Ch.32). He experiences this as a direct affront to Yahweh and an abandonment of the project Yahweh has given to his people. He explodes, filled with the fireball of righteous wrath. Gathering the Levite warriors about him, he thunders:

> Thus says the Lord God of Israel, "Put every man his sword on his
> side, and go to and fro from gate to gate throughout the camp, and slay

every man his brother, and every man his companion, and every man his neighbor" (Exodus 32:27).

The writer adds glumly: "And the sons of Levi did according to the words of Moses; and there fell of the people that day about three thousand men" (Exodus 32:28). Thus, perpetually within our psyches, does Moses introduce the Ten Commandments, one of which declares, "You shall not kill" (Exodus 20:13). Of such stuff is the shadow side of the Judeo-Christian heritage made.

Image-Making and the Serpent's Power to Heal

In the shadow of Mt. Sinai, questioned by an inflamed Moses, Aaron explains what has happened:

> "For they said to me, 'Make us gods, who shall go before us; as for this Moses, the man who brought us out of the land of Egypt, we do not know what has become of him.'
> "And I said to them, 'Let any who have gold take it off'; so they gave it to me, and I threw it into the fire, and there came out this calf" (Exodus 32:23f).

The calf that comes out of the fire is an image born of the firepit, symbolizing the chthonic place of the mothers. Worship of such an image ties the people back into the womb, into the domain of the Goddess, whose earth is not ashen and wasted, but fecund and vibrant with creativity. This is a primitive "heresy," and the sword-slash comes down. The sword-slash, psychoculturally integrated, also comes down a million times a day within each of us; in it we recognize the flaming sword of the Edenic cherubim, guardians of the gates of Paradise.

Edward F. Edinger, a Jungian analyst, finds two places in the Bible where Yahweh reverses his prohibition against images. In Numbers, Yahweh has inflicted the people with a plague of snakes, psychological (eating them up inside) as well as physical. He instructs Moses, "Make a fiery serpent, and set it on a pole; and everyone who is bitten, when he sees it, shall live" (Numbers 21:8). The numinous serpent, then, symbolically takes on and reflects the projected contents of the people's suffering unconscious. Edinger writes:

> The image-making power of man, his imagination, thus has a healing effect on the damage inflicted by God — a most instructive lesson. In psychological terms, it is saying the destructive effects of the unconscious can be healed by seeing the image of the agency of the hurt. The fiery serpents are the anger and resentment that bit the Israelites and poisoned them; to see the image of what has bitten one exteriorizes the unconscious effect and brings a separation between it and the ego. . . .We are released from the poison of the effect if we can see the image that lies behind it.[14]

Jesus' own belief in such "serpent power" for healing is recorded in the Gospel of John. Jesus says, "And as Moses lifted the serpent in the wilderness, so must the son of man be lifted up" (John 3:14). Jung elaborates:

> All opposites are of God, therefore man must bend to this burden; and in doing so he finds that God in his "oppositeness" has taken possession of him, incarnated himself in him. He becomes a vessel of divine conflict. We rightly associate the idea of suffering with a state in which opposites violently collide with one another, and we hesitate to describe such a painful experience as being "redeemed." Yet it cannot be denied that the great symbol of the Christian faith, the Cross, upon which hangs the suffering figure of the Redeemer, has been emphatically held up before the eyes of Christians for nearly two thousand years. This picture is completed by the two thieves, one of whom goes down to hell, the other into paradise. One could hardly imagine a better representation of the oppositeness of the "central" Christian symbol.[15]

In light of the healing function of these objectified images, consider the awesome psychocultural implications of the fiery Apocalypse objectified by St. John! On several occasions President Reagan has stated that nuclear war might be seen as the fulfillment of St. John's dire biblical prophecy; here, certainly, he voices the feelings of millions of our people. From the standpoint of psychocultural interpretation, we are forced to concur, if only because of the dazzling matchup between the phenomenon of St. John's vision and that in the scenarios of our best informed war-gamers.

We must weigh the meaning of the 50,000 brazen serpents wrath-fully coiled in the arsenals and hearts of the Judeo-Christian super-powers. Knowing a serpent when we see one may be the first part of wisdom, but knowing about 50,000 warheads ready to strike dead all of humanity. . . .that is to load the psychocultural system for another Yahwistic/Mosaic dissociation. Alas! The horrifying sight of Medusa's head has turned us to stone.

Systematic Repression
of the Goddess

We have speculated that Adam rebels against a matrist, cow-like harmony, rather than against a patrist, bull-like tyranny. We have noted that, concomitantly with this rebellion, Adam and Eve's experience becomes the experience of the "reality principle": they come to live within the parameters of their knowledge of good and evil, even as they start brooding on the fact that it is their God-given lot in this life to suf-fer and finally to die. Their sons institute rituals of sacrifice not out of love and reverence for Yahweh, but out of the self-interest of the reality principle; the reality principle itself begins its long career of patrist dehumanization when Cain, whose sacrifice Yahweh does not regard, kills Abel, whose sacrifice is well regarded by the Lord. The fratricide *survives*, to use a Darwinian term — even as his brother's blood cries from Mother Earth's womb.[16] Humankind is thus depicted in the Bible as cutting itself off from its own roots in brotherhood, earth, womb, in-stinct; out of this debacle grows the culture of the Judeo-Christian spiritual heritage. For our purposes, this culture may be broken down into two broadly distinguished aspects: 1) the pre-Christian biblical culture; and 2) the culture of Christendom. Both may be studied in terms of their respective spiritual projects. We turn now to an inter-pretation of certain characteristics of these two projects as they bear on the religious pathogenesis of nuclear war.

I. The Contribution of the Ancient Hebrew Project

The pre-Christian biblical culture makes a holy project of living according to Yahweh's will for his Chosen People. Yahweh declares, "I, the Lord your God, am a jealous God" (Exodus 20:5); it has been noted, however, that "another word for 'jealous' is 'insecure.' "[17] As Aho states, the *Kriegethik* of a society and its dominant religion are dialectically related, representing two aspects of a single military-religious value structure.[18] The jealousy that is Yahweh's brand therefore contaminates his followers and is a crucial factor in the holy project:

> Specialness is a lack of trust in anyone except yourself. Faith is invested in yourself alone. Everything else becomes your enemy; hated and attacked, deadly and dangerous, hated and worthy only of destruction. Whatever gentleness it offers is but deception, but its hate is real. In danger of destruction it must kill, and you are drawn to kill it first. And such is guilt's attraction. Here is death enthroned as savior; crucifixion is now redemption, and salvation can only mean destruction of the world, except yourself.[19]

Thus the jealousy of God correlates with the insecurity of his Chosen People. The more utterly the enemy is destroyed, the more self-righteous "we" can feel in meting out what is justly due; the more violent are the means "we" employ, the more devoted our action must be in the eyes of God. Early on, well nigh divine levels of destruction and genocide are projected:

> But in the cities of these peoples that the Lord your God gives you for an inheritance, you shall save alive nothing that breathes, but you shall utterly destroy them . . . . as the Lord your God has commanded (Deuteronomy 20:16f).

Aho comments, "In none of the scriptures of the other major world religions, the Mahabharata included, is there such a terrifying commandment as this."[20] Echoes of the ancient Hebraic dispensation are heard in President Truman's self-righteous explanation:

It is an atomic bomb. It is a harnessing of the basic powers of the universe. The force from which the sun draws its power has been loosed against those who brought war to the Far East. . . . If they do not now accept our terms they may expect a rain of ruin from the air, the like of which has never been seen on this earth. . . [21]

In a balance of terror maintained by nuclear arsenals, the jealousy of God and the insecurity of people together induce structural instability. Yahweh, whether under the banner of Adam Smith or Karl Marx, remains the jealous God of the fireball of righteous wrath. Our presidents have not resisted the urge to capitalize on this. Former White House aide H. R. Haldeman reports President Nixon as saying:

I want the North Vietnamese to believe that I've reached the point where I might do *anything* to stop the war. We'll just slip the word to them that for "God's sake, you know Nixon is obsessed about Communism. We can't restrain him when he's angry — and he has his hand on the *nuclear button*" — and Ho Chi Minh himself will be in Paris in two days begging for peace.[22]

John F. Kennedy played a similar game with this wild card, finessing: "Krushchev must not be certain that, where our vital interests are threatened, the United States will not strike first [with nuclear weapons]."[23] To this day no American administration has been willing to pledge no first use. Russia, for her part, has foresworn first use, but boldly announces that she will respond to nuclear attack by unleashing her entire strategic arsenal. Both superpowers speak Yahweh's language — and apparently each has considerable credibility with the other.

Having repressed the matrist sensitivity to mercy, accommodation, and nurturance of life, America as a superpower pursues a well-rehearsed project. It is puritanical to the core — paranoid, judgmentally flayed, and joyless. Even worse, it is a shadow existence practically devoid of soul, inasmuch as anima has been repressed. Life in America is, to use Norman O. Brown's term, "death-in-life."[24]

II. The Contribution of Christendom's Project

Christendom's project expands the ancient Hebrew project into the magnified dimensions of heavenly space and infinite time. The belief is that one lives in this world in such a fashion that the final judge will find it impossible not to admit one's soul to heaven. Scorn for the body and for this world is dramatically expressed. In Revelation, Earth and mundane creatures are absolutely expendable in the final decisive holocaust — a sacrifice consumed by fire. George B. Leonard comments, "We have had a Secretary of Defense who has written that 'mere biological survival' isn't really as important as whether our good Godly side wins over their evil Godless side."[25]

Orthodox Christian theology nurtures such apocalyptic fanaticism. When we view it through the lens of the nuclear bomb's fireball, we have to agree with Whitehead's statement, "I consider Christian theology to be one of the great disasters of the human race."[26] Whitehead is not referring to exotic religions when he emphasizes, "Religion is the last refuge of human savagery. . . . ; the uncritical association of religion with goodness is directly negated with the plain facts."[27]

Ernest Becker suggests, "most of the evil that man has visited on his world is the result precisely of the greater passion of his denials and his historical drivenness."[28] The devaluation of the physical world is part and parcel of the biblical repression of the Goddess — the unknown but numinous "other" that is neither Yahweh nor his Son.

Do not modern Jews and Christians continue to pursue their established projects, committing Adam's sin against the Goddess? The better they become at the established practice of their sacred traditions, the more the primordial sin is aggravated. By immortalizing this same old sin, each perpetuates and deepens the guilt of the expulsion, soaring ever higher on the wings of self-hatred and salvational fantasy. Due to the skyrocketing career of technology — this may be the final flaw — self-imposed annihilation becomes more inevitable, and more imminent, through repression.

Nuclear war as Armageddon is the logical culmination of Yahweh's means for righting a cracked world: Goddess murder, fratricide, intertribal mayhem, international holocaust, and, finally, planetary ruin.

The person who lives with weapon in hand and heart is fatefully transformed, the Judeo-Christian weapon of choice being the Mosaic sword
transformed into the nuclear missile. Like Moses' God above the crest
of Mt. Sinai, we spiral aloft until we become our own nuclear bomb.

Western civilization has been characterized as Faustian — continually spiralling onward and upward to perilous heights of self-aggran-
dizement, domination, and righteous wrath. This is premised on the
fallacious notion that problems stemming from a crime against the
Edenic deity can be fixed by relentless further repression of the Goddess. The end is in sight, however, for the Faustian, Judeo-Christian
"man": Nemesis' cosmic cure for his dis-ease is Armageddon.

The more compliantly and traditionally we respond to our spiritual heritage, the more securely we may rest in the faith that our misery
will be ended through nuclear folly.

Conclusion

J. Robert Oppenheimer, the chief scientist on the Manhatten Project, said in 1946:

> We have made a thing, a most terrible weapon, that has altered
> abruptly and profoundly the nature of the world. We have made a
> thing that by all standards of the world we grew up in is an evil thing.[29]

We have made ourselves a molten image of hidden things that are
in "The Place" which the serpent would lead us to. We would have
knowledge of them, were we willing to go and see, but our religious
heritage has forbidden us passage to "The Place." Jung warns:

> . . . . in the unconsciousness is everything that has been rejected
> by consciousness, and the more Christian one's consciousness is, the
> more heathenishly does the unconscious behave, if in the rejected
> heathenism there are values which are important for life — if, that is
> to say, the baby has been thrown out with the bath water, as so often
> happens.[30]

Jung continues by tracing a path for those who will follow. As we
shall see, this path is the way of the serpent, and the way to a broadened

and deepened Judeo-Christian heritage.

> The hero, who is to accomplish the rejuvenation of the world and the conquest of death, is the libido, which, brooding upon itself in introversion, coiling as a snake around its own egg, apparently threatens life with a poisonous bite, in order to lead it to death, and from that darkness, conquering itself, gives birth to itself again . . . .The hero is himself a serpent, himself a sacrificer and a sacrifice. The hero himself is of *serpent nature*; therefore, Christ compares himself with the serpent.[31]

There is an empirical reason why Christians might recognize Jesus as a critical symbol for our time: he has uttered words the superpowers need to hear if we are to have a world tomorrow. He has also said these words with an authority more powerful and compelling than any other hero in our tradition. These words are quoted in Matthew 5:44: "Love your enemies." Even as he promises that the Paraclete would be here to inspire and enable us, he notes, ". . . . he who believes in me will also do the works that I do; and greater works than this will he do. . . ." (John 14:12). Aside from the bloodshed, a host of twentieth-century events and movements proclaim — in the Galilean mode of quiet, loving persuasion, a patrist accommodation to the matrist — a humbly redeeming return of repressed matrist strengths. This drama — literally a struggle between choices and their attendant fates — lives within each of us, just as Yahweh, the Goddess, the serpent, and "the hero" all live within each of us.

If contemporary Christians and Jews are going to carry on a dialogue between themselves, and if they would then dialogue with the rest of humanity, they must understand that the fireball of righteous wrath remains the hallmark of their God, whether he be called Yahweh or Father. The only water that can quench this unutterable horror is our common chthonic humanity — the genuine compassion of the *eternal feminine*. If "the sun of righteousness shall rise, with healing in its wings" (Malachi 4:2), then surely, like its prototype of the Egyptian sun-disc, it is eternally upborne by two entwined snakes. However, until we Judeo-Christian folk manage to reintegrate the serpent with the sun in our innermost reality, the sun will continue to run out of control; the fireball of righteous wrath, objectified as the nuclear bomb, will inevitably destroy this world. The apocalyptic fulfillment of the Judeo-Christian expectation has potentially become a betrayal of heaven, Earth, and humankind.

While Christians are challenged to assimilate the "Galilean" force of Jesus' ministry, Jews need to reconnect with the hidden, feminine side of their tradition. *Shekinah* is the feminine presence of God, accompanying the people even in exile. *Shabbat* is the queenly form of every seventh day; *Chokmah* is feminine Wisdom, another Paraclete-like divine manifestation.

The Goddess is the Goddess, by any name. She is falsely served by much that has beset us under the guise of "progress," "security," and "defense." Progress in the making of ever more murderous weapons ill-pleases wise *Chokmah*, who issues the vital warning: "Pride goes before destruction, and a haughty spirit before a fall" (Proverbs 16:18). It is she who declares, "I was set up at the first, before the beginning of the earth. . . . I was his daily delight" (Proverbs 16:18). The whole destiny of humanity is at stake if we — and Father Yahweh within us — continue rebuffing the Goddess who takes special delight in the sons of man (Proverbs 8:31).

The following declaration for the Goddess remains a tribute to Hebrew genius:

> For he who finds me finds life and obtains favor from the Lord;
> but he who misses me injures himself; all who hate me love death
> (Proverbs 8:35f).

As Presence and Wisdom, she counsels as the serpent once counseled, "Keep hold of instruction, do not let go; guard her, for she is your life" (Proverbs 4:13). Her warning is timely, if only we are willing to listen: "Do not envy a man of violence and do not choose any of his ways" (Proverbs 3:31); "The iniquities of the wicked ensnare him, and he is caught in the toils of his sin" (Proverbs 5:22); "By insolence the heedless make strife, but with those who take advice is wisdom" (Proverbs 13:10). She is truly the Goddess who, serpent-like, would guide us unerringly to The Place within us, The Place from whence all life and being issue.

This is not a program; it is not even lame and halting guidelines. It is the expression of a mood, a groping sense that an attitude may change, a situation may transform, and a psyche may reconstellate. The price of mature understanding might turn out to be a painful weaning from comforting but deceptive piety. But to live as avatars of the Goddess carries a promise that more than compensates for the pain.

Endnotes

1. The method of psychocultural interpretation is founded on Jungian archetypal psychology, summarized, e.g., in Jolande Jacobi, *The Psychology of C.G. Jung*, new revised edition, foreword by Dr. Jung (Yale Paperbound; New Haven, Conn.: Yale University Press, 1962). Its critical tenor is indebted to Jung's classic, *Answer to Job*, in Vol. 11 of the *Collected Works*.

2. The terms "matrist" and "patrist" are defined and applied by G. Rattray Taylor in *Sex in History: The Story of Society's Changing Attitude Towards Sex Throughout the Ages* (Harper Torchbooks; New York: Harper and Row, 1973), p.83.

3. The terms are bonded to denote the inherent relatedness of their referrents. Cf. Herbert Read's "Art and Life, " *Adventures of the Mind from The Saturday Evening Post*, eds. Richard Thruelsen and John Kobler, and intro. Mark Van Doren (First Series; New York: Vintage Books, Alfred A. Knopf, Inc., 1959), pp. 158-70.

4. Carl G. Jung, *The Collected Works of C.G. Jung*, ed. Herbert Read, Michael Fordham, and Gerhard Adler; trans. R.F.C. Hull, vol. 9, part 2: *Aion: Researches into the Phenomenology of the Self* (Bollingen Series 20; New York: Pantheon Books, Inc., 1959), p. 194. Jung observes, "The God-image is not something *invented*, it is an *experience* that comes upon man spontaneously. . . .The unconscious God-image can therefore alter the state of consciousness, just as the latter can modify the God-image once it has become conscious."

5. Alfred North Whitehead, *Process and Reality: An Essay in Cosmology* (Harper Torchbook, The Academy Library; New York: Harper and Brothers, 1929), p. 519.

6. Ibid., pp. 520f.

7. Cf. Luis Marden's classic of forthright nostalgia, "Tahiti, 'Finest Island in the World,'" *National Geographic*, Vol. 122 (July, 1962), pp. 1-47.

8. Robert Graves, *The White Goddess: A Historical Grammar of Poetic Myth* (New York: Creative Age Press, 1948), p. X.

9. Jean Shinoda Bolen, M.D., *Goddesses in Everywoman: A New Psychology of Women* (San Francisco: Harper & Row, 1984), pp. 283, 284; cf. Bolen's documentation, pp. 20f.

10. Robert Graves, *The Greek Myths, Vol. I* (Pelican Books; Harmond-
     sworth, Middlesex, England: Penguin Books, Ltd., 1955), p. 13.

11. Graves, *The White Goddess*, p.382; cf. p. 215, FN. 1. The priority and
     primacy of the Goddess in the prehistory of lands giving birth to
     Western civilization is regarded by many as well documented; the
     most impressive evidence discovered in this research is Jacquetta
     Hawkes, *History of Mankind: Cultural and Scientific Development*. Vol. 1,
     Part 1: *Prehistory*, under auspices of UNESCO (Mentor Book; New
     York: The New American Library, 1963), passim. Compare with the in-
     valuable and massive work of Merlin Stone, *When God Was a Woman*
     (New York: Harcourt Brace and Jovanovich, 1976).

12. Graves, *Greek Myths*, I, Chapter 50, "Asclepius"; Fritjof Capra integrates
     this material into his holistic perspective in *The Turning Point: Science,
     Society, and The Rising Culture* (New York: Simon and Schuster, 1982),
     pp. 309-12.

13. The interpretation of the theological event at Mt. Sinai as a "nuclear
     explosion" is Wolfgang Giegerich's; cf. his tape, "The Nuclear Bomb
     and the Fate of God," Chicago, January 18, 1985. Dr. Giegerich is a
     Jungian analyst in Stuttgart, Germany; he is bringing out a book, *The
     Psychoanalysis of the Nuclear Bomb*.

14. Edward F. Edinger, *Melville's Moby-Dick, a Jungian Commentary: an
     American Nekyia* (New York: New Directions, 1978), p. 51.

15. Carl G. Jung, *Answer to Job*, trans. R. F. C. Hull (Bollingen Series;
     Princeton, N. J.: Princeton University Press, 1969 [1958]), pp. 54f.

16. The King James Version at Genesis 4:11 reads "and now art thou cursed
     from the earth, which hath opened her mouth to receive thy brother's
     blood . . . ."; cf. the Revised Standard Version: "and now you are cursed
     from the ground, which has opened its mouth to receive your
     brother's blood . . . ." In the more recent version, the Earth has been
     neutered, excising the suggestion of a naive Goddess-animism. This
     does seem to be a further castration of the Goddess.

17. Quoted from David Viscott, Chicago Talk Radio WIND, November 6,
     1984. Graves identifies the acacia as the bush from which Yahweh an-
     nounces "I AM WHO I AM." (Exodus 3:14), and comments, "The
     acacia is, indeed, a thorny, jealous, self-sufficient tree, needs very lit-
     tle water and, like Odin's ash, strangles with its roots all other trees
     growing near it." (*The White Goddess*, p. 223).

18. James A. Aho, *Religious Mythology and the Art of War: Comparative
     Religious Symbolisms of Military Violence* (Westport, Conn.: Greenwood
     Press, 1981), p. 195.

19. Foundation for Inner Peace, *A Course in Miracles, Text* (Tiburon, Calif.:
     Foundation for Inner Peace, 1975), p. 472.

20. Aho, *Religious Mythology*, p. 175f. In his research, Aho finds at least twenty cities (including those listed by Yahweh in Deutoronomy 20:17) recorded as thusly wasted.

21. From Truman's announcement of the dropping of the atomic bomb on Hiroshima, quoted in Fletcher Knebel and Charles W.Bailey, II, *No High Ground* (New York: Bantam Books, 1960), p.178.

22. President Richard Nixon quoted by Haldeman in H. R. Haldeman with Joseph Dimona, *The End of Power* (New York: Time Books, 1978), p. 83.

23. Quoted in *Newsweek*, April 9, 1962, p. 32.

24. Norman O. Brown, *Life Against Death. The Psychoanalytical Meaning of History* (Middletown, Conn.: Wesleyan University Press, 1959), p. 316.

25. George B. Leonard, *The Transformation: A Guide to the Inevitable Changes in Humankind* (New York: Delacorte Press, 1972), p.44; Leonard quotes from Melvin Laird, *A House Divided* (Chicago, 1962).

26. *Dialogues of Alfred North Whitehead as Recorded by Lucien Price* (Mentor Book; New York: The New American Library of World Literature, Inc., 1954), p. 143.

27. Alfred North Whitehead, *Religion in the Making* (Living Age Books; New York: Meridian Books, Inc., 1960 [1926]), p. 36.

28. Ernest Becker, *Escape from Evil* (New York: The Free Press, 1975), p. 90.

29. J. Robert Oppenheimer, "Atomic Weapons," *Proceedings of the American Philosophical Society*, Vol. 90 (January, 1946), p. 7

30. Jung, *Answer to Job*, pp. 78f.

31. Jung, *Psychology of the Unconscious. A Study of Transformations and Symbolisms of the Libido. A Contribution to the History of the Evolution of Thought*, trans. with intro., Beatrice M. Hinkle, M.D. (New York: Dodd, Mead, and Company, 1963 [1916]), p. 417.

ENCOUNTERS
WITH
ALTERNATIVES

Introduction to Part Two

In this section of the book, we see the mainline traditions through the process of dialogue. Unlike dissolution, in dialogue one maintains one's own identity while reaching out to understand the other's perspective. It is what Martin Buber called "feeling the other side." He writes that he discovered this on his grandfather's farm while caring for a favorite horse. One day, currying the animal, he became aware of feeling this action from the horse's side. That simple experience was central to Buber's understanding of authentic dialogue.

The Western religious tradition understands from Genesis 2:16 that our primordial parents were placed in a garden world with the instructions to serve and preserve it. This is the source of the critical biblical category of justice, the great cornerstone virtue entitling each of Adam and Eve's offspring access to the fruits of the garden. The pursuit of justice in its turn generates dialogue, since it is only through dialogue that we recognize the legitimacy of the other's claims.

In his classic, *The Courage To Be*, Paul Tillich describes three different ways in which non-being assaults our existence: guilt, meaninglessness, and fear of death. We buffer the last of these through a variety of "life insurance" strategies. Guilt is assuaged through the punctilious fulfillment of ritual, whether religious or societal. But even when we have shuttered the windows against the howling winds of death and guilt, how do we keep out the fog of meaninglessness that creeps in through every crevice?

Tillich suggests that our socialized way of handling this is by having "one true faith." This can be a religious faith, which is the essence of all forms of fundamentalism, or it can be a political ideology. Pure believers can be met in the White House or in the Kremlin. They are, however, incapable of dialogue. The process of dialogue necessitates understanding one's perspective as only a perspective, something of which the fundamentalist of any stripe is incapable.

The hope Tillich extends to us is the very courage from which his book derives its title. It requires letting go of our neurotic and culturally-conditioned prophylactic pretenses. There is no effective insurance against death; no ritual protects us from guilt; nor can a dogma mindlessly adhered-to stave off meaninglessness forever. We must let these winds of non-being blow over us, and trust our lives forward towards that ultimate Ground of Being who transcends our most sophisticated thoughts and cherished words. We must trust what Tillich called "the God beyond God," i.e. the mystery beyond all our dogmas, creeds, and scriptures.

Although dialogue characterizes all the articles in this volume, the explicit consideration of alternate viewpoints is a special focus of the six articles in Part Two. Charlotte Kamin uses the hagiographical nomenclature of her own Jewish tradition to describe that extraordinary Jew who became the central symbol of Christianity. The faith generated by the Koran is sensitively explored by a Jesuit priest, Tom Michel, who spends his personal and professional life bridging the two great faith communities of Christianity and Islam. A teacher of philosophy and religion, Stephen Infantino uses categories of Eastern thought to help elucidate some of the darker mysteries of Christian theology, and in return proffers a few gifts to Hinduism and Buddhism from his Christian treasury. Mike Foster boldly suggests that an enigmatic ex-Episcopalian priest might be a primary teacher of Eastern spirituality in our own Western world. A Roman Catholic nun, Madeleine Sophie Cooney, encounters a unique spiritual presence in a Japanese Buddhist roshi with whom she shares "the Buddha's blood." And Buddhist priest Kozan Beck relates his spirituality to our Western world, with all its technological pride and achievement.

Respondeo etsi mutabor. "I answer, even if I will be changed" — this phrase was quoted by the Jewish thinker Franz Rosenzweig as a hallmark of real dialogue. Many discussions are billed as dialogues, yet fail to meet this requirement. The participants merely bide their time, waiting for the other person to finish so they can continue scoring points. True dialogue is characterized by the willingness to change, to respond spontaneously in the freshness of the moment's encounter, not to merely rehash stale stereotypes and old prejudices. The noted historian of philosophy, James Collins, once remarked that it is not given to us human beings to be without prejudice. But what is possible for us is to be aware of our prejudices and to know when we are speaking or acting from them, rather than from other evidences or purposes. In these articles, the reader can sense the authors' efforts to identify prejudices, move beyond them, and respond from the open space of authentic encounter with other viewpoints.

Jesus as Zaddik

by Charlotte Golden Kamin

Gerald Ringer asserts that Judaism and Christianity will fuel nuclear destruction of the world if they continue to promote religious pathogenesis, suppressing the Goddess attributes of compassion, love, and mercy in favor of the demands of God: in Hebrew Scripture the "fireball of righteous wrath," and in the New Testament, apocalyptic fanaticism. The following essay examines a less black-and-white pattern for human living as perceived by the biblical writers and their interpreters in describing the character and activity of the zaddik.

Nineteenth-century research regarding Jesus investigated at length his role as messenger, teacher, pastor, healer, reformer, redeemer and prophet.[1] Contemporary research adds a title: *hasid*, the pious man of God noted for his devotion and legendary healing talents.[2] The purpose of my study is to add zaddik to the list of ways in which Jesus' role can be interpreted. Zaddik is a title used by the sages, those spiritual-religious leaders who compiled the Talmud,[3] to designate a supremely righteous individual who does the will of the Father in heaven; who accepts the Torah; who gives *zedakah* (charity), and in doing these things imitates the deeds of his Creator.[4] In the centuries which bracket the advent of Jesus and Christianity, the sages expanded this description, detailed below, to draw a complete portrait of the zaddik. My study will compare the character, life experience, and teachings of Jesus portrayed in the Synoptic Gospels with the picture of the zaddik articulated by the sages, to assess the legitimacy of adding zaddik to the list of Jesus' attributed roles.

The current state of research on historical Jesus sets the stage for this inquiry. Jewish scholars in the twentiety century have continued a tradition of studying Jesus and his teachings which could only have begun after the time of the Enlightenment, a time which witnessed an escape from the ghettos and a freedom from centuries of Christian persecution, at least in some quarters. The same freedom which promoted birth of the Reform or Liberal movement in Judaism also allowed Jewish scholars to explore Jesus' character and ideas, both in religious history and against his Jewish background.[5]

During the same time period, Christian scholars embarked on a search for the historical Jesus which necessarily included a thorough study of his Jewish roots. In the post-World War II decades, interest and research escalated, and were encouraged by statements in *Nostra Aetate*, Vatican II's *Declaration on the Church and Other Religions*. In addition, Christian interest in Jesus' Jewish roots has been intensified by the theological process known as "Christology from below". Hans Kung provides an explanation of this concept in the introduction to his controversial *On Being a Christian*. He states that to know what it means to be a Christian, one must measure one's self against Jesus — not measure Jesus against the Church or its dogma, leaders, and followers. He suggests that a fresh approach to discussion on Jesus would begin from below, from his humanity.[6] Such an examination of Jesus' character and teachings, from the point of view of the Jewish milieu of his time, would be aided by Jews and Jewish sources.

It has been stated that nineteenth-century research tested Jesus as messenger, teacher, pastor, healer, reformer, redeemer, and prophet. Note the descriptions of Jesus as redeemer or prophet. As a redeemer, he is not the Messiah expected by the Jews; to the Christian, he is Messiah and God-in-Christ. If we define a prophet as neither a philosopher nor a systematic theologian, but as a covenantal mediator who delivers the word of God to the people in order to shape their future, then indeed Jesus should be labeled prophet. Oxford scholar Geza Vermes adds another role for Jesus: charismatic Galilean holy man, a hasid in the tradition of Honi, the Circle-Drawer, and Hanina ben Dosa. These are believed to be first-century *hasidim*, pious Jewish persons of God, noted for their devotion and miraculous healing talents.[7]

While there is scholarly opinion supporting Vermes' thesis of an inevitable tension between hasidim and more orthodox rabbis, one could argue that the element of conflict is exaggerated. Gershom

Scholem, for example, describes a group among the pupils of Yochanan ben Zakkai, sages of the first century who were the *Tannaim* (teachers) of the *Mishnah*[8]. These were not only codifiers of the oral law in Judaism, they were also important representatives of mystical and theosophical thought who left a legacy of spiritual tradition.[9]

In *Jesus and the World of Judaism*, Vermes explains that were it not for the abnormal eschatological and politico-religious fever under Roman domination, conflict between Jesus and the rabbis would have resembled only in-fighting of factions belonging to the same religious persuasion.[10] Certainly, current research which places Jesus in the Pharasaic tradition would support this position, although Vermes himself places the holy people of Galilee in a category distinct from Pharisees, Essenes, Zealots or Gnostics. Of special note for the purposes of this study is the closing paragraph of Verme's conclusion, in which he states that Jesus is clearly recognizable within the Jewish framework of his time as, "Jesus the just man, the zaddik, Jesus the helper and healer, Jesus the teacher and the healer. . ."[11] Since the just man, the zaddik, is the leading title in this list, it is interesting that this was not explored by Vermes in the same depth as was, for example, hasid, the Galilean holy person.

Hasid and zaddik are not identical terms in Hebrew although the definitions and synonyms for each show considerable crossover. The same may be said for the English translations, one-who-is-pious (hasid), and one-who-is-righteous (zaddik). Both refer to one who has reverence for and obedience to God, and thus is faithful to religious duties and observances. Both terms suggest the conformity of life to requirements of divine or moral law. In addition, *zedek* (righteousness) is by definition invested with *justice* (in English, add virtue and integrity); *hesed* (piety) conveys love and compassion. Clearly both are relational terms (person to person, or person to God, and vice versa). This relational aspect of the zaddik will be explored further.

The sages established their views of righteousness, zedek, and of the righteous person, zaddik, by interpreting the variety of characteristics gleaned from Hebrew Scriptures. Many biblical contexts of zedek reveal that it is a concept of relationship: person to God, God to person, or person to person. The zaddik is one who fulfills demands imposed by a relationship; to act righteously is thus to fulfill obligations *due*. It is noteworthy that the Hebrew word for charity is *zedakah*, an entitlement on the part of the needy according to God's revelation, not a choice on the part of the donor (Proverbs 3:27).

In social relations, the zaddik preserved the peace and unity of the community by upholding its physical and psychical wholeness and by fulfilling the demands of the communal and covenantal relationship (e.g. Job, Psalms 15:2-5, Isaiah 33:15). Thus the wayfarer, the poor, the widow, the fatherless, the beast of burden, the land, are cared for by the zaddik (e.g. Isaiah I: 16-17). Psalm 37 details how the righteous comport themselves: they deal graciously, are charitable and wise, have integrity, cherish and pursue peace, and ultimately are protected because they take refuge (have faith) in the Lord.

The zaddik reflects the zedek of God, a righteousness dependent on God's grace, not humanity's action. God's gift of law is pedagogic, to help humanity be holy as God is holy (Exodus 19:5-6, Leviticus 19:2). As the human zaddik insures the rights of fellow humans by fulfilling obligations of relationship, so God insures the rights of humanity by righteous (just) judgments on behalf of the community of Israel. Even apparent punishment has a pedagogic intent for the people with whom God stands in relation.[12]

The portrait of the zaddik painted by the sages is also illuminating. Although rabbinic literature does not make extensive references to righteousness in general, the qualities adhering to righteousness (ideas about and characteristics of the zaddik) are numerous, describing one who is good, free from sin, and who carries out obligations to God and man by obeying the precepts of the Torah.[13]

Ephraim Urbach of the Hebrew University in Jerusalem and his English translator, the late Israel Abrahams, have provided a summary of important talmudic ideas in *The Sages: Their Concepts and Beliefs*.[14] This work and its attendant notes provide a picture of the zaddik. The only person in the biblical narrative expressly given the title of zaddik is Noah: "Noah was a righteous man, blameless in his generation; Noah walked with God" (Genesis 6:9). Noah became the prototypical righteous man and an extensive aggadic literature was woven around him. Urbachs asserts that the motifs in this literature are shared by the Greek man of God:

> He is a man beloved of the gods, mediates between them and mortals, and his life has typical features. His birth is announced

beforehand and mostly takes place in unusual circumstances and conditions. The man of God matures rapidly in body, spirit, and moral understanding, and he arouses, as an infant or child, the wonder of all who see him. His knowledge comes direct from God. He has wonderful powers at his disposal: he hears and sees hidden things; he knows the secrets of the future; he is able to control both animate and inanimate nature. In his youth people persecute him, but subsequently he appears as a savior, counsellor, and pleader, and uses his powers for the benefit of mankind, saving people from the wrath of God, warding off natural disasters, and helping the poor and suffering in everyday life. He dies an unnatural death, either as a martyr or a death accompanied by marvels, and miracles are wrought on his body. His death does not mean the cessation of existence but entering into a higher sphere.[15]

The claim in this essay is that the Jesus of the Synoptic Gospels does indeed fit the sages' description of zaddik.

Basing a discussion on the biblical passage: "The righteous is the foundation of the world" (Proverbs 10:25), the sages declare that the world exists only on the merits of the zaddik (Yoma 38 b; Hagigah 12 b). There are various formulations about the number of zaddikim who sustain the universe: 1, 30, 45, 50, 72. The most popular conception is that there are, in every generation, 36 zaddikim (*lamed-vavniks*) who greet the *Shekinah* (the Divine Presence) daily, by whose existence the world is sustained (Sukkah 45 b).

The righteous, by their deeds, bring blessing and prosperity to the world. The zaddik not only controls the laws of nature (Taanith 23 a), but also God's decrees, which can be annulled (Makshirin 16 b). Zaddikim are allotted two special tasks: to weigh the scales of judgment upon the world in favor of merit, and to influence people who draw near them simply by their existence. Although the disciples may not attain the level of the zaddik, they acquire some of the "fragrance." Such charisma and influence, however, is not enough; the zaddikim must protest against the wicked and advocate for their fellows. The zaddik has the power to transform God's attribute of justice into the attribute of compassion (Sukkah 14 a), but this power is given because of deeds and loyalty to the Torah and its precepts; the zaddik alone does not become a law and precept.[16] The zaddik could desire and become capable of creative acts similar to those of God (Sanhedrin 65 b). Furthermore, the activity of the righteous and the influence of their merit do not cease with their death; rather, their influence for the good of humankind continues, in the manner of the biblical patriarchs, prophets, and zaddikim. (The merit of the patriarchs, Abraham, Isaac and Jacob, has salvific effect).[17]

Another element in the portrait of the zaddik which fits the Jesus of the Synoptics into its outlines is the idea that the suffering and death of the righteous have a redemptive or expiatory value for others. The zaddik is held partly responsible for the sins of the generation (Shabbath 33 b). The righteous suffer for and with their generation, and their deaths expiate for the others' sins (Makshirin 28 a; Ex. R. 43:1; cf. Genesis Rabbah 34:2; Sanhedrin 108 a). By the extent of these references, it is clear that this conception was an important one to the sages, especially post-70 C.E. when the Temple was destroyed and sacrifice was no longer possible. George Foote Moore gives an excellent summary of the sages' viewpoint that expiatory suffering and death create atonement in *Judaism in the First Centuries of the Common Era*, Vol. I.[18] He cites:

> Sufferings propitiate God as much as sacrifices; nay, more than sacrifices, for sacrifices are offered of a man's property, while suffering is borne in his person. Sifre 1 c
> ... make my blood a sacrifice for their [thy people] purification, and take my life as a substitute for theirs. Eleazar in 4th Maccabees 6:27-29

Donald Hagner, in his chapter on "The Religious Teaching of Jesus,"[19] explores at length the level of Jewish belief that expiatory suffering or dying provide vicarious atonement for others. He concludes that Jewish scholars tend to deny that Jesus saw his own death as providing such redemption, relegating pertinent New Testament passages (e.g. Mark 10:45; Matthew 26:28) to a post-Resurrection theology read back into the canon. Some of the reservations cited above are Jewish responses to the concept of a Messiah who suffers, which is not a part of mainstream Jewish theology regarding messianic expectation. If, however, Jesus is seen in the role of zaddik, it is possible to use another lens to view his suffering and death. The letters of Paul are beyond the scope of this essay, but if Paul truly sat at the feet of Gamaliel (Acts 22:3), he was no stranger to the rabbinic concept that the suffering of the zaddik has an expiatory quality. We would speculate that this had some influence on Paul's concept of justification through the death of Jesus (Romans 3:21-26), except for the problem of dating. While the rabbinic conception developed over a long period of time, its importance intensified only after 70 C.E., 12-16 years after Paul's Letter to the Romans.

What do the Synoptic Gospels relate about Jesus that corresponds to the portrait of the zaddik drawn by the sages? Return to Urbach's picture of the zaddik mentioned earlier[20], and note:

> His birth is announced beforehand and mostly takes place in unusual circumstances and conditions.

Jesus' birth was announced beforehand (Matthew 1:18-25; Luke 1:26 38; 2: 1-20) and took place in unusual circumstances and conditions. The story of the "virgin" pregnancy, the explanation given to Joseph and Mary, the appearance of the Eastern star, the arrival of the Magi, and the birth in the manger, form a story which continues to intrigue us.

> The man of God matures rapidly in body, spirit, and moral understanding, and he arouses, as an infant or child, the wonder of all who see him.

The story of twelve-year-old Jesus in discussion with the rabbis, ". . . and all who heard him were amazed at his understanding and his answers" (Luke 2:41-52) would qualify here; also, ". . . and Jesus increased in wisdom and in stature, and in favor with God and man." (Luke 2:52).

His knowledge comes directly from God. Jesus gives thanks to the Father saying that the Father has delivered all things to him, and only the Father and Son know each other — save for anyone to whom Jesus chooses to reveal him (Matthew 11:25-27; Luke 10:21-22).

> He has wonderful powers at his disposal: he hears and sees hidden things; he knows the secrets of the future; he is able to control both animate and inanimate nature.

Jesus' powers as healer are firmly drawn in the New Testament: e.g. the leper (Matthew 8:1-4; Mark 1:40-45; Luke 5:12-16); the centurion's servant (Matthew 8:5-13; Luke 7:1-10); and Peter's mother-in-law (Matthew 8:14-15; Mark 1:29-31; Luke 4:38-39). He also gathers a huge crowd and heals them all regardless of their afflictions (Matthew 12:15-21; Mark 3: 7-12; Luke 6:17-19).

His nature miracles amaze his followers. To name a few: he calms a storm (Mark 4: 37-41); walks on the sea (Mark 6:45-52); and multiplies the loaves and fishes to feed the multitudes (Mark 6:33-44). He predicts the fate of the cities of Galilee (Matthew 11:20-24; Luke 10:13-15). He knows of his future sufferings, death, and resurrection (Matthew 16:21) and that he will be betrayed by one of his disciples (Matthew 26:20-25).

> In his youth people persecute him, but subsequently he appears as a savior, counsellor, and pleader, and uses his powers for the benefit of mankind, saving people from the wrath of God, warding off natural disasters, and helping the poor and suffering in everyday life.

Herod's paranoia about the birth of the king of the Jews challenges him to search out the newborn babe. It is the appearance of the angel in Joseph's dream, warning him to flee to Egypt and return upon Herod's death, which saves the infant Jesus (Matthew 2:1-20). Jesus' authority is consistently challenged as he takes his ministry into his own country (Matthew 13:53-58; Mark 6:1-6; Luke 4:16-20). Jesus has to thwart the tempter (Matthew 4:1-11; Mark 1:12-13; Luke 4:1-13).

The proclamation of the Synoptic Gospels reveals a Jesus who is counsellor (Matthew 6:25-34 and Luke 12:22-31), savior (Matthew 20:28 and Mark 10:45), and intercessor (he casts out demons in Matthew 8:28-34; Mark 5:1-20; Luke 8:26-39). His message is not only for the righteous but for the poor, the prostitutes, the publicans and sinners (Luke 18:9-14). He wards off a natural disaster by calming the winds and sea which threaten to capsize the boat in which he and his disciples are crossing the sea of Galilee (Matthew 8:23-27).

Jesus is martyred and crucified (Matthew 26 & 27; Mark 14 & 15; Luke 22 & 23) and resurrected (Matthew 28; Mark 16; Luke 24) to reappear (Matthew 28:11-20; Luke 24:13-53; Mark 16:9-28) and ascend to his place at the right hand of God (Mark 16:19-20). His martyrdom, death,

and resurrection to a higher sphere of existence complete his qualifi-
cations as zaddik in accord with Urbach's summary of the sages' view,
but this does not exhaust the elements of his life and character which
portray him as zaddik.

The task here is not to outline the history of Jewish theology regarding characteristics of the Messiah, but it is clear that some of those
characteristics apply to a rabbinic view of the zaddik. Post-exilic times
saw a shift from a concentration on dynastic perpetuity (of the House
of David) which was reflected in messianic expectations, to a focus on
the *qualities* of the expected redeemer—qualities first expressed by
Isaiah (16:4-5; 11:1-5) and emphasized by the sages: the foundation of
his throne would be justice, he would be distinguished by his zeal for
justice, and he would be charismatically endowed for sensing the
rights and wrongs of a case and executing justice. This execution of
justice (righteousness) insures the peace and unity of Israel's people
in the Messianic era. The second Temple concept of a Priest of Righteousness (*Kohen Zedek*), side by side with a Davidic King Messiah, continues to be present in literature of the sages and the eschatology of the
Essenes. Jewish Christians (Ebionites) of the first century saw the
functions of Priest (of righteousness), King, and Prophet brought together in the person of Jesus.[21]

It was not a lack of righteousness that made the sages reject Jesus
as Messiah, but the fact that he emphasized the Kingdom of God as a
righteous community in which the important consideration was individual spiritual redemption rather than political-national redemption. Messianic expectation by the sages required that the Messiah
break the yoke of heathen oppression and reign over a restored Kingdom of Israel, to which the exiled Jews would return to live in an era
of peace and justice. The apolitical and anational stance of the Gospels'
Jesus does allow for qualification as zaddik in the sages' perception,
since he is portrayed by the authors as charismatically endowed for
sensing the rights and wrongs of a case and for executing justice (see
below). The thrust of the argument is that Jesus, like the zaddik the
sages characterize, is concerned with observing the *spirit* of the Law,
not its words alone (Matthew 5:17; 7:1-5; 11:20-25; Luke 6:27-38; 41-42).

Donald Hagner understands the Pharisaic thirst for true righteousness as the motivating force behind ". . . their [the Pharisees'] passionate zeal for the minutiae of the oral law,"[22]—an effort to achieve the

kingdom of priests and holy people described in Exodus 19:5-6. Hagner does not draw the interesting comparison between exhortation in Hebrew Scriptures to ". . . be holy; for I the Lord your God am holy." (Leviticus 11:44-45; 19:1-2) and Jesus making a similar demand of his listeners for *imitatio dei*: "You, therefore must be perfect as your heavenly Father is perfect," (Matthew 5:48) or "Be merciful, even as your Father is merciful." (Luke 6:36). "For if you forgive men their trespasses, your heavenly Father also will forgive you; but if you do not forgive men their trespasses, neither will your Father forgive your trespasses." (Matthew 7:14-15).

Jesus describes the unrighteous as not giving food to the hungry nor drink to the thirsty, not welcoming the stranger, not clothing the naked, and not visiting the sick or imprisoned (Matthew 25:34-ff). The unrighteous will be eternally punished, but the righteous will have eternal life (Matthew 25:46). Jesus shares this view in Mark 12:38-40 when he condemns the hypocritical Pharisees who are impressed with status, curry public honor, and oppress widows. The sages say the zaddik does not do good for the sake of reward, he does good for the sake of heaven (Avot I:3).

What of the justice (righteousness, *zedek*) of the zaddik, according to the rabbis? He is just, as God is just; God is known as the "eternal zaddik" or the "zaddik of the world". The Jewish conception of justice has redemptive, not merely punitive, quality. As the Law is pedagogic, teaching humankind how to live in a relationship of faith with God, the righteousness (justice) of the zaddik fulfills the *spirit* of God's will. The zaddik goes beyond fulfilling merely the letter of the Law, a concept known as *lifnim meshurat ha din* (Baba Metzia 83 a). Jesus shares this characteristic of supererogation: when he claims to have come not to abolish the law, but to fulfill it (Matthew 5:17); to warn that unless our righteousness exceeds that of the scribes and Pharisees, we cannot enter the Kingdom of Heaven (Matthew 5:20). He fulfills the concept of *lifnim meshurat ha din* in his exhortations against divorce (permitted in Jewish law), lust, swearing, false piety, and especially in his support of loving your enemies and praying for those who persecute you: ". . . For if you love [only] those who love you, what reward have you?" (Matthew 5:46).

David Flusser states in *Jesus* that there is something problematic for Jesus in his relationship to the law and its commandments. In

Flusser's view, Jesus shares this with most Jews who take their Judaism seriously.[23] Surely it is the Gospels' portrayal of Jesus' attitude to practical *halakah*, the Law, vis-á-vis eating and drinking, Sabbath observance, association with sinners, and the personal authority assumed by him which would make some scholars question the positive assessment of Jesus as zaddik made here.

The sages spoke of the *zaddik gamur*, who, like Abraham, Isaac, Jacob, and Moses before him, fulfills the whole Torah from *alef* to *tav* (Shabbath 55 a). Jesus tells his listeners in Matthew 5:18 that not an iota, not a dot, will pass from the law until all is accomplished. It might well be the intent of the Matthean chronicler to convey a similar totality. A cautionary note regards the question of whether Jesus becomes "a law and precept unto himself" and in so doing refutes the sages' portrait of the zaddik. The weight of evidence presented here allows a new approach to Jesus from a Jewish viewpoint: to see him as a zaddik according to the portrait drawn by the sages in the first centuries of the Common Era.

Endnotes

1. Claude Montefiore, *The Synoptic*, Vol. I (London: Macmillan & Co., Ltd., 1910), cxx.

2. Geza Vermes, *Jesus the Jew* (Philadelphia: Fortress Press, 1981), pp. 58-85.

3. Tradition indicates that the Oral Law co-existed with the Written Law, the Torah, from the time it was received at Sinai, and that it provides elaboration and interpretation of Torah teachings. The Talmud is the collection of books which form the written repository of the Oral Law in Judaism. It is made up of the Mishnah (the code of Oral Laws), whose teachers are called Tannaim and which was codified c. 225 C.E.: and the Gemara (commentary and elaboration of the Mishnah) whose teachers are called Amoraim and which was codified in Jerusalem c. 420 C.E., in Babylonia c. 500 C.E.

4. Ephraim Urbach, *The Sages: Their Concepts and Beliefs*, 2 vols., trans. Israel Abrahams (Jerusalem: Magnes Press, 1979).

5. See in particular: Donald Hagner, *The Jewish Reclamation of Jesus* (Grand Rapids: Zondervan, Academie Books, 1984). Walter Jacob, *Christianity Through Jewish Eyes*, (Cincinnati: Hebrew Union College

Press, 1974). Trude Weiss-Rosmarin, ed., *Jewish Expressions on Jesus*, (N.Y.: Ktav Publishing House, Inc., 1977).

6. Hans Kung, *On Being a Christian*, trans. Edward Quinn (N.Y.: Wallaby Pocketbooks, 1978).

7. Vermes, *Jesus the Jew.*

8. See note 3.

9. Gershom Scholem, *Major Trends in Jewish Mysticism* (N.Y.: Schocken Books, 1961), p. 41.

10. Geza Vermes, *Jesus and the World of Judaism* (Philadelphia: Fortress Press, 1984).

11. Vermes, *Jesus the Jew*, p. 225.

12. "Righteousness," *Interpreter's Dictionary of the Bible,* Vol. 4 (New York: Abingdon Press, 1962).

13. "Righteousness," *Encyclopedia Judaica* (Jerusalem: Keter Publishing House, 1972).

14. Urbach, *The Sages.*

15. Ibid., p. 492.

16. Ibid., p. 495.

17. Ibid., vol. I, Chap. 7, "Man's Accounting & the World's Accounting," pp. 483-523.

18. George Foote Moore, *Judaism in the First Centuries of the Christian Era*, 2 vols. (N.Y.: Schocken Books, 1971).

19. Hagner, *Jewish Reclamation*, pp. 203-207.

20. Urbach, *The Sages*, p. 492.

21. "Messiah," *Encyclopedia Judaica*, 1972.

22. Hagner, *Jewish Reclamation*, p. 172.

23. David Flusser, *Jesus* (N.Y.: Herder & Herder, 1969), pp. 44-46.

Faith in Islam

by Thomas Michel

In the previous article, Charlotte Kamin describes the Jewish sages' rejection of Jesus as Messiah as a result of his announcement that the Kingdom of God is a righteous community based on individual spiritual redemption rather than political-national salvation. The tension between faith as a solitary pilgrimage of the believer, versus faith as a communitarian phenomenon with sweeping societal implications, affects not only the Jewish and Christian communities but also the third major branch of the Abrahamic tree of faith: Islam.

Throughout its history, Islam has seen many individual thinkers and societal movements which have viewed faith as either a path to achieving personal perfection, or as a comprehensive societal program in accord with the designs of God. Islamic faith has led individuals to the highest reaches of mystical experience; it has also given directives which form the basis of various cultural, economic, and political systems. In Islam, as in Judaism and Christianity, the polarity between faith as a call to individual righteousness and sanctity, and faith as a liberating, redemptive force of human society, can and should probably never be resolved. In this article I would like to present the bases, or *pillars*, of Islamic faith in order to demonstrate the fundamental content of revelation with which the Muslim faces the challenges of modern life.

Islam is a religion about which most non-Muslims have relatively little factual information. We may think of a chanted call to prayer from minarets, of dark-veiled women moving silently through the streets, of a graceful but forbidding arabesque calligraphy lining the walls of mosques. With the aid of Hollywood we might picture sword-wielding armies hurtling across desert wastes crying forth the name of their prophet. Beyond this, we may find ourselves short of ready facts to explain the "Islam" that forms the reality behind these scattered and often conflicting images.

Ironically, the first term of my title — "faith'" — indicates the vastly different directions from which we approach Islam, or any other religious phenomenon. How each of us views and judges faith in Islam directly depends on the notion of faith carried by each of us individually. How would you define faith for yourself? An intellectual acceptance of truths about God? A personal acceptance of Jesus or someone else as your personal savior? A blind leap of trust in an unknowable deity? The acknowledgment that you have been chosen by God or that you are a member of a people chosen by him?

A closely related question concerns the image which faith gives to our lives and our universe. It has been argued that it makes a great deal of difference whether a people views life as a banquet, a pilgrimage, a dream, a labyrinth, a carnival, or a prison sentence. In this article we will try to discover what faith-image of life Islam offers to Muslims, and how Muslims attempt to pattern their lives in accordance with this vision.

The Quran

The central formative religious experience for Muslims — comparable to the Exodus for Jews, to the death and rising of Jesus for Christians, and to the enlightenment of Buddha under the Bo tree for Buddhists — is God's handing down to Muhammad the prophetic revelations which form the Book of Recitation, the Quran. These revelations took place over 22 years and transformed their recipient, Muhammad ibn 'Abdullah, from a prominent seventh-century Mecca businessman with a fairly good family pedigree into the Messenger of God, the cornerstone of a new society, the final seal of the prophets, and the bearer of a new book, a new law, and a new outlook on life.

Because the principal formative event of the Islamic religion is the revelation of the Quran, and concurrent with it the prophetic mission of Muhammad, Islam is a much more explicitly scripturalist religion than either of the other two great traditions that look back to Abraham as their father in faith. In the Judaic tradition, we see a God acting through historical events to reveal himself to a people, thereby creating a salvific community. In Christianity, this history is compressed into the life of one man, and his experience is considered definitive and communicable to his followers. The event that forms and imprints the everlasting shape on the Islamic community is the Book, the Word of God, handed word for word directly from its divine author to its messenger and prophet, Muhammad.

For this reason, it is imperative that our study of Islamic faith begin with its Quranic roots. We need to explore the faith of Muhammad and the message announced in his preaching. Let us review the social situation into which these revelations came, to see what they were warning against and what vision of life they were trying to form. Finally, and most importantly, let us look at the development of Quranic faith, as it grew and adapted itself to new and unforeseen crises.

Muhammad

We can begin our exploration of Quranic faith with its messenger, Muhammad, when he was in his early forties. The year is approximately 610 C.E. As mentioned before, Muhammad was a respected business figure in the thriving commercial and caravan center of Mecca in Eastern Arabia. But this prosperity and social respectability had not always been a part of Muhammad's life. He was an orphan, raised by his uncle. He had traveled with his uncle's caravans to Syria in his youth, and because of his responsibility and honesty was hired by a wealthy older woman of Mecca, Khadija, to manage her trading firm. They later married, and Muhammad was monogamously faithful to her until her death many years later.

With his economic security and social status assured by his partnerships with Khadija, one might expect that his life would follow the pattern set by the other successful burghers, enjoying what could

anachronistically be called "the Meccan miracle." Mecca was something of a boomtown for two reasons. First, to the north the Byzantine
and Persian empires had been locked in a half-century of warfare, their
armies criss-crossing greater Syria in advance and retreat, thus im-
periling the traditional trade routes between Byzantium and the East.
In the decades preceding Muhammad's birth, the Byzantines circum-
vented this by setting up a government favorable to their interests in
Yemen, in south Arabia, and by using the western littoral of the peninsula as their new caravan route. Thus the semi-nomadic tribesmen
along the trade route were able to transform their traditional areas of
sovereignty into booming trade centers. None were more successful in
this than the Quraysh of Mecca.

A second and almost equally important reason for the pre-emi-
nence of Mecca was the presence of a shrine, a cubical structure called the *Ka'ba* in Arabic because of its shape. In this were placed images
of the various tribal deities, as well as pictures of the prophets of Judeo-
Christian tradition: Abraham, Moses, Jesus, etc. The finest examples
of poetic literature of the time were also housed in this shrine. Thus
Mecca was the most important site of pilgrimage for the nomadic
peoples of the peninsula, and because of this it was a *haram*, a protected area where bloodshed, warfare, and tribal vendetta could not be
carried out. This of course served to enhance its role as the leading en-
trepot in western Arabia.

All of the social abuses traditionally associated with the nouveau
riche were exemplified by the situation in seventh-century Mecca.
Many people were eliminated from the prevailing prosperity. The
traditional victims of abuse and neglect — the widows, orphans, handi-
capped, outcasts and strangers from their tribe — had no claim on
anyone's good will or sense of responsibility. Slaves and women had no
rights. The latter were particularly helpless. A woman's dowry at marriage was kept by her father. She could be married and divorced at will,
and had no right to alimony and no basis for financial security. Female
infanticide was common.

It was obviously his repugnance for these prevailing social conditions that pushed Muhammad out of the comfortable berth in life for
which he seemed destined. He began to withdraw from Mecca for
periods of solitude in a hilly region just north of the town, and it was
during one of these nocturnal retreats that the first revelation came to

him. He was terrified and confused by it, as would be any reasonable person, and he kept it a secret from everyone but his wife. She had an old relative who was conversant in Christian and Judaic scriptures; when informed of the revelation, the old man stated that this type of experience could be identified as within the Mosaic tradition.

A Mission

Some months later, the second revelation came. This one included a mission: to preach and denounce the prevailing evils of Mecca — their pagan polytheism and their social injustices. It is here that the prophetic genius of Muhammad can be seen, in his perception that these two issues were indissolubly linked. The oneness of God and the call for an ethically-based social order were the twin foundations on which the first ecstatic outbursts of Islamic faith relied, and it is these same twin goals that Muhammad would be working to achieve during his prophetic mission in Mecca. His later attempts to build a society in Medina according to the Islamic ideal would be informed by the same vision.

Muhammad's insight was to see that the comfortable polytheism which revolved around the Ka'ba was working hand-in-glove with its business oligarchy. It had no ethical code to limit oppression, to encourage generosity or social responsibility, to protect the powerless, or to make men judge their actions by anything that transcended their empirical pragmatic concerns.

Certainly there were Jews and Christians in the Arabian peninsula, but their foreign scriptures and strange customs were alien to the spirit of this essentially desert people. On the other hand, the peninsula had produced a native prophetology of its own — men like Hud, Salih, and Shuayb. It was to the prophets Moses, Noah, Hud, and Salih that Muhammad felt most spiritually akin in his early preaching.

The faith he was preaching — the oneness of God and the necessity of social concern — met first with ridicule and then with active animosity from the leading personalities of Mecca. He was accused of being a sorceror, of being possessed, and of associating only with the worst class of people. It certainly seemed to be true that his early followers were predominantly the disenfranchised: slaves, women, and outcasts; but they also included a number of young men from better families who would take on important roles of community leadership in the future.

A Warning

At this point, still very early in his prophetic career, a new element entered Muhammad's preaching. It was that of warning: those to whom a prophet has been sent but who do not change their ways, and rather scoff and lay verbal traps for the messenger, will be held accountable on the Day of Judgment. A particular judgment passed historically upon unbelieving peoples also began to be preached, and the stories of Noah and the people of his time, and Moses in Pharoah's court, were recounted with details which indicated their relevance for the situation at hand. The well-known destruction of earlier peoples, whose ruins had often been a source of wonderment to the local Arabs, was attributed to the people's rejection of messengers who had been sent to preach monotheism and justice to them.

Of course, along with these severe warnings of Final Judgment and painful hellfire for the unbelievers, there was good news of the rewards of paradise for those who believed and did good works. These word-pictures of paradise in the Quran, often caricatured by Westerners as gross and sensuous, are actually images carefully tailored to the harsh realities of life in the central Arabian desert. Paradise is a well-watered garden where the precarious elements of sustenance are abundantly supplied.

The very precariousness of life in such an inhospitable region of the earth prompts one of the most important elements of Islamic faith — the teaching of *qadar*. This all-important term in the Quran is often translated as predestination, but this reflects later theological controversies rather than the Quranic teaching itself. The highly sophisticated Arabic poetry of Muhammad's time frequently points out that there are some elements of a person's life over which one has no control — birth, sustenance, death. If the rains come, the marginally desert areas bloom and man reaps an abundance; if there is no rain, hard times and even starvation inevitably follow. Similarly, life could be going along perfectly for someone, when his camel becomes hurt on a desert journey and his own death quickly follows. This sudden intervention from the unknown which instantly alters one's plans was known by pre-Islamic Arabs as *dahr* or fate. It was not predestination, but an acceptance that a person's life was measured by something beyond knowledge or control, whose decisions could not be altered. To this the Quranic message brought both a consolation and challenge. The one who brings life and death, the one who gives sustenance, is God. The one who has power over their lives, the one who sets the measure of their possibilities, the one who created not only the universe but each individual person, is not some impersonal, blind, unconcerned fate as they had thought, but is one God who is described in the Quran as the compassionate, the merciful, the protecting friend, the one rich in forgiveness, the loving, the refuge. He is also described as the all-seeing and all-hearing judge, and in this lies the challenge. For it is only those who are unbelieving and have produced no good deeds who have to fear.

Muslims

As years passed in Mecca, Muhammad continued to gain converts who would surrender their lives to God's will, for that is what *Islam* means. They would become *Muslims*, that is, those who surrender themselves to God and his judgments, who actively strive to make their personal and societal lives conform to his will. Simultaneously, the persecution by Meccan leaders increased. At the beginning, they apparently felt that this was a fad which would quickly pass; as it grew obvious with the passage of time that this was not the case, they became determined to crush the movement by force. The weaker members of the small community were tortured and killed; Muhammad's clan was boycotted in an attempt to put pressure on him to cease his preaching. Some of the Muslims fled to Ethiopia. Muhammad was offered a compromise: that the traditional divinities be considered angels in the new scheme. At times Muhammad himself wondered whether these revelations were all from God or whether he was possibly deluding himself.

During all this, the revelations kept coming. One theme began to exert itself more strongly than the rest, and to dominate the messages.

It is what might be called the Abraham motif. Abraham emerges as the true man of faith, who turned his back on the idolatry of his father and his people, who set his face firmly fixed towards the path of true worship of the one God. Thus Abraham is called a *hanif*. Scholars still dispute the exact significance of this word, and whether it was used before Muhammad's time or was a technical term appearing first in the Quran. Either way, its meaning in these Abrahamic passages is clear — it stands for the person who worships only the true God and follows his commands. In this he is distinguished from the pagans as well as from the majority of Jews and Christians. The latter two groups, who are called the *People of the Book* — that is, people with revealed Scriptures — had split into various parties and sects, and had divided up the divine message. This truncated and distorted message was used by each group as a club against the other. Muhammad saw himself rather as being in the direct prophetic line from Abraham, a line that included patriarchs like Ismail, Isaac, Jacob, and Moses; the classical Hebrew prophets, David; the traditional Arabian prophets; and Jesus and his mother Mary. These prophets were disassociated from their wayward followers and were revered as Muslims — that is, people who had surrendered to God — and who all brought essentially the same prophetic message. In all this we see another element of Islamic faith which distinguishes it from that of Jews and Christians: the acceptance of the messages and books of all prophets up to and including Muhammad.

After his emigration from Mecca to Medina, Muhammad set himself about the task of building a society according to the ideals enunciated in the revelations. The revelations were still coming, but they began to be more and more concerned with the legislation by which this new community was to be formed. Muhammad had not forsaken his prophetic call for the more attractive and rewarding role of political leader. In Medina, as previously in Mecca, his goal was to call people to the building of a society which would be guided by God's commands rather than by human whims. The twin pillars of that society in Medina would remain what they had been in Mecca — the worship of God alone, and the establishment of a moral social order.

As was probably inevitable in the formation of such a society, its separateness and individuality became stressed. Conflicts with the Jewish tribes of Medina, and later disputes with Christians, led to polemical rejections of these peoples. However the story is not clear-cut, for the Quran also contains unmistakable references to a type of universal salvation, at least for monotheists. It is stated that Jews, Christians, and Arab monotheists will be judged by their own books, and that those who believe in God and the Last Day and who do good works will have nothing to fear and will not suffer.

I have summarized the most important elements contained in the faith represented in the Quran. But fourteen centuries have passed since the revelation of this book. Our study must be balanced and completed by reference to the constant exegesis which this book has received at the hands of Muslims since that time. The oral reports of the things Muhammad said and did, and the legal decisions he made, have added an authoritative extra-Quranic corpus of literature which specifies and amplifies the message of the Quran.

The Five Pillars

A Muslim today would describe his surrender to God as having five pillars. I would like to offer a brief examination of these so that we can see how they carry on the vision announced and commanded in the Quran.

The first pillar of Islamic faith is the witness that there is no God but God alone, and that Muhammad is his messenger. This formula expresses an uncompromising monotheism and accepts Muhammad as messenger, and thereby the message he brings. It is the true creed of Islam and is included in every prayer. It forms, along with "God is the greatest," the most popular graffiti on the commuter stations of Cairo and Damascus, and is the subtitle of many newspapers and magazines in the Islamic world. By accepting the second part of this witness, that of the messengership of Muhammad, the Muslim also accepts all the previous prophets and messengers, and their messages and books.

The second pillar is the public prayer. This is performed by every conscientious Muslim five times a day, and its form is strictly fixed by Islamic tradition. The prayer (*salat*) must not be considered empty formalism, however, as each prayer requires a specific act of intention; if thoughtlessly performed, it does not fulfill the obligation. Similarly, it is not meant to be an oppressive duty, and Islamic law allows a great deal of latitude in regard to times, places, and exemptions for those unable to gather with the community at the proper time. Moreover, life in the Islamic world has adjusted itself admirably to a schedule where the prayers form an integral part of the day, rather than acting as alien interruptions. The function of the prayer is to sacralize life according to the Quranic ideal, so that at morning, noon, and night all Muslims remake their surrender to God, facing the direction of the ancient shrine, the Ka'ba, which since the Quran has symbolized the presence of the transcendent God on earth.

It is the third pillar of faith which specifically commands the major impulse of Quranic teaching, that of a responsible social order. This is the poor tax which must be paid by all Muslims for distribution to the disadvantaged in the community. The beauty of this concept is that it is not an uninvolved generosity by which the wealthy, out of the goodness of their hearts, help the poorer among them. Rather it is a duty, a strict obligation upon each Muslim, such that if one did not give according to the standard set by law, one could not be considered a true Muslim before God. The poor-tax, then, is a measure to balance the inequalities of economic life; it is a matter of justice demanded by the religion itself, as many of the more socially oriented Muslim thinkers of our own time have pointed out.

The fourth pillar of faith in Islam is the month-long fast during the month of Ramadan. During the period of fast, which is from dawn until sunset, Muslims abstain from all food, drink, stimulants such as cigarettes, and sexual relations. The religious purposes of this fast are variously explained, and each bears part of the truth. Ramadan is a time for religious renewal, and in addition to the daytime fast, evening prayers are doubled in the mosques, and many of the more pious spend the night in prayer and reading the Quran. Ramadan is a month of celebration for the gift of God's word, the Quran, since it is believed that the first revelation took place during this month. The fast is the principal Islamic communitarian experience, and the sense that everyone is doing something difficult together for God has the effect of heightening a Muslim's consciousness about belonging to a people. It is this communitarian aspect of Ramadan that most strikes a non-Muslim in the Islamic world, for the counterpart to the daytime fast is the evening of family celebrations. Unlike the annual fasts for Jews and Christians, atonement for sins is not a central element in the Ramadan fast, although God's ever-available mercy and forgiveness are felt to be especially abundant during Ramadan.

The fifth and final pillar of Islam is the pilgrimage. This again is a great communitarian experience, as anyone who has read the account in Malcolm X' s autobiography can testify. It is a once-in-a-lifetime event, and obligatory for those who can afford it. Its most spectacular ceremony is the circumambulation of the Ka'ba, long since cleansed of its idols by Muhammad; the essential act, however, is the whole group of pilgrims standing in the presence of God on Mount Arafat. This moment is meant to crystallize, in the space of one afternoon, all that the Islamic faith stands for. It is God who is the beginning and end of our lives, the one who sets the standards by which we live, the one who decides our ultimate destiny, the one who has called the pilgrims to this desert mountain in obedience to the divine will. Life is not a labyrinth where humankind stumbles about, trying to piece together some meaning for itself; rather, it is a standing in the presence of one transcendent being and submitting to the compassionate, forgiving, guiding, supportive, and merciful will.

Thus, in conclusion we have returned to the place we started. What image of life does Islamic faith give to those who accept it? The labyrinth with its twists and turns and dead ends must be rejected, as must the bright and illusory but ultimately superficial carnival, the banquet with its sense delights that instantly please but are soon forgotten, and the dream with its insoluble questions about reality and existence. The image of a pilgrimage comes closer, but the actual image envisioned by Muslims is that of the straight path — the highway that leads directly to the goal, from which deviation to the right or left may land one in spinning sand, impenetrable forests, and unmarked trails. The opening chapter of the Quran forms part of each Muslim's daily prayer. It is a prayer to God to show people the straight path, the path for those on whom blessing falls, not the path of those who earn God's anger or who have gone astray. This straight path for Muslims is the faith of Islam, their trusting surrender of themselves to God's merciful will, and their commitment to build life and society accordingly.

The Principle of Complementarity and World Religions

by Stephen Infantino

Comparisons, whether objective or subjective, often stress the differences and divisions among religions. In a nuclear world which is already politically and economically divided, healing the divisions created by major religions of the world has become more urgent. Some people, like the Reverend Thomas Keating, even believe that world religions have an obligation to heal their divisions:

> The world religions have a special obligation to contribute to the cause of world peace. For in the past, their confessional differences have led to violence, injustice, and persecution. If they would pool their spiritual resources and give witness to the world community of mutual respect, compassion, and understanding, political and nationalistic divisions might more easily be overcome.[1]

If the divisions are to be healed, however, differences among the religions must be taken into account and not merely glossed over. Past ecumenical movements have stalled because the various faiths engaged in dialogue have been shocked by the threat of having their identity absorbed into some super-religion. In other instances, denominations have even refrained from any dialogue because they feared the creation of some vague, all-inclusive type of faith.

Complementarity

The concept of complementarity recognizes differences as real, and yet sees these differences not as creating divisions but as balancing and enriching each other. One such use of the principle of complementarity can be found in an article by scientist, mathematician, and educator, Dr. Warren Weaver. Weaver writes that it was Niels Bohr's principle of complementarity that enabled him to accept both a humanistic/deistic concept of God, as well as a theistic one.

> Therefore, when I ask myself what I believe about the nature of God, and when I do this within an impersonal, intellectual framework, I find it satisfying to say that God represents the moral purpose of the universe and that He is the author of the great, grand design. On the other hand, when I am in trouble or frightened about the safety of those I love, or when I am wrestling with very personal problems, or when I hear the cry of a child in the night, or when I am moved by a well-remembered hymn, then my view is paradoxically different. Then He is the ever-dependable friend, the loving and protecting father.[2]

Just as Bohr saw no inconsistency in accepting the fact that light can be both a particle and a wave under separate experimental conditions, so Weaver sees no difficulty in God being both non-personal and personal. This notion of complementarity is commonly expressed by the phrase, "two sides to the same coin." God is both personal and non-personal. There is Saguna Brahman and Nirguna Brahman — two aspects of the same reality. Krishna, Rama, Gautama, and Jesus can be different appearances or incarnations of the same eternal logos or ultimate reality.

This, however, is not the type of complementarity on which this article will focus. In a certain sense, this idea of complementarity emphasizes the oneness, and unity among religions. It is found in Hinduism, and often enables religions to focus on a common ground from which to begin a dialogue. The other type of complementarity is one that involves balance or completion of one belief by another. It is the type in which one belief helps another out of some logical difficulty. It is the complementarity meant when one says that spouses or friends should complement each other. It usually comes at the end of a dialogue rather than at its beginning. In fact, one of the major works dealing with this type of complementarity is entitled *Beyond Dialogue*.[3] Quentin Lauer and Roger Garaudy speak of it in their book, *A Christian-Communist Dialogue,* as a "sympathetic understanding of disagreement." On this "third level" of dialogue ". . .each position constitutes for the other a significant counterbalance. Atheism plays a purifying role for the Christian by preventing him from adoring a false, man-degrading god; and Christian faith for its part awakens the atheistic humanist to the necessity of remaining open to transcendence — if not of God, at least of man."[4]

There are further advantages to using this second sense of complementarity when dealing with the philosophies of major world religions. These advantages are especially applicable to those who are just beginning to come in contact with other faiths. A 65-year-old Jewish-Italian ex-boxer and former student of mine, when asked if he would feel threatened by studying different religious philosophies, replied, "Oh no, I can admire another beautiful woman and still love my wife." In other words, differences — even attractive differences — do not necessarily imply contradiction or conflict. One can admire a different religion without feeling unfaithful to one's own belief. By lessening the threat posed by religious differences, the attitude of complementarity helps to de-polarize those newly exposed to religions other than their own.

Another advantage to the attitude of complementarity is that concepts from other religions may be used to help one's own religion out of some logical difficulty. To carry out the former student's analogy, a husband might learn something from the other woman that would prove helpful in dealing with his own wife.

A third benefit is that we may see that it is possible to do something for people in other religions besides converting them. We can offer others our beliefs as a tool to better understand their faith.

Last of all, complementarity may help us obtain a more comprehensive view of our own faith by discovering something that we had never known before or that had been underemphasized.

Showing how all of the major world religions could complement each other would be a lifetime task. However, the following exposition offers examples in which three of the major world religions — Hinduism, Buddhism, and Christianity — complement each other. The first three examples have been worked out in some detail. The other nine are presented in summary form.

Eternal Hell

One of the theological problems long vexing Christianity has been the question of how God can be all-loving and merciful, and yet punish people with eternal hell. Some Christians have solved this problem by denying that hell is eternal. Apart from being too facile a solution (one could just as easily deny the infinite love and mercy of God), this denial of eternal punishment does not seem to do justice to the normal meaning of the Greek word *aionion* in Matthew 26:41,[5] or to the way in which this passage, and Luke 16:26, have traditionally been interpreted by the majority of Christian denominations.

From classroom experience, I have found that the more traditional Christian has responded to this problem by simply saying that there is no problem: "The person did wrong; the punishment is his fault; there is no reason to blame God for the punishment." The normal definition of punishment, however, is "retributive suffering, pain, or loss" — which is administered or exacted in recompense.[6] Punishment in the strict meaning of the term implies a dual cause. Both the wrong-doer and the one who administers or exacts the suffering are responsible for the punishment. God as the judge can commute the sentence.

The law of karma found in Hindu belief can offer a way to reconcile God's infinite love and mercy with a belief that persons can eternally suffer in hell for their sins. Briefly put, the law of karma is the law of cause-and-effect in the moral order. There are three distinctions between the idea of punishment and that of cause-and-effect. Firstly, if I put my hand through a window and the hand is cut, I do not say that I was punished for putting my hand through the window, but would say that this is an example of cause-and-effect. If the word *punishment* were used, it would be in the broad or figurative sense. A second distinction is that cause-and-effect or karma dictates that the effect of putting my hand through the window is the same whether I did the act deliberately or unintentionally, whereas ignorance and insanity can be extenuating circumstances for punishment. Thirdly, when there is a question of cause-and-effect, the only one responsible for the effect is the agent; there is no judge who either allows the effect to take place or prevents it. In short, there is no judge to share the responsiblity for the effect.

The traditional Christian response to this problem is actually an attempt to remove all responsibility from God for the harm that the wrong-doer suffers because of his own misdeed. The drawback to this traditional response is that as long as the harm is conceived of as a punishment, the responsibility of the judge cannot be completely removed. This traditional response explains punishment in terms of cause-and-effect, but punishment involves two responsible agents producing an effect, whereas karma involves only one.

Speaking of karma rather than punishment, total responsiblity for the eternal separation from God can be placed on the agent. Eternal separation would be the result of a person's constant rejection of God's love and will. God continues to offer mercy and love, but the person persists in refusing, for whatever reason. Someone might object that no people in their right mind would continue to reject God's love if they knew that accepting it would end their pain. However, it is not far-fetched to think that some people would choose to suffer rather than admit to being wrong and accept forgiveness. There is the stubbornly proud person who is extremely angry with God because of the problem of evil. There is also the extreme skeptic who could never be convinced of the existence of God no matter what sounds, visions, or situations were experienced. These types of people might find it psychologically impossible to accept forgiveness from an all-loving God.

Human Freedom

A second logical problem, found not only in Christian belief but also in Judaism and Islam, is the reconciliation of God's will and omnipotence with a belief in human free will and responsibility. The problem is that God wills people to love God and each other, but this is often made ineffective by human free will. This ineffectiveness seems to imply some limitation in the power of God's will. The standard solution is to say that God could force a person to do the divine will but is restrained so that the person can exercise free will. God has the power but chooses not to use it.

This solution, however, still gives us a God who is limited in power— although self-limited. Suppose we conceive of an all-powerful ruler who could bring world peace but chooses not to exercise the power to do so. Such a ruler would probably not be called all-powerful in the fullest sense of the word, i.e., actually exercising unlimited power. In fact, such a ruler might even raise doubts about being all-powerful at all. While this solution may satisfy those who already believe, or want to believe in, an all-powerful God, it still describes a God with de facto limited power and is not too convincing for those who are neutral or skeptical regarding the omnipotence of God. To the skeptics, this solution seems more like a lame excuse—"Oh, God could, but just doesn't want to."

The Hindu belief in reincarnation may offer a solution which, if not easier for the skeptic to accept, at least does not appear to be as evasive as the solution traditionally offered by Christians. The attempt to reconcile God's omnipotence with human free will, however, is not enough to justify the concept of reincarnation; we must also clarify what it is that God wants which human free will prevents. If we assume that God wants people to make free decisions that are morally good and then take the consequences, we have started towards a solution. When we add the belief in reincarnation to this assumption, we are led to explain the dilemma of God's omnipotent will and human freedom in the following manner. Most people exercise free will, learn from their mistakes, gain greater knowledge over a series of lifetimes, and eventually come to the decision that the best thing to do is to live a moral life by loving God and each other. The divine way prevails, and God is therefore omnipotent. Human beings eventually decide to use God's way because they have learned from the consequences of their free decisions that it is best for them to do so.

Reincarnation

Christians should have little problem incorporating the notion of reincarnation into their belief. Reincarnation had been accepted in

Christianity until it was condemned in the sixth century. Quincy Howe in his book, *Reincarnation for the Christian*, makes a good case for its compatibility with Christian belief.[7] The reasons presented for its condemnation in the past are no longer very strong. Howe even refers to the story of the man born blind[8] to indicate that the apostles entertained a belief in reincarnation and that Jesus at least tolerated such a belief.

Reincarnation can also help Christian theology out of the dilemma of reconciling a belief in Jesus as the only way to the Father — "For of all the names in the world given to men, this is the only one by which we can be saved"[9] — with divine fairness and God's universal salvific word. All have not come to a knowledge of the truth nor to a knowledge of the name of Jesus. Granted that Christian writers have dealt with this problem in other ways[10], the use of reincarnation is as good as the others and has the merit of avoiding relativism, and at the same time creating a bridge between Christianity and one of the other major religions of the world. Through belief in the name of Jesus, one will ultimately obtain release from the cycle of reincarnation and enjoy complete union with God.

Other Examples

I would like to spend the remainder of this article briefly sketching some further areas of complementarity. In some instances, it will be Christianity that is complementing another religion. It is with some reservation that I offer certain Christian beliefs as an aid to other religions. Since I am a member of the Christian faith, I am more comfortable pointing out how other religions can complement Christianity than in pointing out how Christianity can complement other religions. Someone on the inside of a religion is more acquainted with that religion's problems and has more of a right to be critical. An outsider offering help is often likely to discover that he has seen some problem, when the group to whom he is offering the help sees none.

Hinduism, with its belief in karma and reincarnation, can complement Christianity. Christianity, with its belief that death and judgment come "like a thief in the night" and its consequent stress on the importance of this present life, can offset the passivity sometimes created by a belief in reincarnation. In short, Christianity offers a sense of urgency about the present life that can prevent the belief in reincarnation from creating complacency and stifling the incentive to make as much progress in this life as possible.

Since the time of Arius, Christianity has had difficulty trying to explain how God can become human, how the infinite can become finite. The Hindu concepts of monism, emanation, and *maya* may offer some help to Christian thought. There would have to be a slight modification, however, of Hindu monism in order to maintain the total otherness of God. Rather than the world being an emanation of the Godhead or Absolute, the person of Jesus would be the emanation of the eternal Logos. Jesus is finite and human only on the superficial level of reality called *maya*. Jesus is infinite on the deeper level of reality. Just as Atman appears finite but is, on a deeper plane of reality, Brahman — infinite being, knowledge, and bliss — so Jesus appears finite but is, on a deeper plane of reality, the infinite eternal Logos.

Both Paul Knitter and John Cobb must be given credit for exploring the complementarities between Buddhism and Christianity.[11] As Cobb points out, the Buddhist doctrine of non-attachment and right-mindedness can keep Christian faith from becoming a selfish clinging to God and Christ. He writes, "Perfect faith is complete letting go, not holding fast. Instead of controlling and directing attention, it is openness to whatever happens."[12]

Cobb also sees the Buddhist doctrine of no-self, i.e. no substantial self, as supporting and encouraging the commandment of Christian love, rather than making it problematical as would a belief in a self that is individualized substance.

> The problems of mutual externality and isolation and the sense of the radical difference between the relation to the neighbor and the relation to the self have all been accentuated in the past by Western substantialist conceptualization. If each were in truth a separate substance, then indeed the relations to the self would be wholly internal whereas the relations to the others would be wholly external. The love commandment would then fly in the face of metaphysics![13]

On the other hand, Cobb suggests that the Christian goal of transcending the personal self, rather than dissolving it as Buddhism seems to imply, can give Buddhism less of a nihilistic character and make it more attractive to Orientals as well as Occidentals. I have been fortunate to hear two teachers from the Buddhist Temple of Chicago speak about the Buddhist doctrine of no-self. The Reverend Saito spoke of "breaking down" the shell of personalized ego that separates one from the rest of reality and prevents harmonizing with the world. The Reverend Kubose, however, spoke of transcending the individualized self. Whether the Reverend Kubose was influenced by Christian thinking, I do not know, but his conceptualization was more personally attractive to me than the more traditional conceptualization presented by Reverend Saito.

Cobb also encourages Christians to use the concept of "emptiness" to conceptualize God. This concept would prevent them from thinking of God as static or anthropomorphic and help return Christian thought to a God who is "ultimate actuality."

> God must be conceived as lacking substantiality. . .God must be the complete, unqualified, everlasting actualization of the *pratitva-samutpada*, dependent origination. It is precisely by being perfectly empty that God, like a Buddha, is perfectly full. That is, God must be totally open to all that is and constituted by its reception.[14]

Cobb appears to be suggesting that Buddhism helps Christianity return to St. Thomas' concept of God as *actus purus*.

In a section entitled, "What Buddhists Can Learn From Christians," Cobb suggests that the Christian belief in Christ not only acting upon the world, but also responding to it, could make Amida Buddha even warmer and more personal. This belief could also give a Buddhist believer a feeling that life is of importance to Amida, since Amida would hear prayers and respond to them.[15]

Furthermore, Cobb sees Christianity contributing to Buddhism by giving it a focus on a "trans-social norm by virtue of which society is judged."[16] Cobb does not mean to imply that Buddhist societies are less moral than Christian ones. In fact he states just the opposite. Goodness is certainly present in Buddhism, but Amida's grace could be complemented by expanding it to include a call to social criticism and social justice. It is such a call that is emphasized in both the Hebrew Bible and the New Testament.

During the first official Naropa Institute Buddhist-Christian Fellows' Dialogue,[17] one participant who had journeyed to Buddhism from Christianity through Judaism said that social concern and criticism were part of her Judeo-Christian heritage that she has retained as a Buddhist. Another Buddhist participant added that the stories of Gautama's miracles on behalf of other people could form the foundation for a more explicit social concern in Buddhism, just as the miracles of Jesus do in Christianity.

In comparing world religions of today, a unique component of Christianity is the ideal of self-sacrificing love symbolized by Jesus' death on the cross, and by his words, "A man can have no greater love than to lay down his life for his friends."[18] The Buddhist monks who burned themselves in protest against the Diem regime during the Vietnam War were examples of this self-sacrificing love. Therefore, it is certainly possible for a Buddhist to come to awareness of such love. Although such examples of self-sacrificing love are found in Buddhism, it has no prominent symbol for this love. Jesus as the Bodhisattva could be such a symbol, and might enhance the Buddhist doctrine of selflessness and compassion.

Conclusion

As our Earth becomes smaller, as people travel more, as businesses become more international, as theologians, scholars, and teachers increase their dialogue, and as the human spirit seeks to expand itself and to embrace all that is true and good, the people of this planet Earth will have a greater opportunity to be enriched by each other's beliefs. Differences will definitely remain. Some may even be irreconcilable, but an open spirit can enable us to unite as one global community, just as our basic humanity unites us in one human race. May this essay be both an attempt and an invitation to help realize this hope.

Endnotes

1. Reverend Thomas Keating, O.C.S.O., *In Search of the Ultimate Mystery — A Proposal*. A paper presented to the Buddhist-Christian Fellow's Dialogue, Naropa Institute, Boulder, Colorado, August 3-10, 1984.

2. Warren Weaver, "The Religion of a Scientist," in *Religions of America*, ed. Leo Rosten (New York: Simon & Schuster, 1975), pp. 304-305.

3. John B. Cobb, Jr., *Beyond Dialogue — Towards a Mutual Transformation of Christianity and Buddhism* (Philadelphia: Fortress Press, 1982).

4. Roger Garaudy and Quentin Lauer, S.J., *A Christian-Communist Dialogue* (Garden City, New York: Doubleday & Co. Inc., 1968), p. 14.

5. See both *The Greek-English Lexicon* by Henry George Liddel, M.A. and Robert Scott, M.A. (New York: Oxford University Press, 1968) in which *aionion* is translated as "lasting, eternal," and *A Greek-English Lexicon of the New Testament*, William F. Arndt & F. Wilbur Gingrich, (Chicago: University of Chicago Press, 1979) in which the word has the meaning of either "without beginning, without beginning or end," or "without end."

6. See *The Merriam-Webster Dictionary* (New York: Pocket Books, 1974) for definitions of punishment and retribution.

7. Quincy Howe, *Reincarnation for the Christian* (Philadelphia: Westminster, 1974). Also, Barbara Clow's article in this volume.

8. John 9:1-3

9. Acts 4:12

10. Lucien Richard, O.M.I., *What Are They Saying About Christ and World Religions?* (New York: Paulist Press, 1981).

11. See Paul F. Knitter, "Horizons on Christianity's New Dialogue with Buddhism," *Horizons*, vol. 8, no. 1, 1981; also John B. Cobb, Jr., *Beyond Dialogue, Toward a Mutual Transformation of Christianity and Buddhism*, (Philadelphia: Fortress Press, 1982).

12. Cobb, p. 104.

13. Cobb, p. 109.

14. Cobb, p. 113

15. Cobb, pp. 130-132.

16. Cobb, pp. 132-136.

17. Boulder, Colorado, August 3-10, 1984.

18. John 15:13

A Western Bodhisattva

by Mike Foster

It seems clear that philosophical, religious, and cultural dialogue is of fundamental importance in uncovering the *Principle of Complementarity*, described by Stephen Infantino as an intimate sense of connection with the world lying beyond the skin. This openness to dialogue, however, is often absent in our modern world. As Chuang-Tzu[1] maintains, we tend to view the world as if we were standing at the bottom of a well, for we mistake that small circle of sky at the top for the cosmos as a whole.

There are, of course, those few teachers who seek to enlighten us and to expand our narrow view of reality. However, these counter-cultural leaders often die as victims of the very societies they challenge. Mahatma Ghandi and Dr. Martin Luther King, Jr. actively opposed injustice, yet were martyred in doing so. These are the true heroes whom the ancient Buddhists of China and Japan praised as enlightened and compassionate souls, deserving to be called sages, saints, and

Bodhisattvas. Is it possible to find in the enigmatic figure of Alan Watts another Western Bodhisattva?

Prior to Watts' death in 1973, he had been drinking heavily. To his many friends and acquaintances from over the years, he was hardly recognizable: a pale, thin frame only faintly resembling the laughing, dancing, singing chief guru of the California counterculture of the late 1950s and early 1960s. It was obvious by then that he had been replaced by younger, better-versed students who had troubled to learn the Eastern languages thoroughly, and to study extensively in India, China, and Japan.

In every way, Alan Watts was failing, destroyed by the exuberant lifestyle he chose for himself. Who was this enigmatic spiritual teacher? In his own words he was a shaman, bridge-builder, teacher, scholar, and lover of the philosophy and psychology of esoteric religions, especially those of the Far East. His enemies, on the other hand, labeled him a charlatan and a popularizer. But to his close friends, students, and many readers from over the years, he was a most unique person, a man far beyond simple categories.

The Man and His Life

Alan Wilson Watts, the son of Laurence Wilson Watts and Emily Mary Buchanan, was born in the village of Chislehurst, Kent, England, in the early hours of January 6, 1915. Quite early in his life, the Watts family
realized Alan was different from most boys his age. They felt he possessed enough intuitive sense and intellectual promise to make him a true scholar. As a result, at the age of seven and one-half, the young Watts was sent off to St. Hugh's School — a most prestigious English grammar school. Already he was demonstrating some of the characteristics that were to remain with him for the rest of his life: love of movement, color, and, of course, love for anything Asian.

In 1930, through mentor/friend Francis Crowshaw, Watts was led to the Buddhist Lodge of London, where he met his lifelong friend, Christmas Humphreys. Humphreys directed the young afficionado of Buddhism to the voluminous writings of D.T. Suzuki, the great transmitter of Zen to the English-speaking world. On all school holidays and weekends in 1930 and 1931, Watts escaped King's Secondary School to go to London, where he involved himself with Humphreys and the Buddhist Lodge. In 1932, Watts prematurely departed from King's School and embarked upon a lifelong trek along the Zen/Taoist Way. Soon thereafter, while working closely under Humphreys' tutelage, Watts composed his first book of real importance, *The Spirit of Zen*. Alan Watts, author, was but 20 years old.

D.T. Suzuki's visit to London in 1936 was a climax to the young Watts' enthusiasm for Eastern thought, for it was Suzuki's works that formed the backbone of Watts' early writings. Suzuki provided Watts with a broad enough philosophical background to establish a whole new outlook, one he could embrace as his own. For example, while traditional Japanese Zen centers around the practice of *zazen*, or sitting meditation and contemplation, Watts' philosophy was one of constant and harmonious movement where, in his own words, there was no room for "sitting on one's ass."

Through his own experiences, Watts realized that the traditional Zen of Japan could never be accepted on its own terms in the West. Westerners were forever on the move, yet went nowhere; the Japanese, on the other hand, proceeded with a more patient attention and appreciative awareness of what was available in the moment. Hence, Watts sought to establish a bridge between East and West, a theme reflected in his second major work: *The Legacy of Asia and Western Man, a Study of the Middle Way*. In this rather presumptuous book, he attempted to sort through the varying interpretations of Eastern mysticism, comparing them to different areas of scholarship in the West. The mystical teachings of Buddhism and Taoism, in relation to Western psychology, philosophy, and religion, provided a major focus for Watts, one spanning his entire life. In *Psycotherapy East and West* he writes:

> This subject has been "in the air" for at least thirty years, and during this time there has been an ever-growing discussion of this or that parallel between Western psychotherapy and Eastern philosophy. The latter are not, perhaps, psychotherapies in the strict sense, but there is enough resemblance there to make the comparison important.[2]

These works were addressed to a wide variety of people: the Christian, the psychologist, and of course, the lover of Eastern mysteries. They all shared one basic conviction: that a bridge could be established between the ways of the East and West. Watts formed what he called a *middle road*, where he spoke of such concepts as *complementary opposites, sexual union,* and *passive resistance.* More importantly, what he thought would take a thousand years to happen would begin within his own lifetime — East and West would start to merge.

While we may legitimately argue that Watts failed at the task he undertook, and that East is still East and West is still West, we must reconsider his primary ideal. He believed that the Western approach is incomplete, and that a synthesis of East and West would provide us with a more holistic perspective. As previously noted, *zazen* never appealed to Watts in the least. However, the basic idea behind sitting meditation — letting the mind quiet itself by addressing each moment as a completely new experience — can be embraced within our own culture.[3] While Zen as it exists in the West today is clearly dissimiliar to what it is in Japan, it is nonetheless *Zen.*

Watts' life was one of chronic turbulence, but the late 1930s were perhaps the most chaotic. During this time he met the first of three wives, Eleanor Everette, an American Buddhist enthusiast touring with her mother in England. Alan and Eleanor fell madly in love, and after gaining approval from Mr. Everette, the two were married in the Church of England.

Alan had established himself as a successful writer in England, and because of his deeply felt pacifism, left England with Eleanor to escape the war, and headed for the United States. After some work and play in New York City, and after publishing *The Meaning of Happiness,* his third major work, Watts began to explore the possibility of participation in the American religious scene. This difficult task seemed achievable only through his entrance into the ranks of the clergy, since theological freelancing would not provide him with sufficient financial security. This, in turn, entailed locating a religious body which would both tolerate his liberalism and grant him the freedom he needed to keep exploring and writing about Eastern mysteries. After some deliberation and contemplation, he somewhat ironically chose the Episcopalian Church, the American form of the Church of England. Watts found himself an ordained priest and a respectable member of the clergy after five years of diligent study.

Stationed at the Episcopalian chapel on the Northwestern University campus in Evanston, Illinois, the Reverend Watts tried to stimulate

churchgoers with stories and teachings about issues he believed important. His sermons were not boring talks on traditional dogma, but
challenging reflections on how one can truly find contentment in life,
or artfully shared insights into the mysteries of the East in relation to
the Western mind. Here Watts developed many close friendships, since
the small chapel was a busy center for searching people. Alan Watts,
priest, really had not changed much from Alan Watts, philosopher.

By 1948, however, he was already growing tired of organized Christianity. His marriage with Eleanor fell into a shambles, and in August
of 1950 he resigned from the ministry. While restraints placed upon
him by the church and testimony from his ex-wife were undoubtedly
part of the reason for his resignation, it was apparent that Watts did not
have faith in this path. Ultimately, he did not believe.

Shortly after resigning from the church and dealing with some of
his own problems, Watts wrote *The Wisdom of Insecurity*—a significantly
new book. Out of the catastrophe of his involvement with the church,
his first marriage, and the desertion of many friends, came something
of much greater value: Alan Watts was finally himself, something he
had never quite been. This was an exciting book, for it was Alan's first
chance fully to exercize his maturity as a philosopher and religious
thinker. It grew out of a philosophical ideal which he tried to follow for
the rest of his life, one which captured the hearts of many American
young people in the early 1960s: life in its fullest is *right now*. This
openness to the *Eternal Now* was what he understood as the heart of
Zen Buddhism. In his own words:

> If my happiness at this moment consists largely in reviewing
> happy memories and expectations, I am but dimly aware of this pre-
> sent. . . I shall have formed a habit of looking behind and ahead, mak-
> ing it difficult to be here and now. . .[4]

This was truly Watts. It was creative, and it discarded all the philosophical baggage which was so much a part of his earlier works. Actually
it is quite a simple philosophy, yet one which is truly difficult to exercise. Simple, in that life consists of "being here and now," but most difficult because so much of our life is spent in an attempt to attain a happiness which seems to reside everywhere else but now.

Soon after his first divorce, Watts stepped into a second marriage, this time with an intensely practical woman named Dorothy Dewitt. Alan and Dorothy then headed for California, where Watts accepted a teaching position at The American Center for Asian Studies, a graduate program exploring the cultures and philosophies of India, China, and Japan. Along with busily getting the school off the ground, he traveled about San Francisco teaching and lecturing, in addition to being involved with a series of television and radio programs. As a result, it was not long before he was quite well known. This was the Watts of the California counterculture, guru of the West, who advocated free love, drink, and, of course, the Eternal Now.

Soon after its inception, the Academy found itself deep in financial troubles. Most administrators and teachers did all they could to make the Academy a success— Watts was no different. The time he spent lecturing and administering did take its toll, though he continued to immerse himself in the workings of the Academy through 1955.

Through the end of 1956, while Watts was filling the unaccustomed role of administrator, he studied, drank, and involved himself in discussion after discussion on the similarities and differences between the East and West. As a manager, however, Watts enjoyed only limited success; when he accepted this administrative position, he absorbed a whole new set of restrictions— ones he neither wanted nor needed. He was finally making a sufficient income from writing and speaking, so at the end of 1956 he left the Academy to live the free life for which he had always yearned.

Soon after his departure, Watts completed *The Way of Zen*, without doubt his most scholarly work. Beginning with the Chinese philosophy of Taoism, and tracing the path of Buddhism through China and Japan, he gave his readers an insightful account of Zen in all its ramifications. *The Way of Zen* was labeled a "best-seller." Watts himself swallowed his ego a bit, calling it a "minor best-seller." Nonetheless, this success clearly catapulted him to the status of chief guru for the Western world. By today's standards, this book is highly informative, but general. But we must remember that there were only a few major works on Zen available to those outside the scholarly circle. We must admire Watts, for he did not simply try to import Japanese Zen into America, but instead forced Western readers to realize their own incompleteness, while integrating some of the basic ideas of Zen into their culture.

The last years of Watts' life were clearly the most crucial. People began to look to him for guidance along their own spiritual paths. These were times of great success, which in itself brought great tragedy. His public life began to conquer him, and he retreated to alcohol as an escape. Zen, in the meantime, began to blossom in our culture. Naturally, within this expansion came different interpretations of Zen, some better than others. Hence Watts felt it necessary to throw light upon the secrets of Zen. He emphasized that the Zen of the hippie/ drug culture, with its occasional dropping of Zen phrases and substitution of psychedelic drugs for the true *satori* (enlightenment) experience, was hindering the serious Zen movement in the West. This of course is an ironic turn of events since it was at about this time that Watts himself began to suffer from substance abuse.

In looking at the Alan Watts of 1959, we seem to see a content man. But he harbored within him a secret longing to be free from a large family and off meditating in a Zen temple in Japan. He was financially secure, but Dorothy continued to pressure him to settle down and live "practically," something which kept Alan miserable most of the time, dulled his style, and threw him into depression after deep depression.

He spent his weeks traveling and lecturing for budget stipends, continued his writing, and practiced his Chinese. He soon moved out on Dorothy, and in February of 1962 the two were divorced. Not too suprisingly, as was his style, Watts entered into a completely new life. Soon after, he married Mary Jane "Jan" Yates, and set up a house boat off Big Sur in California, where he spent time with Aldous Huxley and various other prominent philosophers. Mentally, he had never been more alert. His marriage was happy. Jan suited him well, since she too wished to be freed from the restraints of modern Western society. These later years, however, wore heavily on Watts: three marriages, public demands, heavy alcohol consumption, and over forty years of smoking were beginning to take their toll.

Watts' health began a rapid decline. Hence his death on the morning of November 16, 1973 did not come as a complete surprise to those close to him. There are those who consider his efforts at East-West unification a failure. In many ways it was. Many of his books, ideas, and beliefs have essentially disappeared, and East is still East as West is still West. However, without the help of scholars like Alan Watts, our present understanding of the Far East would certainly be reduced. More importantly, though, with constant and rapid destruction of our environment, the specter of nuclear war in space, and increasing conflict in Third-World countries, Watts' message is perhaps even more appropriate today than at the time of his death.

The Bodhisattva Doctrine

The Bodhisattva doctrine arose from a disagreement about proper interpretation of the teachings of the historical Buddha, a conflict which led to the division of Buddhism into two separate schools. The first, the Theravada ("school of the elders") is a strict monastic path, one supposedly leading the practitioner to his or her own personal enlightenment (*nirvana*). This is achieved only when one destroys all egoistic desire, for it is the desire to cling to various materialistic elements of existence that hinders our experience of ultimate reality. Not surprisingly, this is a path for the very few. Its disciples must join a monastery, give up all worldly possessions, and spend their lives in study, meditation, and contemplation in hopes of someday attaining nirvana.

Mahayana Buddhism is the second major branch evolving from the teachings of Siddharta Gautama. While Theravada Buddhism maintains that the quest for nirvana is a personal quest, the Mahayanist holds that no one person can enjoy spiritual release until all people have. To pursue nirvana as a personal goal is itself egoistic and meaningless when we consider the greater spiritual teachers, who reject their own enlightenment in order to aid all sentient beings along their paths. Here we uncover the primary difference between the two traditions: while on the one hand the Theravadin maintains that nirvana is the chief end for all individuals, the Mahayana Buddhist argues that it is the eventual awakening of the cosmos as a whole which is the ultimate task of the spiritual healer.

This idea is reflected in Mahayana philosophy in terms of the Buddha/Bodhisattva dynamic. Purely out of compassion, the Bodhisattva turns away from the doors of nirvana, so as to aid all humankind along the way. Har Dayl writes:

> The Bodhisattva ideal was taught in order to counteract this
> tendency to a cloistered and inert monastic life. A Bodhisattva is

empathetically one who criticizes and condemns the spiritual egoism of the *Arhat* ("enlightened one" in the *Theravadin* tradition), with whom he should always be contrasted . . . A Bodhisattva was defined as one who strove to gain *Bodhi* ("enlightenment"), as he wished to help and succor his fellow creatures in the world of sorrow, sin, and impermanence.[5]

The Bodhisattva possesses three basic characteristics separating him/her from those who are less spiritually advanced. The first, compassion (*karuna*), is not a new notion in Buddhist thought, as it is often ascribed to the historical Buddha after his enlightenment. In Mahayanist literature, however, the idea is given greatest priority, for it is the driving force behind the actions of the Bodhisattva.

The second general characteristic, skill in communication (*upaya*), can be understood as the means by which the Bodhisattva conveys the apparently complex and difficult teachings of Buddhism so as to make them accessible to people at all levels of understanding. The Buddha, for example, was especially good at simplifying his teachings depending on the size and abilities of his audience. For an audience of ten thousand, he would keep his message relatively simple (e.g., the Four Noble Truths and the Eightfold Path to enlightenment). To his disciples, on the other hand, he was able to present a much more complex philosophical analysis.

The final characteristic of the Bodhisattva is wisdom or intuitive insight (*prajna*). While *karuna* and *upaya* stand out as concrete and self-explanatory, true wisdom is much more difficult to grasp, and is certainly beyond rational definition. Perhaps it can best be understood as an intuitive and trans-rational awareness of what is really going on in the world and in the cosmos as a whole. It is that rarefied ability to see what others cannot, and actually to experience life in a deep and intimate way.

The Bodhisattva embraces and becomes the word of ultimate reality, and promptly brings it back for all people to marvel at and to heed. Moses, Christ, Muhammad, and Buddha, as well as a host of other figures in spiritual history, all fit into the basic mold of the Bodhisattva, since even though they had reached a deep spiritual and mystical understanding, they still chose to teach and to serve on earth to aid in the eventual enlightenment of all humankind.

A Western Bodhisattva

The life of Alan Watts similarly stands out as a model through which people could begin to grapple with the deeper mystical teachings of East and West. Through his charisma and his eloquent articulation of these deep philosophical ideas, he sought to put everyone "in the know." However, to force people to pay attention to their own spiritual processes, Watts had to go completely against the scholarly norm and articulate his ideas in a more simplistic fashion, one that everyone could understand. This is not to say that the ideas he set forth were not themselves still very complex, but rather that he communicated them with such ease and simplicity that even a child could understand:

> . . . the interesting aspect of Watts' philosophy is its reduction to simplicity: that is the way he wanted it, the old Zen masters were always pointing towards simplicity in the anecdotes they told again and again. Now Watts was making up his own analogies and putting them in terms familiar to twentieth-century American society.[6]

It was because of this simplification of terminology, however, that Watts gained a reputation as a popularizer among members of the scholarly community; they believed his interpretations diluted the deepest meanings of the ancient Eastern philosophies. We must, however, reemphasize that it was Watts' conscious objective to simplify this extraordinarily difficult material. In the same manner as the Bodhisattva attempts to articulate ultimate reality to all people, so did Watts try to communicate in terms that everyone could understand.

The Bodhisattva character of Watts' career involves much more than this. If the Bodhisattva is really to influence the norms which guide an entire culture, he or she must act as countercultural leader, as someone who in varying degrees takes a stand against the oppressive status quo and against commonly accepted misconceptions of the truth.[7] Watts was such a figure for the twentieth-century Western world; his uncanny ability as one of the acting chief gurus of the recent counterculture seems to support this idea. Just as the Bodhisattva often rebels against societal ignorance, so Watts was active against what he considered the great faults of our own society.

An apparent problem arises in this treatment of Watts as a Bodhisattva: while the Bodhisattva is a mystic, one who has attained a truly enlightened state of consciousness, many see Watts as completely selfish and egoistic, and certainly do not perceive in him the characteristics ascribable to the Bodhisattva. While the Bodhisattva seems a perfect being, in that she/he acts with great compassion, Watts was perhaps a drunken bum who lived off his charismatic image. He abandoned his country at the very time he was called to protect it, and he left two wives and five children to fend for themselves. How could we possibly contend that he was compassionate? Compassion was once defined as "feeling another's ache in your own heart."[8] Watts felt the ache of an entire world, one that saw four wars, poverty, environmental disaster, and nuclear madness, all arising from the human ego. He wrote and spoke about all of this, and in the end he was victimized by the very ego he spoke against. He was not perfect by any means, but only a cynical world could doubt his capacity for compassion.

To understand the Bodhisattva as perfect, however, is completely misleading. Only one who has fulfilled his/her Buddha nature has achieved perfection. In the Buddhist tradition, such an achievement often results from the Bodhisattva's exaggeration of personal weakness. Frances Cook remarks:

> The Bodhisattva *Marga* ["path"] is conceived as being a very long, heroic endeavor, covering many lifetimes, marked in each life by the total commitment of the Bodhisattva to emancipate all beings even at the expense of his own life. But in order to do this, he must take pains never to actually reach the final stage of his career, perfect enlightenment. . . . According to *Fa-tsang*, he prevents this by retaining some moral and intellectual faults *(Klesha)* which will bind him to rebirth, thus enabling him to be perpetually reborn in the evil paths in order to aid suffering beings.[9]

Har Dayal maintains that there are ten *kleshas* in Buddhist literature:

1. Greed
2. Hatred
3. Delusion
4. Pride
5. Speculative opinion

6. Doubt

7. Stolidity

8. Excitement, exaltation

9. Unconscientiousness

10. Shamelessness/disregard for social censure[10]

While it is certainly not our responsibility either to apologize or to justify Watts' personal faults, this deeper analysis of the characteristics of the Bodhisattva certainly affords powerful insight. Indeed, some of the ten *kleshas* could serve as perfect adjectives with which to describe Watts: perhaps he was proud in the sense that he demonstrated a need to occupy center stage; certainly he was opinionated, as his writing and his public pronouncements testify, and he was an especially shameless man who held little regard for social convention and censure.

An implicit paradox seems to arise. The Bodhisattva is simultaneously the representative of perfection, yet she/he is imperfect. We must remember, however, that *nirvana* is planetary awakening, rather than just the enlightenment of the individual practitioner. Thus the apparent contradiction can be resolved. The imperfection is not with the Bodhisattva but, conversely, with the faults of the particular society as a whole. In essence, the weaknesses of the Bodhisattvas constitute a reflection and personal embodiment of their culture.

It is precisely in this light that we may discover Alan Watts as a Western Bodhisattva, for Watts truly did personally manifest and indicate many of the major characteristics of our society—both positive and negative. In the words of Al Chung-Liang Huang, Watts' close friend: "He reminded us by his own successes as well as failures how perfectly natural life's imbalance is to all of us."[11] Both Alan Watts and much of Western society suffer from the same disease: the conflict of internal imbalance. As balance is of fundamental importance in the martial arts, so is achieving a psychological balance instrumental in realizing contentment. We must consider, however, how balanced Alan Watts could possibly have been. In one sense, he was in perfect balance with our culture. On the other hand, Watts' life was actually in precarious imbalance, remaining stable only through the consumption of alcohol:

> . . . Alan was able to forgo many of his Victorian inhibitions and
> create for himself and others a curious kind of balance which some-
> how sustained him. In later life. . .constantly pulled by outside
> demands, he was too successful to stop — and too brilliant to submit
> to his own nature. He became the perfect example of the Western
> man as a victim of the *yang*-dominant world.[12]

Yang, of course, is the Chinese configuration for "positive." Analogous to the operation of a battery, one cannot realize contentment
until he/she has grappled with, experienced, and accepted the negative. For Watts this yin/yang polarity was without a doubt the most
necessary balance within his own life and the life of every individual.
It can be seen as good/bad, black/white, East/West, life/death, or
male/female. The trick, as Watts consistently emphasized, is to balance
these complementary opposites.

Through all his game-playing and entertainment of his audiences,
through his lucidity and great wit, Alan Watts provides us with an ideal
vision of reality: a time and place in which we can exercise our individual freedom without loss of our concern for the whole. He was
convinced that people could rid themselves of the incessant need to
identify themselves as other than human, yet not lose the wonderful
uniqueness of each individual. Watts challenges us to live together,
rather than hiding behind our ego masks and illusionary sub-cultures.
Perhaps most importantly, Watts asks that we stop analyzing, categoriz-
ing, and philosophizing about the nature of reality and begin to participate and rejoice in it. For only through experiencing the natural
reality will we not destroy it.

Clearly, the beauty of human civilization arises from the mind, but
it also embodies a dark element with which we all must begin to contend. We humans tend to group experiences, individuals, and all other
elements of existence together, as if each were not a unique expression of the natural process. Racism is an obvious example. As Watts
saw it, it is only through the "other" that we can possibly come to know
ourselves:

> You are yourself the universe which you are observing. You are
> trying to get at yourself when you love/hate other people. I am going
> to leave it to you to work out the connection between frustration and

its implication (it's a wonderful trip), and add only that the aspect of yourself which you cannot see is obviously not any idea, image, or opinion of yourself that you have not already formed.[13]

By treating this opposing factor as completely separate, we have ignored the fact that only through this aspect or idea can we really ever come to know that as part of ourselves. In a sense, we cannot get at the root of ourselves without first embracing the other.

This is in many ways analogous to a jig-saw puzzle, for only when all pieces are in place do you know where yours fits. By placing that final piece in, you come to the sudden and simple realization that it was actually one picture in the first place:

> How is it possible that a being with such sensitive jewels as the eyes, such enchanted musical instruments as the ears, and such a fabulous arabesque of nerves as the brain can experience itself as anything but God?[14]

Whether or not Alan Watts actually came to realize himself as part of this whole we will never know, but he certainly left this ideal for all of us who follow in his footsteps.

Endnotes

1. Chuang-Tzu was a Chinese poet and philosopher during the first century, B.C.

2. Alan W. Watts, *Psychotherapy East and West* (New York: Vintage Books, 1962), p. ix.

3. There is, for example, a long history of walking meditation in Zen Buddhism, which is perhaps more easily applied than *zazen* for the average Westerner.

4. Allan W. Watts, *The Wisdom of Insecurity* (New York: Pantheon Books, 1951), p.35.

5. Har Dayl, *The Bodhisattva Doctrine in Buddhist Sanskrit Literature* (Delhi, India: Indological Publishers, 1932), p.3.

6. David Stuart, *Alan Watts* (New York: Stein and Day Publishers, 1976), p. 176.

7. Christ provides us with a classical example of the rebel tendency of the Bodhisattva, since he was surely murdered because he was seen as a threat to the government.

8. From a lecture delivered by Professor R. H. Miller at Lake Forest College on March 19, 1986.

9. Francis K. Cook, *Hua Yen Buddhism* (University Park: Pensylvania State University Press, 1981), p. 110.

10. Dayl, *Bodhisattva Doctrine,* p.109.

11. Alan W. Watts, *TAO: The Watercourse Way* (New York: Pantheon Books, 1975), p.127.

12. Ibid, p.125.

13. Alan W. Watts, *Cloud Hidden Whereabouts Unknown* (New York: Vintage Books, 1968), p. 199.

14. Alan W. Watts, *The Book on the Taboo Against Knowing Who You Are* (New York: Vintage Books, 1966), p. 143.

One Day, No Day, Each Day, Zen Day

by Madeleine Sophie Cooney

When I read Mike Foster's article on "A Western Bodhisattva," I recalled my own encounter with a Japanese Buddhist abbot who seemed to me the epitome of an "Eastern Bodhisattva." It would be difficult to imagine two more different human beings than Alan Watts and Naka-gawa Soen-roshi, but each possessed the art of cherishing the *Eternal Now*.

On January 15, 1970, I had an experience that changed my life in a way that is still more a matter of mystery than history. The dynamics of the event and its results are easy to describe, impossible to ration-alize. Together, they compose a koan whose meaning is so obvious that I cannot decipher it. Seventeen years later, that day at Ryutaku-ji re-mains one of those moments outside time that resist logical analysis and objective evaluation. Only a straightforward description is pos-sible, and through description, perhaps a sharing of the teasing, elusive quality of Zen.

During several months of teaching in the Graduate English Division of the College of the Sacred Heart (Seishin Gakuin Daigaku) in Tokyo, I was invited to go once each fortnight to Susono, near Mt. Fuji, to lecture on English Literature to the novices of the Society of the Sacred Heart. I traveled up by bus, gave my class, enjoyed the hospitality of the Japanese community, stayed overnight, and returned to Tokyo via the Tomei highway, made famous in Hiroshige's *ukiyo-e* prints of the traditional Stations of the Tokkaido. In these days the old Tokkaido Road is a super-highway, but the superb mountain scenery is as magical as it was portrayed in hundreds of "pictures of the Floating World."

One day in mid-January, I had gone to Susono to lecture, when I was invited by the mistress of novices and the principal of the school to accompany them to a Buddhist monastery in Mishima City, Shizuoka Prefecture, just a few minutes by car from our convent. An appointment with the abbot, Nakagawa Soen-roshi, had been arranged by two Japanese ladies — his disciples — whose children attended our school at Susono. At the time, I had never heard of Ryutaku-ji or its revered abbot, and I had never read Philip Kapleau's book, *The Three Pillars of Zen*.

I accepted the invitation enthusiastically and looked forward to an entire day at a Zen Buddhist monastery, whose main shrine is devoted to the goddess Kannon (in Chinese, Kuan-Yin), Mother of Mercy. Japanese Christians, in times of persecution, used to stand reverently before representations of Kannon, while really directing their prayers to Mary, the Mother of Jesus. Like the Virgin, Kannon is often depicted holding a small child.

The five of us set off early for the Monastery of the Pond Dragon and soon arrived at the foot of a very high, wooded hill on which the monastery buildings sat, overlooking rich farmlands worked by the monks. Some monasteries had become quite commercialized, and offered souvenir shops selling everything from cotton candy to little figures of Daruma, the god of luck; but Ryutaku-ji, which had been founded some two centuries ago, kept the Buddhist traditions of quiet awareness and meditation.

We climbed slowly up the many rustic steps set among beautiful groves, feeling already the peace of Zen Buddhism. On top of the hill, in a large clearing, stood the simple and elegant old monastic buildings, all in pure Japanese style. They were surrounded by typical gardens, swept scrupulously clean, and were musical with running water. Even in winter, with its damp, penetrating cold, they looked springlike, since birds were singing, the white and pink plum blossoms were already in flower, and oranges hung on the trees. We proceeded to the main building, removed our shoes, and substituted soft socks which we had brought with us. At once, a young monk appeared, bowed low, and led us around the veranda, up more rustic steps, and into a tea ceremony room, where cushions were set out on the tatami mats. We were invited to sit once we had knelt at the *tokonoma*, or sacred alcove, to admire the flower arrangement, the scroll, and the New Year's offerings — seven figures of dogs, to initiate the Year of the Dog.

At each place was a ceramic charcoal burner, as the room was cold. Small fires were obviously meant to give off some heat, or at least to suggest warmth, but since the buildings were made of thin wood and the windows filled with paper panes, the houses were extremely chilly. The monks were all barefoot, their hands and feet swollen, and in some cases purple with cold.

In a few moments the abbot appeared and bowed low to greet us with a most charming welcome, full of ease and poise and simplicity. I can never hope to describe adequately the appearance or the gentle power of Nakagawa Soen-roshi. No one else in my life has impressed me so profoundly. He was quite an old man — or so he seemed — and his shaven head was long and thin, like a weathered gourd. His face resembled an old wood carving, except when he laughed, which he did quite frequently with delight and spontaneity. He radiated happiness and peace and joy, and reminded me of the words of Jesus, "Unless you become as little children . . . ." But there was in him, too, a kind of mischievous, elfin spirit, so that he never seemed conventional, nor did he say and do what was expected, but instead always what was natural, unpremeditated, and perfectly suited to the occasion. I have since reflected that it would be as impossible for him to do or say anything awkward or tactless as it would be for a daisy or a star. He was as close as I have ever come to total simplicity.

While we were trying to absorb the impact of the abbot, one of the Japanese ladies retired to make preparations for the tea ceremony. With the young monk's help, she then carried out the prescribed ritual with grace and perfection. First, small lacquered trays were passed around with cakes decorated in a white crane motif. The sweets were little works of art made with the ubiquitous Japanese bean paste. Their function was to condition the palate for the bitter tea. Meanwhile, the hostess, in formal kimono of course, was brewing the green tea and stirring it with a bamboo whisk to create froth on the surface. The first bowl went to the roshi, as master of the house, and then one went to each of us. The tea ceremony, when done in proper spirit, with full attention to details of ritual and perfect balance between formality and simple sharing, is a real communion. At the beginning of a day of extraordinary giving and receiving, it bonded the seven of us into a community of friends.

My bowl had twelve zodiacal animals in Chinese characters around the rim, and I was shown by the young monk which one was the dog, so that I would be sure to drink from that spot. After swallowing the tea in three appreciative gulps, we were to finger the bowl lovingly and compliment the host on its structure and color harmony. Experts, of course, would refer to the provenance of the bowl, since tea masters often possess works of art from the famous kilns of past centuries. The conversation was carried on in a leisurely spirit, and followed a familiar pattern within which there emerged a surprising amount of freedom.

When we had finished the tea, and the closing ceremonies of cleansing and removing the tea utensils had been scrupulously carried out, the abbot said, "In a Zen Buddhist monastery, one of the main forms of entertainment is the peace and tranquility. Let us for awhile amuse ourselves with this tranquility — all right?" Whereupon we all fell silent and listened to the birds in the plum trees, to the unseen water trickling down the hillside, and to the gong that accompanied the chanting of a sutra as the monks in another building were offering newly cooked rice before statues of Buddha and the Bodhisattvas. On his cushion, with his spine absolutely straight, and ceremoniously garbed in the special light brown that marks him as head of the house, the roshi sat alert and completely at ease, listening and teaching by saying nothing. Presently he said, "Later, we shall have discussion. But — I disgust with discussion. The best discussion is no discussion." We all burst into laughter, because after all the committees and questionnaires and "dialogue" following Vatican II, many of us felt the same way but lacked the roshi's "special English" in which to express ourselves.

After awhile, the abbot informed us that we were invited to lunch at 11:00 with the monastic community. He added that the monks had all risen that morning at 4:00, shared an hour of public prayer and chanting of sutras in the main shrine, moved to the zendo for an hour of zazen in the lotus position, had a simple breakfast, and done their cleaning; now the cooks were preparing the main meal of the day. He explained to us the etiquette of the refectory, where not a single word is spoken during meals, "of course." He said that servers would take our bowls and fill them with rice. While they were so doing, we should put our palms together, rub our hands back and forth, and with a swift movement, shoot one hand ahead of the other to indicate when the bowl was full enough. Unless we did that, he warned, the server would simply continue to ladle rice into a mountain, which we would then be expected to consume. The servers would come around three times. If, on the third time around, we found that we had reached our limit, we should bow profoundly to indicate "thanks, but no, thanks." He asked me if I could manage chopsticks, and I said that I could, but the young monk stopped me in the procession into the refectory to give me a fork and spoon.

The dining hall was apparently set up and removed before and after each meal. It was simply a series of low benches arranged in two lines along a corridor, with cushions on the floor behind the benches. I saw the younger members of the community putting them out about five minutes before dinner. Then we all filed in. The superior and two others (his council, I assume) sat at a bench across the top of the two lines. One of these monks had two blocks of wood which he clapped together with a startling amount of noise, whereupon they all began chanting a sutra. This continued the whole time the servers were bringing in huge wooden containers of steaming rice, vegetables, and seaweed soup, as well as pickles and other condiments for the rice. Each of us had a nest of five black lacquered bowls. The servers were strong and acrobatic young monks who got down on their knees and made a profound bow while holding a heavy bowl, served two people, stood up without moving their feet from the original spot, moved down the line, then repeated the performance with an agility, grace, and muscular coordination that would have done credit to the Bolshoi Ballet. While everyone else seemed to keep what we used to call in the noviceship "custody of the eyes," I followed this masterly choreography with fascination.

Not until everyone had been served with everything: a heaping bowl of rice, a bowl of soup, a bowl of vegetables, and two small bowls of assorted pickles and other flavor-filled condiments, did the monk at the head table again clap his signal to end the grace before meals. Before beginning to eat, each monk took a tiny portion of rice and placed it on the table near the edge. Later we asked why, and were told that this rice is for all of the people of the world who want to possess something — not just the hungry, but even the rich, who suffer from a hunger for greater wealth. The monks say, in effect, "All right, if you want something, take this; we'll share."

Then everyone fell to eating, and my worries about their starving to death faded away at the happy sound of men crunching away at their copious, if not very exciting, rations. (Their supper, by the way, is at 4:00 or 4:30, and is a very simple meal.) The servers, meanwhile, were busy getting ready for the second onslaught, during which nearly everyone had seconds, and quite substantial ones as far as I could observe. The third time around, most people bowed, but one monk at the end of the bench grabbed the sleeve of the departing server and had another portion of rice. Then the servers came in with boiling water and poured it into each person's main bowl, and everyone proceeded to do dishwashing, using their fingers and the towels which each one had brought in a little packet. Great care was lavished on the ritual of washing, drying, and stacking, and the stowing away of the towel. A server collected the nests of clean bowls, we stood for more chanting, and the acrobatic young servers slung a stack of three heavy benches under each arm, carrying out the entire refectory at one fell swoop. By the time the sutra was over and the final clap of the signal resounded, there was no sign that a dining room had ever been there.

Nakagawa Soen then took us for a walk through the gardens, where we met some arriving visitors. They turned out to be the famous Yasutani Hakuin, perhaps the best-known Japanese Zen master, who is very much loved in the United States and looks infinitely old and wise; his disciple, Yamada Kyozo, whom I had heard of as Father Hand's roshi; and a well-known woman novelist, Koyama Ittoko-san. They had come to pay their respects to the abbot, and we all went together to visit the tomb of the monastery's founder. There we were all given joss sticks to burn, and the three Zen masters chanted a sutra.

We then climbed a hill dotted with charming little shrines, and statues of Buddha and the Buddhist saints. Our roshi gathered some dead leaves and twigs, and gave me a match, asking, "Would you like to light a fire in a Zen Buddhist monastery?" I would and I did, and we all stood around and warmed ourselves at the fire, sharing its mystery and beauty, enjoying the color and crackle and comfort for perhaps ten or fifteen minutes. I saw some pieces of bamboo growing near the fire and asked if I could take one home. The abbot answered, "You may, and you may make yourself a bamboo flute." Yamada-roshi remarked that it would be nice if we had some sweet potatoes to roast in the fire. Children in Japan love to buy roasted sweet potatoes from a man who cries out the word "O-imo" in a melodious little musical phrase. He is a regular street peddler, like the Good Humor man. In the meantime, our roshi went off and changed his elegant brown habit for working clothes, and came back with a bucket and dipper. He made a ceremony of putting out the fire with the water, although perhaps the action was practical as well, since Japan had not had rain in more than forty days. Fire in Japan can be tragic, since most of the smaller houses are fire traps.

As we returned to the veranda of the shrine, the abbot stopped us and said, "Listen to the sound of the water." We all paused, stood very still, and listened intently for several minutes. Then he clapped his hands and went on. We were taken to the rooms of his predecessor, a man whose memory he so venerated that he kept these rooms just as they had been under the former abbot. One was a homey little shrine of Kannon, with a graceful wood carving of the goddess, a hand-wrought book of sutras, and several examples of the older monk's calligraphy on the walls. These characteristic calligraphy works often consist of one Chinese character, perhaps the word meaning "dream" or "mother," or some other word full of emotional suggestion. The character is done very spontaneously with a brush in sumi, or black ink, and is simply itself, having no other meaning than the repercussions stirred in the heart of the beholder. Nakagawa Soen showed us one of his own creations. At one time he had made a Zen Buddhist foundation on the Mount of Olives in Jerusalem, leaving behind a disciple to care for it when he returned to Japan. With some olive wood from the Mount he had made a pair of clappers. On one he wrote the words "O live" and on the other "Dead Sea." He clapped the wooden blocks together and said, "The sound of life and death. It is one sound." Then he brought in a large metal tray from Jerusalem holding a jar of water from the

Dead Sea and seven wooden chopsticks — six for us and one for his absent old teacher, whose cushion was kept in its usual place. We all sat around the tray, put our chopsticks together into the jar of water, and then tasted the brine. Said the roshi, "It is a very sweet taste, the taste of the earth." He called this salt water from the Dead Sea the water of life because Jesus was baptized in the Jordan, which flows into the Dead Sea.

We then had a tour of the inside of the monastery. At the shrine of Hakuin, the founder, the abbot asked us to say a prayer in English. We said the Our Father, which pleased him. He recited a sutra, ending with something in English about the cosmos, past, present, and future. "Who is not a cosmic man?" he asked. "Each man is breathing the universe in and out at each moment of his existence." He showed us a beautiful bronze bell which Hakuin had used, and asked us to listen as he struck it, and to keep silence, bending our heads so that our ears would catch the very last reverberations of the sound as it died away and ceased. The tone of the bell was deep, sweet and penetrating, and the experience of listening with all our attention for the very last vestige of vibration, which was felt rather than heard, was a true Zen experience. When there had ensued a few moments of complete silence, Nakagawa Soen said quietly, "Never stops — only spreads — to infinity." On our way back to the tea room, we paused at the zendo where the monks pray, study and sleep — one to each narrow tatami mat. "One monk, one mat. This is the life of simplicity and perfect happiness."

When we returned to the tea room, the abbot said, "I want you to listen for a few moments to the sound of the kettle boiling." Meanwhile, he brought out a large, bright orange, lacquered bowl. In the alcove hung a long, gnarled gourd filled with sake. Our roshi announced, "I am going to give you the blood of Buddha to drink." The five of us held the big bowl as he tipped the gourd and poured out some of the golden sake. Taking a large bamboo whisk, he stirred the surface of the rice wine, creating bubbles like those in the green ceremonial tea. Then he said, "These are not bubbles of sake; they are the constellations of the universe, and this is the spirit of the rice, the blood of Buddha." We tipped the great bowl and each in turn drank from it. It was potent, and sweet, and warming.

We moved once more, to an even smaller and more delightful room, where the roshi talked about the "seven happy dogs," little canine

figures offered to the monastery for the new year. He gave us tanger-
ines, delicious dried persimmons, and boiling water poured into an old
tea bowl which had supposedly belonged to the monk who began the
tea ceremony centuries ago. One last special moment was spent with
Yamada-roshi and Yasutani-roshi in the small shrine of Kannon, where
we had an opportunity to ask questions about Zen. Yamada-roshi said
that his favorite scriptural quotation is, "The kingdom of God is within
you." He said that beyond the universe of phenomena is God. Someone
started to say, "Yes there *must* be. . . ." He corrected her and said, "Not
must be. . . *is*." He explained the elementary principles of zazen: breathing, bodily posture, inattention to ideas and concepts. He then con-
cluded, "One seeks and seeks for God; when the seeking finally stops,
that is when we find him." He told us about going to a Catholic retreat
house in Kamakura. At night he used to go into the chapel, lighted only
by the sanctuary lamp, and he added, "Jesus and I sat there together."

Again we found ourselves in the tea room where we had begun the
day. This room, like every room we saw, was artistically correct. Everywhere were classical flower arrangements, worn but precious ceramic
pieces, and a few select objects arranged in accordance with the Japanese custom of having one or two perfectly chosen accessories, frequently changed, for simple contemplation and enjoyment. The roshi's
whole day had been spent in making us feel perfectly at home, in
showing us everything, and revealing to us the beauty of Zen Buddhism; yet at the end of the day I was amazed at how leisurely and
uncluttered it had been, and what simple things we had shared: water,
fire, sake, the sound of a running stream, the smell of woodsmoke, our
hands around a pottery brazier filled with charcoal, the spring of the
tatami mat under our feet when we came in chilled from the outside.
Every once in a while, the abbot would tell us to stand up and move our
feet to restore circulation. He himself enjoyed the simplest things and,
without appearing to do so, taught others this art. He was a great master of the art of education, saying very little, but showing the way by
"the method of direct pointing."

We accompanied Nakagawa Soen as he bade farewell to the other
two roshis. We all knelt on the veranda to witness and take part in the
many ceremonial bows and farewells. The departing guests turned
back to bow several times as they went down the path. The host knelt
for some time after they had disappeared, with motionless concentra-

tion, and finally bowed in their direction. As we prepared to leave, we returned once more to the shrine of Kannon, where a young monk was reciting a sutra. Our beloved roshi came with us while we changed into shoes and put on coats. He let us take his picture, surrounded by the five of us. He placed his hands on my head and gave me a blessing, then continued bowing as we went down the path, often turning back to see his beautiful, kindly, wise, and gentle face, his old eyes sending a benediction after us. I am sure he thought, "Never stops. Only spreads. To infinity." I know now this truth for sure.

Because of what I learned about prayer from Nakagawa Soen-roshi, even though I am not even sure he is still living in this world, I know that I still meet him in the only One where we, still a teacher and still a student, are one.

Postscript. As this essay was in preparation for publication, and on the very day I learned of its inclusion in the projected volume, I heard that Nakagawa Soen-roshi had moved into the plentitude of life.

Buddhism, Existence, Technology, and Daily Life

by Steven Kozan Beck

We spend a lot of time trying to understand ourselves, the meaning of life, the nature of existence, and the way everything works. We work equally hard to get what we need and to obtain well-being. We each perceive our needs a little differently, and the ways we achieve them can be even more varied. Some people give to others; some rob banks.

Our understanding affects how we perceive our needs and therefore, what we perceive them to be. As Sister Cooney's evocative piece so clearly suggests, the simplicity of our needs is intimately linked to the clarity of our perceptions. Our understanding of the way things work determines what we must do to get what we want. In a complementary sense, what we need and what we want affects the way the world looks to us, which in turn reflects our understanding of it.

In our efforts to comprehend, we customarily divide the whole of existence into categories. Formal education treats experience as a variety of separate subjects. Only rarely do we see existence viewed as a single whole. The closest we usually come is to look at one half at a time.

One way of looking at things is scientific, analytical, objective: the intellect examines objects of experience. It focuses outwardly on the world around us. It makes possible the technologies which support our lives.

The other way of looking is subjective, introspective, and intuitive. This way is concerned with purpose and meaning. It confronts the phenomena of birth and death from the inside. It is the gateway to serenity, compassion, love, and wisdom. This approach is the way of spiritual practice and experience.

These two approaches sometimes seem diametrically opposed and mutually exclusive. When we see only from one of these viewpoints, we may think we are seeing the whole picture. Religion and science each have a way of assuming that they alone possess the whole pie.

However separate and disconnected our ways of understanding are, all people unconsciously strive to integrate experience from the moment of birth. Subjective and objective perception remain inseparable within us and in our living of daily life. Even our unconscious approach assumes a basic unity of existence.

Within existence itself, subjective and objective are also inseparable. Science and religion are each concerned with the nature of existence, and the principles by which it works. As a single whole, the principles which underlie each cannot be very different.

This article is about existence as a whole, viewed in terms of the four facets already mentioned: 1) subjective spirituality; 2) objective technology; 3) living of daily life subjectively and objectively; 4) the underlying nature of existence.

The only model I know which recognizes the unity of existence is the "medicine wheel" of the American Indian spiritual tradition. The medicine wheel recognizes existence as a single mandala. The Buddhist counterpart is the "wheel of dharma," but its traditional understanding is primarily focused on spiritual practice alone. It is interesting to note that the word *dharma*, which means spiritual teaching or voice of the heart, is often translated as "the medicine which cures all ills." My use of the medicine wheel is from the Buddhist perspective. Although it is inspired by the Native American tradition, it does not presume to be a traditional presentation.

These four facets interrelate in many ways, but there is one sequence which seems particularly useful: (1) turning within, through spiritual practice, we are able to let go of attachment and uncover our original nature; (2) original nature is the nature of existence, and the inherent principles by which it unfolds and functions; (3) technology seeks to utilize these principles and their patterns of energy exchange to provide the means of supporting life; (4) our actions together with our use of technology create the conditions and problems we experience in daily life.

In everything we do, from using a typewriter to driving a car, success depends on our understanding and acting in accord with the principles of existence. Even something seemingly as simple as sweeping the floor requires that we act in harmony with the way a broom works, the way our body moves, and the way dust flows. It may be that the problems we experience are the result of misunderstanding the way in which existence works. Solving problems, whether individually or collectively, requires understanding that is not just spiritual and not just technological, but whole.

Contemplative Action

Pure awareness — the sound of the bell, the crackle of burning twigs, the perception of this moment — is the basis of contemplation. Through contemplation we return to the root of existence, the ground of being, from which springs life itself. The living of life brings the challenge of survival. We develop technologies to support life and social relationships which we hope will lead to well-being for all. Contemplation and action could not be more different. Contemplation involves stillness and letting go. Action involves movement and deliberate purpose. One is subjective and spiritual, the other, objective and material. Yet the living of life is an intertwining dance of the two. Together, deep awareness and skillful movement create contemplative action.

All of us live face-to-face with the misery of life and death. Who are we? What is the fundamental nature of existence? At root, they are both the same question and can only be satisfied through direct subjective experience. Conceptual answers are not enough. Science deals with phenomena and cannot penetrate the essential nature of existence. Objective analyses cannot provide meaning or elicit value. The search for answers and meaning directs our attention inwards.

If the mystery of life and death turns us within, then the living of life draws our attention outwards. We are all engaged in some fashion with the process of survival. Beyond survival, we all seek well-being. For these we need sufficient air, water, food, shelter, protection, creative activity, recreation, social interaction, emotional support, and rest.

The process of survival requires both mental and physical action, and technology becomes our most basic tool. We use it to harvest and modify the resources we need and want. Technology functions within the wider context of the environment and its ecosystems. The way we develop and use technology is not only determined by what is possible, but by our specific purposes. Hence technology also functions within the context of social and economic conditions.

Contemplative practice begins for many with the experience of suffering. It may be suffering in connection with change, loss, illness, injustice, or death. Suffering in this sense is not the physical or emotional pain itself. With insight it becomes apparent that suffering results from the way we relate to our experience.

Technological development and social concerns begin for many with the experience of insufficiency. Insufficient water, food, shelter, employment, medical care, freedom, peace. Some 500 million people are starving. One billion people lack adequate housing. The functional balance of many of our ecosystems is threatened and the potential for nuclear extinction exists.

Suffering is subjective and, according to Buddhist teaching, is cured through transcendence: accepting and letting go of our desire for conditions to be other than they are. In other words, through contemplation. Insufficiency, on the other hand, is objective, and is cured through access to, and use of, technology and resources to provide the necessities of life. Which is to say, through action.

The problems of suffering and insufficiency are cured in very different ways, and often experienced in very different contexts. We may be lacking in necessities without suffering. We may suffer in the midst of good health and abundance. Yet there can also be strong interconnections. The need to cling, which sets the stage for suffering, is greatly reduced when the necessities of life are assured. Physical pain can be reduced, or even alleviated, by letting go of anxiety and resistance.

In practice we sometimes mistake suffering for insufficiency and insufficiency for suffering. It is all too easy to try and solve the problem of suffering by consuming more, or to try to solve a problem of insufficiency through introspection or detachment alone, leading to avoidance and denial. Within our lives as a whole, suffering and insufficiency are frequently intertwined. The challenge of life is to solve both. To do so requires contemplative action.

Buddhist Practice

Contemplative action begins for most people with the recognition that sufficiency does not cure suffering. In the midst of our discontent we encounter a deep but elusive sense that we are not just body and mind, that we are not just the changing content of awareness. From within comes a longing for that which we truly are. Suffering and longing lead to inward attentiveness.

Contemplation or meditation is the practice of mindfulness. Or, more simply, the practice of paying attention. Formal Buddhist contemplation involves sitting quietly and alertly with the back straight, breathing in a relaxed manner from the abdomen. The attitude of mind is one of nonjudgmental awareness. Neither grasping after nor pushing away thoughts, feelings, sensations, or intuitions. Neither deliberately thinking, nor trying to exclude or repress thought. Meditation is relaxed energetic awareness. It is not dreamlike, trancelike, or hypnotic. It is simply acceptance of whatever comes along without preference or aversion. This acceptence allows whatever is present simply to be as it is. It allows us to rediscover the freedom of not reacting, of not being caught up in the content of our perception. This is a freedom known by all infants and forgotten with age.

The receptivity of acceptance is a prerequisite for the deepening of awareness. We cannot become aware of something if we are unwilling to accept its presence. And we cannot let go of an attachment we do not recognize. If suffering is caused by attachment it would seem a powerful motivation for letting go! When we come face to face with our own clinging, however, the situation proves somewhat more complex. We may encounter the feeling that clinging is necessary for survival. Through meditation we begin to remember the experiences which led us to cling in the first place.

The newborn infant floats in an ocean of undifferentiated unity with all that is perceived. There is no distinction made between environment and organism. Early childhood involves the process of developing a sense of separateness, which permits functioning as an autonomous organism. Undifferentiated awareness must become focused through and identified with the apparatus of bodymind in order to exercise volition. Functional autonomy develops for the sake of survival.

This functional separateness does not in itself cause us to forget our original oneness with all things. The events that do cause us to forget are different for each of us, yet there are broad similarities. We may learn from an experience of (apparent) rejection, abuse, abandonment, or ridicule that we are unlovable or inadequate in some way. The flow of life and love which constitutes our being becomes "saddened." If we do not accept and let go of it, it functions like a grain of sand inside an oyster. It becomes a hurt which we close up around, forgetting our original openness. This creates a much deeper sense of separation than is required for functional autonomy.

This is also where confusion is initially created in the course of contemplative practice. For the sake of survival we need a functionally autonomous sense of self capable of exercising volition through holding on and pushing away. For the sake of transcending suffering we need to find out how to let go of the attachment and rejection that maintain it. At first we are almost unable to distinguish between these two types of separateness. It is extraordinarily difficult to let go of the self that assures survival. We end up struggling against ourselves. At this point in contemplative practice, it becomes important to take meditation into daily life, for it is there that we are able to recognize the ego or selfish self and the cycles of cause and effect creating and maintaining it.

In becoming identified with this person who is unlovable or inadequate, our sense of what we are becomes limited first to the body and mind, then to mind only, and finally to the ego — the limited portion of the psyche we can accept and identify with. Our ego, bound by self-imposed limits of rejection and acceptance, becomes subject to limitations on success and failure. We may feel adequate only by achieving success or superiority in some measurable form. We may feel a need to struggle with inadequacy, pain, loss, fear, defeat, death, and thus fight against existence itself.

When we feel inadequate or unlovable, we tend to assume that acceptance and adequacy are achieved through competition or struggle. The specifics are different, and actually quite complex, for each of us, but they include strategies and behaviors developed in an effort to cure the original hurt and misunderstanding. These may range from a frantic demand for attention to a shy avoidance of interaction, but the result is the same. Whether we are actively a nuisance or passively withdrawn, others tend to respond as though we were indeed unlovable, unlikeable, or inadequate. The initial assumption is verified.

Unfortunately, strategies based on a misunderstanding cause the very failure they seek to avoid. As long as we do not recognize the underlying misrepresentation for what it is, the more we perpetuate the failure — in a sincere effort to correct it.

The result is a self-validating, self-perpetuating cycle, in which misunderstanding begets and is confirmed by failure. The cycle can be particularly tenacious because it filters our perception of our sense of self, our identity, and even our worldview. Consequently, within the overall context of the cycle of misunderstanding and failure, there is no solution.

The "formal" *koans* of Zen Buddhism are expressions of this spiritual dilemma and its causal cycles. Each one is a formalized recorded version of a trainee's own "natural" personal koan. They are not literal analytical expressions, but serve to point directly to the all-encompassing unsolvability of the dilemma itself.

The only solution to our spiritual dilemma, koan, or, cycle of misunderstanding and failure, is to let go of and convert the cycle itself. To leap beyond the limiting and illusory constraints of misunderstanding and apparent insufficiency.

The first requirement, however, is to remain still, alert, and accepting, within the center of confusion. Only nonjudgmental stillness can penetrate the misunderstanding and hurt, and bring gentle acceptance. Acceptance allows pain and misunderstanding to be present, and brings freedom from suffering and the ability to let go. Letting go, sometimes experienced as forgiveness, releases old pain, grief, separation, and misunderstanding. Forgiveness lets go of the resistance which keeps ourselves and others out of our hearts. It reveals our inherent and inalienable adequacy, acceptability, and lovability.

The heart of all things embraces everyone and everything without exception. However unacceptable some action or person may seem, there is nothing which is not lovingly embraced by the eternal.

Opening the heart means opening ourselves to the original nature of things — unborn, undying, unconditioned, unbounded. It appears gradually and is at first unnoticed, like a fog lifting or a slow dawn, although sometimes it appears in a flash. This eternal nature is all things and it is no-thing, remaining empty, immaculate, and eternal. We experience its facets as compassion, love, and wisdom. We label it as: Buddha nature, God, Allah, the Great Spirit, the Supreme Brahman, the Tao. Nevertheless, it cannot be encompassed by words or concepts.

We cannot positively "know" our original nature with the cognitive mind. And yet with gratitude and respect, we can relax into and move in harmony with it. We can listen, as the Quakers say, to the "still small voice of the heart." It is all that we are, and is awareness itself. Yet, as functioning human beings, "we" are not "it."

Having begun to let go, the next step is to find alternatives so that cycles of failure do not reappear in other guises. We must make the effort to convert misunderstanding.

Buddhist contemplative practice is to live an ordinary life — from the heart. To live from the heart of existence is to act in harmony with all beings and all things.

Original nature — the nature of existence — is inherently adequate in the most optimum sense and naturally gives rise to conditions which manifest this adequacy. Since all is one, all facets of existence are in harmony with all others and in the fullest sense, function to benefit others. The greatest variable is human behavior. If we fail to act in harmony with the way existence works, adequacy becomes failure once again.

Conditions of Existence

Our collective social and technological problems bear many of the earmarks of the personal spiritual dilemma. Such problems as hunger, poverty, housing shortage, civil and national conflict, resource depletion, environmental destruction, and nuclear weapons, continue to proliferate in spite of our best efforts. In some cases they have been exacerbated by the measures intended to effect the cure.

If their existence is indeed the result of the causal cycle of internal misunderstanding and external failure, then they are only symptoms and have no isolated solution. They are a result of the misunderstanding of the nature of existence, so taken for granted and seemingly self-evident that it goes unnoticed.

Our collective problems are extraordinarily complex and interconnected when examined in detail. We hold many different and sometimes conflicting opinions as to what they are and how they are caused. Yet I would suggest that there is one root misunderstanding from which all others spring. This misunderstanding is the belief that existence is a struggle for survival *against* others and the very nature of life, a struggle that only the powerful and wealthy can win.

Sometimes the belief that it is a "dog eat dog world," in which "good guys finish last," appears overtly, and sometimes it appears subtly and unconciously. Our experience often seems to confirm this belief, as our problems of insufficiency convincingly suggest that there are not enough of the basic necessities to go around. It seems self-evident that survival requires that we obtain the necessities by being stronger, richer, smarter, faster — even if someone else must lose. From the moment of conception, life can seem to be a race against death.

On a deeper level, however, the struggle against other people, the environment, and death implies that the nature of existence itself must be inherently inadequate. This original inadequacy must be overcome in order to achieve sufficiency and survival.

Herein lies the point of failure. If existence is not inherently adequate by nature, we, as products of existence, can do nothing to make it so. Adequate conditions are only possible if they exist as potential, and sufficiency and well-being can only be achieved by recognizing and acting in accord with the way existence actually works.

When we struggle against existence itself, we are fighting against the way it works, guaranteeing failure. When we attempt to dominate or exploit others, they tend to fight back. Then life does become a struggle for survival. When we act on this misunderstanding, it becomes self-validating and self-reinforcing. Ultimately, however, it is only us fighting ourselves. As the products of existence, when we fight against it, we are fighting against our very nature, our very being.

This does not mean that life is all sweetness and light. Life can be dangerous, and death is certain. From the standpoint of the ego, death is a considerable threat. From the standpoint of our true being within awareness, death is merely part of the flow of existence, a dropping away of this present body and mind, and another ever-present opportunity to open and relax into original enlightenment.

Survival requires effort. Biologically, survival is won by the "fittest"—those organisms which most successfully fit their ecosystem and function in accord with it. Human survival is achieved by working in cooperation with our ecosystems, other people, and the underlying principles of existence.

Existence is inherently adequate in the fullest and most optimum sense. As original oneness, it unfolds as all things, and they remain one. Each facet of existence naturally functions to support every other, because oneness always functions in harmony with itself.

Existence, in a rather literal way, does everything with nothing. It achieves the optimum with the minimum, creating abundance. Conversely, what is achieved is only optimum when it is achieved with a minimum. Objectively perceived, existence unfolds as space, time, and energy. Subjectively experienced, the eternal unfolds as compassion, love, and wisdom.

Since they are a single whole, all facets of existence naturally work in synergetic cooperation. Synergy is that which is more than the sum of its parts. It is a single whole which differentiates into separate aspects, just as a fetus in the womb differentiatingly unfolds its parts from bodymind. Synergy is the basic principle of inseparable oneness that does the most with the least, in harmony with itself.

The balance of nature is such that no organism or species can profit over another without undercutting the basis of its life-support process. Each organism feeds on and, in turn, is food for others. Competition for profit is the tip of an energy-exchange process which overwhelmingly depends on cooperation. When competition exists, it is competition with others, not against, and helps assure that the minimum is used optimally without waste.

The recognition of underlying principles is not enough to convert the causal cycles of failure. It is the conditions themselves which convince us that life is a struggle. The causal cycle of conditions has a number of distinct steps, the first being the most significant and the least noticeable. In forgetting that existence is inherently adequate, our approach to survival is to develop and use technology as a weapon. We create technologies that strive to conquer nature and produce maximum profit from others.

When our first priority is the production of profit, however, we are no longer able to produce what we need efficiently. Profit is maximized by taking something simple and efficient and making it more complex and luxurious (expensive). Generally speaking, it is more profitable to sell a luxury item than an equivalent product that is less expensive (unless you can sell significantly more of the inexpensive version). It is also more profitable to sell the same thing several times rather than just once. Planned obsolescence makes money.

These strategies for maximizing profit increase wealth for the producers, and increase the consumption of energy and natural resources required for the product. In the case of planned obsolescence and over-packing, the result is waste. Our insufficient and wasteful use of resources has nearly depleted a number of industrially important, non-renewable elements and compounds. As they become more difficult to obtain, their price goes up.

In addition to competition for resources, we also experience competition for jobs. This allows wages to be kept lower, and increases profit. This in turn leads to the individual struggle not only for employment but for a life-sustaining wage. Our struggle for maximum wages or profit is both individual and collective.

Wage and profit concerns, however, are relative to the costs of our necessities and the way we obtain them. For most people, housing is the most expensive necessity, especially when related energy, service, maintenance, insurance, and financing charges are added. For a majority of people today, not only in this country but worldwide, housing has become unaffordable.

To pay for unaffordable housing, we must produce and consume an ever-increasing quantity of goods and services. We have created, and are caught in, a cycle in which we must use energy and resources wastefully in order to maximize profit. We must do the least with the most. It is not that we deliberately set out to waste, but that we have created markets for products and services that are unnecessary, solely to make profit.

This cycle does not seem too objectionable at first glance, as long as we can afford to consume resources at our present rate. It appears to increase wealth and the number of jobs while providing more goods and services for consumption. It allows us to obtain the necessities of life by producing and consuming luxury items. What a deal! We are drawn in by our fear of losing the struggle on one hand and our desire to consume on the other.

When we look at this cycle from the viewpoint of existence itself, however, we begin to see that it results in failure because it is precisely backwards. Existence creates conditions of optimal adequacy by doing the most with the least. From the misunderstanding that survival requires domination and profit, we have created a cycle in which it becomes necessary to do the least with the most. We have created an upside-down world in which we must produce and consume increasing quantities of luxury items just to obtain the necessities of life. Worst of all, this cycle is at the expense of the majority. The result can only be failure.

Our collective survival and well-being can never be achieved through struggle, but only, as Buckminster Fuller put it, by doing "ever more with ever less." We must use the technology and the life-support process to produce what we need *first,* and the profit-making luxuries we want *second.* (Although there is nothing wrong with luxuries of profit, unless they assume a higher priority than the necessities of survival.) We must be able to provide the basic necessities in an affordable, efficient manner before we can do the most with the least. In fact, we are able to do so for all the necessities of life — except housing.

Housing is the only necessity which remains unaffordable for many, even when produced cooperatively. We are very good at building luxury housing and very limited in our ability to provide good basic housing.

Our collective cycle of failure is perpetuated by many aspects of the total situation. Yet the cost of the housing alone is enough to maintain it. Until we can produce and acquire truly affordable, energy self-reliant, high quality, *basic* housing, life will indeed remain a struggle which only the wealthy can win.

Housing Technology

Housing is our most basic means of life support. Shelter is the place in which most of our other basic needs, including food, water, and sleep, are met. Housing technology is developed according to our inner concept, model, or understanding of what a dwelling is and does. Beyond necessity however, our housing model reflects our dreams and aspirations. It reflects what we want, and our view of the nature of existence.

Our inner housing model begins from what I believe to be a primal, archetypal sense of dwelling-nest. Nest-building animals manifest an inner concept of nest that achieves the most with the least, in appropriate response to their environment. So pre-industrial indigenous housing traditions from around the world reflect universal patterns that achieve the optimum with a minimum. Our innate housing models, however, are further conditioned by our actual experience with different types of housing, economic and environmental conditions, and learned cultural attitudes.

Based on the ideal dream house imagined by most people, our primary housing model appears to be a mansion. Average house size has increased 40 percent since World War II. We have come to associate quality with quantity. In a world where survival requires wealth, the mansion is the ultimate symbol of success. Larger, more expensive housing also profits the designer and builder. The small contractor today simply cannot afford to build compact, truly low-cost housing, unit by unit, on-site. With the conventional construction process and worksite preparation, time and labor are nearly the same regardless of building size (within limits). But the profit margin is much less. On the whole, in the United States, our attention, effort, and marketing have gone into the development of mansionlike housing.

Since a mansion, by nature and intent, is a conspicuous display of wealth, it does not need to make efficient use of space, structure, or energy. In practice, most of our dwellings are not mansions, and we would like to use space, structure, and energy efficiently. Unfortunately our housing model is not able to do this, and we have a conflict between what we want, and what we are able to do. Ironically, and yet inevitably, our mansion ideal has led to conditions in which only mansionlike housing is fully adequate.

Necessity, however, can be a powerful agent for change, and a strong motivation to find alternatives which work. There is evident today a revived interest in compact, efficient, high-quality housing. In addition, there is a growing recognition of the need for housing which can be "clustered" together to reduce the amount of land required, while continuing to provide private outdoor space for each unit.

True affordability, however, requires the utilization of all the other basic strategies for affordable housing. Applied individually, as they usually are, they help a little. But a real reduction of cost is possible only when they are used together.

These are the basic strategies for affordability recognized by most designers:

1) Reduction of size, and therefore of material and labor costs;

2) Clusterability, reducing the land needed;

3) Construction by owner, reducing labor costs;

4) Factory building, utilizing industrial efficiency;

5) Wholesale purchase of materials in bulk, reducing cost;

6) Mobility, required for factory production, allowing home owner-ship without land ownership, and permitting resale when a larger or smaller dwelling is needed;

7) Core housing, which provides the basics and is able to be added to in the future when finances permit;

8) Cooperative, corporate foundation, or government financing to reduce interest rates; the lower the cost of the dwelling, the less that needs to be borrowed, and the easier it is to borrow the needed sum;

9) Energy conservation and solar collection to facilitate energy self-reliance, reducing the operating costs;

10) The synergetic integration of function, space, structure, and energy in overall design, so that the optimum configuration of each (in response to specific requirements) is simultaneously the optimum pattern for all the others.

Combining these strategies leads to an approach which can result in a uniquely alternative housing system.

Community Relationships

Housing and technology are not only the basis of life support, they also condition larger economic patterns that in turn affect environ-mental and social relationships.

With truly affordable housing, we no longer need to spend up to half our income on housing. A compelling urgency for maximum wage or profit is removed. Life is not a struggle for survival. We have time to do some of the things we had to pay others to do when we were working full-time, thus further reducing our reliance on a money-based life-support process. As a result we can live more self-reliantly.

At one time, of course, almost everyone lived with a great deal of self-reliance, building their own shelters, growing their own food, making their own clothes. It was a lot of work, and it left little margin of safety when times were hard. This was especially true in Europe, and later in colonies worldwide, when people were forced to give large portions of their produce to landlords and kings. The development of technology made it possible to harness large amounts of energy and produce more, but it also meant greater specialization. It led to a market-based economy requiring either barter or money. It also provided a means for producing even more profit.

When the necessities of life can only be obtained by buying them from others, our life support becomes subject to a limited number of available jobs, which in turn are subject to a fluctuating economy based on the non-necessities for profit. However, technology need not be used only for the production of profit.

As our technologies have become more sophisticated in utilizing principles which do more with less, they also bring us back full circle. They have made it possible to live far more self-reliantly with far less effort than ever before. "Appropriate" technology combines the best of both worlds. It is effective yet simple, decentralized and small-scale, emphasizing livelihood rather than profit. Together with truly affordable housing, it once again allows us to produce and acquire what we need independently of the production of luxuries.

The truly affordable, energy-collecting dwelling is the basis of a cooperatively self-reliant life-support system. When combined with a greenhouse, it can produce all of the fresh vegetables required year-round. It functions, in effect, as a homestead, even if it does not provide full self-sufficiency. It allows us to work part-time for what we want, providing much more freedom to do the work we want to do. While many people would not wish to be food self-sufficient, this also becomes a possibility. Approximately one-quarter acre will provide all of the grains, legumes, and vegetables for a family. Although profitable small-scale commercial farming is increasingly difficult as a result of agri-business, gardening for self-reliance is an altogether different matter.

Affordable, energy self-reliant housing is just as important in Third-World countries as it is in developed nations. Subsistence farming remains the life support for many. However, in the poorest countries, where three to five percent of the population own eighty to ninety percent of the farm land, and forty to sixty percent are landless, those who need it most are denied the means of producing food. At this point it is almost a cliché: land reform is prerequisite for survival — for the vast majority of the world's population.

The powerful insight of the American Indian tradition, and the biblical concept of commonwealth found in Leviticus and colonial New England communities, is that land cannot actually be owned or possessed by anyone. It can only be used by the community for the common welfare. It follows that each household has the right to use a basic plot of land, or "freehold," for the purposes of life support, without charge.

The practice of "owning" land is a functionally useful way of determining who has the right to use land, and how they acquire that right. The control of large areas of land is in itself a profitable resource which should be paid for and taxed. All this tends to obscure the broader truth that land control, by whatever name, is only by collective agreement. Land is the environment and its ecosystems, which support all life. In the most real sense, it cannot be possessed by anyone, only shared by all.

The combination of individual ownership of homes, and the collective ownership of land on which they are sited, has been done through land co-ops and community land trusts. Nevertheless, there are potential conflicts and confusions about rights of use which are eliminated when the dwelling is movable.

If the option of truly affordable housing, and the cooperative non-profit production of bare necessities, could potentially guarantee survival only for a few, then the rules of the game might reasonably give the victors the "right" to profit over others. If, on the other hand, there are sufficient necessities for all, and survival does not depend upon winning at the expense of others, then no one has the right to exploit other people, monopolize resources, or destroy the environment.

On the positive side, reasons why the wealthy should benefit include their facilitation of access to land, and the nonprofit provision of basic necessities. Quite simply, the poor cannot consume luxuries and increase the wealth of large corporations unless their survival is first assured. The energy-efficient, cooperatively self-reliant, nonprofit provision of basic necessities is in everyone's best interests, even those of big business.

The way we relate to other people, and the way nations relate to each other, is largely determined by economic patterns. When survival is based on the process of struggle, we relate to others in the same way. Sexism, racism, classism, ageism, and national chauvinism are based on fear and make it possible to exploit other people. Prejudice also gives us a socially approved target for venting anger and allocating blame. Without these prejudicial attitudes to filter our perception, we would all too easily see that other people are just like us. It is not possible to exploit someone with whom you identify. It is also not possible to fully reunite with our innate enlightenment, and our original nature, while exploiting and disidentifying with some aspect of it.

When twenty percent of the world's population consumes over sixty-six percent of its wealth, and thirty percent live on three percent of its wealth, there is a tendency for the poor to feel helpless and exploited, or at least upset with economic and political systems which make this extreme disparity possible. At present rates of growth, the poorest will never benefit from a profit-making world economy.

At root, the extreme frustrations which give rise to terrorism are fueled by this overwhelming inequity, experienced within the context of a belief that survival is won by the wealthy and lost by the poor. Specific political differences and conflicts are only catalysts within a far more basic context of struggle for survival. While desperation does not excuse immorality, it does make it more understandable. It is precisely this wider context in which the conflict between capitalism and communism exists, in which right-left polarization occurs, and from which the nuclear arms race has resulted.

Capitalism clearly sees the repressive, totalitarian side of communism. Communism believes that centralized ideological control of people is necessary to prevent the capitalist greed, lying within each person, from flaring up and exploiting others. A fair distribution of wealth to assure collective well-being is the Marxist ideal.

Communism clearly sees the exploitive side of capitalism that historically has subjugated others for the sake of profit. Forms of sub-jugation have included colonial imperialism, taxation, slavery, sweat-shop working conditions, extraction of natural resources from unde-veloped nations, monopoly of economic and technological power, and appropriation of land and resources from native peoples. Capitalism is blind to this, since its existence seems to require the making of maxi-mum profit for survival. We are simply playing by the rules of the game. On the positive side, the personal freedom to pursue spiritual and material well-being in a free market commonwealth are demo-cratic ideals associated with capitalism.

Capitalism and communism each tend to be blind to their own weaknesses and the other's selfless strengths. We each see the other's shortcomings as proof of their evil intentions. Psychologically, this phenomenon is known as "projection." What we deny or refuse to see in ourselves we project on to others. They appear to be evil or inade-quate. If the other side is evil, and armed with nuclear weapons, then in spite of our best intentions and most rational thought, we must re-main more powerful.

War is the ultimate expression and verification of the struggle for survival. Nuclear annihilation is the ultimate expression of war. Within the context of conditions created by our cycle of misunderstanding and failure, there is no solution. The opposite of war is not peace but sub-jugation. Peace is not something which exists simply in the absence of war, but in the absence of exploitation.

War and exploitation exist within a cycle of struggle, one against the other. To cease struggling does not mean that we become passive doormats, only that we cease to be active aggressors. The martial arts of tai chi and aikido prove the strength of this third position. They re-spond to conflict and attack by moving with the situation and redirec-ting the energy of the opponent, rather than magnifying it through opposition. The attack is converted by overturning the situation and dissolving it, not by overwhelming it. The problem is cured by ceasing to create it in the first place.

Our spiritual and collective problems are created by the way we live, and solved by the way we live. When we struggle against others economically, socially, or militarily, the overall result is failure. On the other hand, when survival is based on a process of non-profit coopera-tion, harnessing the power of technology, it ceases to be a struggle against others.

Communism and capitalism are each half-wrong and half-right. They are each based on one of the two complementary principles of life support: necessities through cooperation, and luxuries through competition. Like the principles involved, each needs the other.

Beyond the cycle of misunderstanding and failure, it becomes apparent that in reality, survival and well-being require acting in cooperation with other peoples, our ecosystems, and the nature of existence. In a world as interconnected as ours has become, we can only flourish or perish together.

Conclusion

To solve our spiritual and social problems personally and collectively, we need both contemplation and action. As important as they are to each other, however, a caution is in order.

Contemplative spiritual practice and social technological action have distinctly different purposes. For those engaged in a spiritual practice, involvement in social concerns can lead to entanglement in external conditions, and loss of sight of the original purpose of transcendence.

On the other hand, social and technological concerns evolve and change over time and are inseparable from our personal opinions. History is replete with examples of the disaster which follows equating divine insight with personal bias, religious institutions and political interests. The same thing is true here. My own views on social issues should not be confused with Buddhist teaching.

The place for contemplative insight and social action to come together is not within the discipline of doctrines, but within people. This is not to say a more formal union is always inappropriate. Many religious orders successfully combine spiritual practice and socially beneficial action. Even so, the balance remains tenuous. It is difficult to prevent the truth of spiritual teaching from being diluted by social or political interests. The quiet voice of the heart is all too easily obscured by the clamor of passing urgencies.

Yet, if in the interest of preserving the purity of contemplative teaching and practice (a major priority in Buddhism) we fail to acknowledge serious social concerns of our time, we only perpetuate ignorance of their root misunderstanding and causal cycles. Life and spiritual practice are not always easy, safe, or separable. While it is often appropriate to maintain a distinction externally, it is unnecessary to perpetuate the separation within our own awareness.

When contemplation and issues of daily life are united within the person, the divinity of transcendence and of existence becomes apparent. Rather than subduing and conquering nature, our emerging role as human beings is to serve as caretakers of the planet. Mother Earth is revealed as sacred life, the manifestation of the eternal. Nowhere is this recognized more clearly than in the American Indian spiritual traditions, and nowhere more completely than in the Southwest.

If we exploit Mother Earth, it should not seem surprising that we exploit women in general. Sexism and patriarchal control are found worldwide. The view that existence is a struggle for survival won by the strongest is a view held primarily by men. As we have seen, our conditions of life often seem to verify this view. Men, responsible for protecting the family and the nation, learn it from hard experience — not out of malice.

Women, on the other hand, are the primary nurturers of life. They are innately in touch with its sacredness and purity, and the fundamental adequacy of existence. Consequently, women tend to recognize more readily that survival and well-being result from cooperation, trust in feelings, and subjective insight.

Feminist indignation is the wisdom and energy required by all of us for change. To utilize it, we must recognize that it is not directed at the biologically male animal per se, but at the mistaken view of struggle traditionally learned by men and resulting in behavior which dominates and exploits women. While we have not created the problem, the way we live either perpetuates or helps to cure it.

We are not the roles and beliefs we come to identify with. We are the original nature of all things first, human beings second, female or male third, and our limiting self-image a distant fourth.

The challenge before us is to bring the conditions of life on our planet back into balance. The work before us is to reunite with opposites. To discover that they are complements, and inherently one from the beginning. This cannot be achieved by eliminating one side of the pair. Mind and body, spirit and matter, life and death, female and male, subjective and objective, contemplation and action — each pair comprises the two sides of that which is.

In reality, there is no inside and no outside, no subjective, no objective. Only empty immaculacy, inherently adequate in the most optimum sense, unfolding and manifesting as the phenomena of existence.

The union of contemplation and action brings detachment to insightful feeling. It allows us to act skillfully without tripping over our own feet. It allows us to act without attachment to either the doing or the outcome.

> To act without attachment is to leave no trace.
> To flow with the situation is to be undefeatable.
> To be undivided is to move in harmony with all things.
> To move in harmony is contemplative action.

Afterword

To see the whole medicine wheel of existence requires two eyes. One looking within. One looking without. One recognizing inherent potential. One recognizing existing conditions. By bringing subjective and objective together we find they are not opposites. There is no within or without, only what is in front of us. Yet either alone is only half of the picture. Talking about this is like trying to describe not only a panoramic view, but depth of field as well. We need to look through both eyes to see in stereo for ourselves. No one else can do it for us. It is only by seeing the whole panorama as a single tapestry, with our whole being, that the straightforward causal pattern emerges.

The value of the medicine wheel of the American Indian spiritual tradition is that it is a way of both recognizing and expressing the interrelated wholeness of ourselves and existence. It helps us see that the social, political, environmental and economic problems we face, along with the potential for nuclear annihilation, are problems which are simultaneously spiritual and technological. They are the result of causal cycles of internal misunderstanding and external failure. They become self-validating and self-perpetuating when we fail to see the connection. The value of the medicine wheel is that in recognizing all of this as a single whole, we open the way for healing to take place. We allow the vast inherent adequacy of our true nature, and of existence itself, to dissolve misunderstanding and manifest in harmony as conditions which benefit all.

Our life itself is the whole wheel. Turning it in the direction of compassion, love, and wisdom, benefiting ourselves and others, we are already home, sharing our common ground with all beings and things.

NEW AGE MODELS

Introduction to
Part Three

"New Age" thinking takes us beyond the encounter with interesting and provocative ideas to the embodiment of radically new visions of reality, and the personal transformation inherent in such an experience. The real essence of this revolutionary movement lies in a central concept: that of interdependence. Whether we meet the beliefs and practices of the New Age in interfaith dialogue, in new approaches to health or healing, or in planetary political thinking, the resonant theme is the same. In a sense, the truth of holism lies at the heart of the esoteric teaching of holiness animating all of the world's religions.

Michael Hugo communicates the flavor of his own experience living in an alternative spiritual community, Shantivanam, which is directed by a Roman Catholic priest, and which reveres and celebrates the sacred expressions of all the world's religions. Jane Lukehart shares the vibrant melody of mysticism and gives us a glimpse of "the path with a heart." The path which she describes transcends differences that isolate one seeker from another. Dave Lothrop connects disciplines as diverse as psychology and religion in their attempts to chart the course of human discovery and growth. Barbara Clow's article points to the perennial interest in reincarnation as the heart of the contemporary spiritual quest. Her argument is that this theory has significant roots in Western religion and can play an important part in today's spirituality. Jim Kenney maintains that we are indeed living in an age of revolution, whose most characteristic feature may well be the dynamic convergence of science with religion in a shared awe of the universe and a renewed faith in the transformation inherent in existence. Bea Briggs explores the provocative comparison of Western science with the yoga tradition. Finally, Brian Swimme locates the essential task of the Earth community in the context of a powerful reappraisal of natural selection in the developing cosmic story.

Each of the authors in this section affirms the belief that in the search for a faith for the twenty-first century, no single perspective is entirely adequate. The reality of this shrinking planet, our Spaceship Earth, deprives us of what was once the luxury of "truths" fervently clung to in myopic isolation. Our age demands that we grasp the vision of convergent truth and embody it in every dimension of our individual and community existence.

Shantivanam: Vision and Model of Contemplative Prayer

by Michael Hugo

Kozan Beck sees an integration of Buddhism, existence, technology, and daily life. While sharing that holistic vision, I would like to develop it with specific reference to the concept of community. It is my belief that a religious or spiritual conceptualization of the human aspiration to dissolve misunderstanding, and to manifest in harmony conditions which benefit all, must be incarnated in community if it is to have the capacity to transform one's self. This is, of course, consistent with the role of the *sangha* (community) in the Buddhist tradition.

In the Catholic Christian experience, the communal life has stood throughout the centuries since Jesus lived as the primary witness of God's presence among men and women of faith. This communal development has led to well-established institutions under the myriad banners of their founder saints, e.g. Benedictines, Franciscans, and Dominicans.

The communities of the past were limited to celibate men and women vowed to lifelong commitments in particular groups. They tended to live in isolation from other world spiritual traditions. In 1963, however, a new model of interreligious dialogue and community worship was introduced in the Second Vatican Council's declaration on non-Christian religions, "Nostra Aetate." With the Catholic Church's recognition of God's truth existing in religious traditions outside Christianity, the way was opened for exploring non-Christian forms of community and worship. This article testifies to some of the changes occurring in Roman Catholic models of community life.

By the time the doors closed on this history-making Second Vatican Council in the early sixties, a creative zeal had been loosened in Catholic minds that would transform the nature of Catholic spirituality and worship for years to come. The most evident and immediate impact Vatican II had upon Catholics was visible in the weekly, central act of worship, the Eucharist. Catholics living in the early to mid-sixties saw the once-familiar Mass rapidly undergoing a metamorphosis. The most obvious changes were the shifting of the altar to face the people and the use of vernacular instead of Latin as the liturgical language. The transformation of the Mass was symbolic of the much deeper changes that many Catholics were experiencing. In the years that followed the alterations of the Sunday liturgy, different perceptions of the theology behind this restructuring emerged. The rite was less frequently described as the "sacrifice of the Mass" and more frequently as the "celebration of the Eucharist." In the emphasis given by theologians and parish priests, the risen Christ began to preempt the crucified Christ as the paradigm of Christian life.

In the language of Matthew Fox, a contemporary Catholic thinker, the theological development seen in the rite of the Mass reflects a movement away from a "redemptive spirituality". For example, I see redemptive spirituality as anti-sensual, despising the pleasures of the flesh and obsessed with the fallen nature of humankind. Fox understands creation-centered spirituality as centered in the Hebrew Scripture's concept of God—a sensuous God who takes pleasure in creation.

It is by way of this brief historical sketch that I have chosen to introduce a creation-centered community of prayer and worship. The community, after all, can embody the best practices developed from the teachings of Vatican II in the areas of worship and ecumenism. Even today, it is largely in communities that Catholic Christians continue to refine and explore new ways of offering the Christian message while deepening their respect for the religious practices and perspectives of other major religions.

This creation-centered theology became real for me in a very specific community of prayer and worship. It is a place that I believe is continuing to perfect and revise the Catholic style of prayer and worship begun during Vatican II. The name of the community is Shantivanam, a Sanskrit word meaning "Forest of Peace." The original Shantivanam is an ashram in northeast India; its spiritual leader is an English Benedictine monk, Bede Griffiths. A site near Easton, Kansas is the location of the American Shantivanam — not an ashram, but officially entitled a "spiritual life center." Its founder is an Irish Catholic priest of the diocese of Kansas City, Kansas: Father Ed Hays.

Father Ed Hays was a well-established, activist priest in the Kansas diocese in 1970, when the precipitant of Shantivanam began to move in his life. Hays, in addition to carrying the duties of his rural pastorate, was also active in the affairs of the Potawanamie Indians and an outspoken opponent of the Vietnam War. By all liberal standards of Vatican II, he carried the credentials of a good, socially aware, and conscientious priest. But even such good practices as these did not leave him immune to criticism.

Ed was challenged one evening by a college student. The young man had done some drinking prior to this encounter and began vehemently to lambaste Ed and his priestly lifestyle. Though acknowledging Ed's social activist role, the man condemned his approach to the gospel as being highly selective. Ed's young friend argued further that the gospels are not a smorgasbord in which you take what you want, eating what tastes good and disregarding the rest. Rather they are spiritual prescriptions demanding a total commitment and practice of all their teachings. The young man continued, pointing out to Ed that though he took the activist role, the anti-war, pro-Indian stance from the pulpit, he is never without three square meals a day, cigarettes, the best scotch, a housekeeper, two cars (one a recreational vehicle), an opulent rectory lifestyle, vacations every summer, and a well-furbished wardrobe.

This encounter provoked a crisis of significant proportions for Ed Hays. Though the young man, after sobering up, tried to retrieve the gauntlet he had tossed before his pastor and friend, it was too late. Whether induced by a wine-bibber or by a sage, Ed felt that what was said to him was indeed the truth. Ed was extremely distraught by the challenge presented to him, but he did not back off from the crisis of faith confronting him. Rather he pushed through it to a whole new vision of church, prayer, and worship, something which was soon to take concrete form in the creation of Shantivanam.

Two equally important factors were at work in transforming Ed's crisis into a truly generative experience. Firstly, it was not Ed's inherent nature to curl up in his rectory and forget about an unsettling conversation. Always the seeker, he went about the business of finding some resolution to the anxiety he now felt. Secondly, there was Ed's superior, Bishop Strecker. Strecker's understanding of Ed's personal dilemma, and his active support in helping him to honestly resolve it, were essential ingredients in the birth of the house of prayer. The bishop, in a roundabout sort of way, became Ed's patron. It was the bishop who granted Ed a year's sabbatical and suggested that he travel around the world. With this important blessing and direction received, Ed moved into this sabbatical year with the zeal and spirit of a true pilgrim.

Father Hays' travels took him to all the major spiritual centers of Europe and Asia. Ed approached all these sacred places as a pilgrim and not as a tourist. He spent time at Taize, France, a center of ecumenical worship and community. A Christian community in Jerusalem became a rendezvous point for Ed with some very prayerful and ascetical Christians. Ed also had time to visit and pray at some of the medieval monasteries in secluded parts of Europe. Sickness overcame him as he was traversing the Middle East, and he flew back to the States, never reaching India's Shantivanam. But he did something better; he transplanted it to America's Midwest.

Upon his return, Ed met with his "shepherd" bishop for a debriefing. Bishop Strecker was obviously impressed by the transformation he witnessed in his brother priest and suggested to Ed that they establish a place in their diocese solely for prayer It would be a place set aside as a service for the people in the area. Within a relatively short time, this inspired duo was able to locate and purchase some land in the rural, rolling farmland of eastern Kansas. The bishop could have found no more apt and creative a "lieutenant" to establish this envisioned place of prayer than Father Hays.

Shantivanam claimed a 120-acre plot of gently rolling wooded farmland. The only structure on the original site was an old horse barn, made of bright aluminum. This building, still called "the Barn," was eventually transformed into the community building where quarters for cooking, dining, and bathing were established. The construction workers who developed Shantivanam were a motley crew of local farmers, Protestant ministers, and a coterie of old acquaintances and friends of Ed. While living in tents for three months, they built seven 12-by-12-foot cabins for staff members and four 8-by-12-foot cabins to house retreatants.

After the structures were completed, some of these people stayed on with Ed, forming the first community. From the very beginning, both men and women, lay people and clergy, inhabited the woods of Shantivanam. A chapel, windowed on three sides and thus open to the full beauty of the woods, fields, and valley before it, was next added to the Barn. Most of the materials for these structures were donated or salvaged from nearby farms. Ten years later, with minor changes and with careful maintenance, this same layout still remains.

Since those first days of Shantivanam, much has evolved that has made it a model community of prayer and worship. Under the tutelage and guidance of Ed Hays, Shantivanam has progressed toward fulfilling his original desire to provide a place of prayer for the diocese. In fact, in a period of ten years, Shantivanam has become a place of retreat and residence for people from all over the United States. Reservations are booked eight months to a year in advance. Shantivanam's fame has spread in spite of Ed's insistance that the media not be allowed to do stories on Shantivanam, to prevent curiosity seekers from disrupting its seclusion. That so many people now know about and utilize Shantivanam is indicative of the attraction such a lifestyle offers.

Constitutive elements of the community include: (1) community composition and commitment, (2) the cell, (3) spiritual direction, (4) ritual, and (5) rhythm. Each of these components are described in light of the Shantivanam model, but I believe they are universally applicable to other settings of prayer.

The true mark of the post-Vatican II Church is visible at Shantivanam in both its composition and the commitment required of the six staff members. From its earliest days, Shantivanam has housed both male and female staff members, an equal balance being essential to its composition. As staff members, they are there for both their own spiritual needs and to provide for the management and maintenance of the "Farm" itself (another name for Shantivanam) and retreatants who frequent it weekly.

Another novel feature about the staff is that it includes both lay people and members of religious communities. This is another sign of a post-Vatican II Church that is seeking to break down a class structure that has fostered two distinct spiritualities — one for lay people and one for priests and nuns. Shantivanam stands on the assumption that the various paths to holiness and wholeness are applicable to clergy and laity alike.

The short-term commitments to Shantivanam required of staff people (6 months to a year or more — one can always negotiate for more or less time) have provided a monastic experience for lay people never before available to them. A lay person, such as myself, can live there for a year, contribute to the community as a staff member, and utilize its structure and lifestyle to assist in sorting out and deepening spiritual values. Afterwards, they can re-enter the "marketplace", renewed and invigorated. Many nuns and priests have taken their sabbaticals there, to reacquaint themselves with lost or forgotten spiritual practices and to learn new ones. With these two departures from the norm of the Catholic monastic experience — the inclusion of male and female members plus the shortened time commitment — Shantivanam holds exciting potential for spiritual pilgrims.

Both the novice retreatant and the veteran staff member of ten years residency would likely agree that it is the *cell* which makes Shantivanam the attractive and enriching center it is. The cell, irreverently referred to by some retreatants as a "shack," is one of the twelve separate, primitive, wooden cabins scattered throughout the 90 acres of forest. A cabin is the Shantivanam version of what the Benedictines traditionally refer to as "the cell." It is the tiny arena in which a person engages himself with God in prayer, meditation, or more conscious living.

Thomas Merton points out the significance of the cell in the following way:

> The right order of things in the solitary life is this: everything is centered on union with God in prayer and solitude. Therefore the most important "ascetic practice" is solitude itself, and sitting alone in the silence of the cell. This patient subjection to loneliness, emptiness, exile from the world of other men, and direct confrontation with the baffling mysteries of God sets the tone, so to speak, for all other actions of the solitary.[1]

As was true of the cells of the early monks, the cabins at Shantivanam are sparsely but aesthetically furnished. Water must be carried to the cabins daily in a plastic milk carton, and little metal chamber pots are provided for washing and toilet purposes.

The cell, or cabin, is a spiritual teacher whose primary lessons are the isolation and seclusion provided. It is the temporary dwelling of those who step out of the mainstream to regain perspective on life. For many, the few days in the cabin is a first experience of being alone. The perspective this gives them often provides the first realistic view they have ever had of themselves. In keeping with one of the most ancient spiritual practices of solitude, after the example of Moses on Sinai or of Jesus in the desert, Shantivanam continues to cherish the cell as the premier principle or discipline in its community of prayer.

Closely akin to the function of the cell in the life of the contemplative forest dweller (for Shantivanam is truly set in a forest), is the concept of *spiritual direction*. What is prayer if not the most basic means of maintaining one's inner movement toward God? The style and intensity of prayer constitutes the most basic form of spiritual direction. By means of mantras, mandalas, breathing, walking, forms of yoga, or various non-cognitive methods of meditation, individuals discover the daily practice which keeps them "directed" toward the one God. Most, if not all of those who live at Shantivanam, are people hoping to reapply themselves to habits of prayer that have become meaningless or all but forgotten.

Spiritual direction at Shantivanam hinges upon the experience of creation, a phenomenon that is witnessed in its fullness in this remote area of rural Kansas. Coming to Shantivanam can be likened to a return to the primal forest, where life was simple, and "true men breathed from their heels."[2] Though Ed provides an excellent service in directing people during private conferences, homilies, and writings, his final word is to encourage them "to stay in the forest, for it will teach you what you need."

When this enigmatic response of Ed's was offered to me, I was baffled by it and distrustful of its somewhat Zen sound. Yet after a relatively short time as a staff member living in my forest haunt, my initial three months' commitment became a decision to remain for twelve months in these magical woods. Through the simplicity of a daily regimen of work, prayer, and play, I slowly came to find sufficient direction for the various needs I had. The concept of finding direction from simply being in the forest (or cell) does not preclude the ancient monastic practice of having a "confessor", i.e. spiritual director. Every person truly seeking to deepen his or her life of prayer needs a guide to help negotiate possible pitfalls. Ed does provide such practical spiritual direction on a consistent basis to staff; at least one conference is given to each of the retreatants during their stay. In addition, a library is available to supplement these conferences. However, it is the time apart from the "normal run of things", the solitude, wandering over the footpaths, the mindful, simple living and the expansive space to "breathe from one's heels" that ultimately guides one ever closer to the Source.

Though Shantivanam is committed to providing the optimum environment for the hermit, it is first and foremost a community. As such, staff and retreatants come together daily to communally ritualize their lives. When people decide together to set themselves to the task of holiness through the contemplative life, there needs to be a daily method of affirming their mutual purpose. Undoubtedly, the life of prayer in the Forest of Peace is not without turbulence. Yet this never totally obfuscates the sense that one is ensconced in the lap of creation. Accompanying this is a consistent sense of quiet, ineffable joy. With Moses, one yields to the Lord and pulls off one's sandals.

The ritual life of Shantivanam is what I recall most about my time there. In rite we daily commemorated the fact that life was a series of sacramental moments and encounters. José Argüelles would describe the effect of this lifestyle as a "grounding of human consciousness through the reestablishment of a reverent relationship to the earth below and the heavens above."[3]

Rather than getting lost in this ecstasy of being bonded so closely with the Earth — the rocky paths, autumn trees, hail and windstorms, verdant hay and wheat fields, blue Kansan skies, winter silences and summer symphonies of birds — we sought to honor these daily moments ritually. Ritual was the fabric that held it all together. Anthropologist Harry Turney-High defines a rite as:

> . . . any standardized procedure used by groups to enunciate or
> strengthen a belief and thereby to produce some desired end, or to
> forestall an undesirable one, or to restore the homeostasis of per-

sonalities or groups of personalities which has been broken or disturbed by crisis. It is the basic technique for expressing and satisfying the collective wish.[4]

For those at Shantivanam, the "collective wish" is a union with God in every act of life. Every rite, whether at the dinner table for meals or in the chapel for meditation and liturgy, attempts to express the collective prayer of the community, the ancient Hebrew *Shema*: "Hear, Oh Israel, the Lord Our God, the Lord is One."

In order that this unity, this collective prayer, should not be mere lip service to the idea of interfaith dialogue, the rites at Shantivanam incorporate many of the major religious traditions of the world. A stalwart bridge has been established between Christianity and Judaism. All major Jewish holidays are celebrated at the Farm. In addition, the Sabbath, or *Shabbat,* is honored every week by this community of Christians All of this is due to Ed's insistence that as Christians, we must be aware of our Jewish roots. To step into another's religious experience ritually is an important step towards removing barricades of ignorance and prejudice. Ed also uses a gift from his friends in Jerusalem, the *tallit* (Jewish prayer shawl), in personal meditation.

In addition to becoming grounded in Jewish roots, readings are selected every day from the sacred texts of Buddhism, Taoism, Hinduism, and Islam, as well as Christianity. On occasion, ancient festivals of the Celts or Saxons are remembered, and members dance around a maypole or a fire-pit in the fields or forest. From the esoteric and forgotten religions, to the common religions of today, all ritual is an effort to pierce the cultural and religious ignorance isolating people from one another and from our transcendent source and goal.

The chapel is the center of the communal rituals of eating, working, and praying. Ed often said that we prayed communally six times a day — three times in the chapel and three times at meals. The chapel is visually stimulating and instructive. It speaks of all of God's people. Icons of Our Lady of Guadalupe and the Risen Christ are placed side by side with statues of Buddha, Lord Vishnu, and Moses. These objects are only artistic reminders of the pluralism of a universe united by one God. Ultimately, these sacred art pieces are ancillary to the overwhelming natural beauty viewed through the large picture windows on three sides of the chapel.

Contrary to Catholic practice in most parishes, Mass is celebrated only three times a week. This could be disconcerting to the guest who seeks to order prayer life entirely around the Eucharist. The intent of limiting the communion liturgy is to discourage people from a dependency relationship on this sacrament. Also, because the Lord's Supper is the primary act of worship for Catholics, reserving its celebration to just a few times a week prevents it from becoming routine. When denied this option of a daily Eucharist, many guests are prompted to search within themselves for other meaningful forms of prayer.

One integral component of the rites practiced at Shantivanam is silence. During our three periods of daily prayer held in the chapel every morning, noon, and evening, a lengthy silent period was included. Silence truly unites doctrinal and religious differences. We can acknowledge the sentiment of the Psalmist: "Be still, and know that I am God!" (Psalms 45). Since the religious backgrounds of our guests vary, on many occasions silence becomes the only unifying rite. What rubrics and liturgy fail to do, silence can often achieve. As the ancient book of Chinese wisdom, the *Tao Te Ching*, professes, "Stillness and tranquillity set things in order in the universe." If Shantivanam maintains any strong link with ascetic traditions, it is its value on silence in spiritual growth. Beyond the rite of silence itself, no one way of being silent is prescribed. People who are novices to this are given a mantra from Father Hays as part of their spiritual direction, if together they decide it suits their prayer development.

Helping to establish the proper ambience of the rituals are a variety of architectural, aesthetic, and sensory aids. Simple rugs cover the interior of the chapel. Guests and staff are given a choice of sitting on a *zazen* stool (a short, slanted stool designed to help one sit comfortably in the straight-backed kneeling position) or on a soft pillow. Both of these encourage the optimum meditative posture. Incense burns for every act of prayer in chapel. It is an excellent reminder of prayer, spreading a sweet aroma throughout the chapel. Fresh flowers and candles are always present on the altar. The altar itself is an unassuming old horse feeder, turned upside down, and resting upon a small patch of earth, left bare of floor covering. The intent of this architectural novelty is to ritually symbolize our rootedness in the earth, just as our link to the heavens is marked by the rising incense.

Throughout all the rites and liturgies of my year at Shantivanam, whether Passover and Succoth or Easter and Christmas, whether at the dining table or in the chapel, music contributed importantly to our worship. Simple chants and refrains were the predominant forms of song during these services. It was hoped that impediments to prayer, often caused by lengthy, wordy, or orchestrated music, would be alleviated by simple melodies and words. Chuang Tzu comments on possible pitfalls of ritual and notes that liturgists and musicians like festivals in which they parade their talents. The silent majesty of God seems best revered not in the ostentatious and the bold, but in the simple and humble songs of faith.

The foundation of Shantivanam is a rhythm and balance that produces the harmony of this unique contemplative community. The many rituals already discussed are aligned with the natural rhythm of the day, week, and year. The rising, the zenith, and the setting of the sun, held sacred by religions both ancient and modern, are points of prayer at Shantivanam. Time in the late evening and early morning is often utilized by staff members for the practice of yoga, reading, crafts, or other centering activities. For the staff member, the week holds 4 to 4 ½ working days—Tuesday, Wednesday, Friday, Saturday, and part of Sunday. Thursday is Forest Day. It is a day when all community activity ceases. People are encouraged to fast and practice silence in the seclusion of their cabin and in the forest. It is a reminder, even to people already embracing a deep commitment to prayer, that the spiritual life demands such a weekly discipline.

Saturday evening is the Shabbat meal, bridging the Jewish and Christian weekly holy days. A truly festive meal and ceremony mark this time as a high point of the week. Tuesday evening and Friday morning Masses are celebrated with long silences and few guests. Sunday liturgy concludes the week, a festive celebration with the prepared homily by Father Hays attracting people from neighboring farms and towns. Finally, Monday is set aside as a day of rest for the staff.

Shantivanam's weeks, months, and years become a flow and rhythm of work, prayer, and play. To preserve its own soul from being locked into step with the 365-day work year, Shantivanam is closed down for four or five one-week periods during the year. This gives the community additional space for free time. Rhythm becomes both a function of the natural cycle of day and year, as well as a response to the contemplative needs of a community of people. Insuring such a predictable rhythm offers assurance that the lifestyle one seeks at Shantivanam, as guest or staff, will be maintained.

The preceding description of the Shantivanam Spiritual Life Center serves as a prototype for future centers. It is a fair question to ask, "How applicable is this model?" and "What is it in this community that is being held up for emulation?"

One component of Shantivanam that is neither easy nor necessary to transfer is its rustic, sylvan environment. Though much of the beauty this community held for me lay in its location, it was not the primary feature which captivated me during my year's residency. People could authentically capture the spirit and soul of Shantivanam in an environment other than a rural one, for the spirit of the forest and the cell can be brought to even the most urban environment.

Shantivanam's most readily applicable characteristic is the value it places on contemplative prayer, creative interfaith dialogue, and innovative ritual. I believe that when a group can bring these three dimensions of the spiritual life into practice, then it has begun to move in harmony with Shantivanam. Though these components are related to the personal history of Father Ed Hays, they are not limited to him. He has creatively explored them, as permitted in the parameters of his diocesan priesthood. If others adapt these features, related but unique phenomena of spiritual life would emerge.

There are two different approaches which could be taken in developing a spiritual life center, based on either a homogeneous or heterogeneous group. For Catholics, the natural boundaries of dioceses and parishes might make the homogeneous approach most practical. If the leadership in the diocese is adventurous enough to develop a spiritual life center, then it might be the best basis from which to grow. Even a cluster of parishes within a diocese would be a sufficient base for uniting people in the common goal of establishing such a center.

The means for establishing retreat centers in the other religious traditions would depend upon the systems they utilize as an organization. Possibly a few Reform Jewish temples could pool their resources, or all Bahai's or all Muslims in an area could combine finances to establish a common house of prayer. I believe the means will fall into place once the end, a place totally devoted to prayer, is agreed upon.

In the second model of a heterogeneous community, the challenges are greater, but not insurmountable. Though the people at

Shantivanam made, and continue to make, great inroads toward developing a creative expression of interfaith life, they ultimately can fall back on a common Catholic Christian faith experience when differences in vision occur. The Eucharist is still the primary ritual for the community of Shantivanam. No such common link would be easily available for Jews, Muslims, Christians, and Buddhists who would band together in community. To work with such a heterogeneous group would demand another kind of creativity not found in the Shantivanam model. However, with the increase in intermarriage today, it not only has become more likely for such heterogeneous religious centers to arise, it has become urgent that they develop.

It was need that gave birth to Shantivanam. Shantivanam did not create that need but responded to it. Ed, through his own personal crisis, uncovered a need common to many people. Ten years later, after extensive involvement in parish ministry, work as a professional counselor, marriage to a Jewish woman, and the birth of our two children, I still see the need for such a style of contemplative life. Though my wife and I obviously have different theological opinions and beliefs, we also have a very common faith in one God. Our prayer and ritual life at home is focused on beliefs common to both of us. During our moments of prayer in the morning and evening, when we say the *Shema* and the Lord's Prayer together, or on Friday evenings when we celebrate the Sabbath meal, or during the times we attend Sunday Mass, we are brought closer through our differences. Our wedding ceremony was witnessed by a rabbi and a priest, a sign of our desire for unity in pluralism. As Ed said in the wedding homily, our marriage was not a loss to either of our faith communities, but a budding sign of what can strengthen both.

From people who are religiously intermarried to people who are intent upon broadening their religious practices, the need for creative spiritual life centers is becoming more evident. The next step for many of these people would be to move outside the sanctuary of their homes to new centers of spiritual growth. It is to such people that Shantivanam has something to say.

Endnotes

1. Thomas Merton, *Contemplation in a World of Action* (New York: Doubleday, 1971).

2. Thomas Merton, *The Way of Chuang Tzu* (New York: New Directions Publishing Corporation, 1965), p. 38.

3. José Argüelles, *Transformative Vision* (Berkeley: Shambhala, 1975), p. 84.

4. Harry Turney-High, *Man and System* (New York: Appleton-Century-Crofts, 1968), pp. 253-254.

Falling in Love with the Divine: The Magic of Mysticism

by Jane Lukchart

Many people are yearning for a different way to live. Their hearts desire a sacred way of existing on the Earth. This great vision is being variously explored, as for example in the community of Shantivanam discussed in the previous article. A growing number of people are realizing that we have reached the limits of an exclusively technological, rational, scientific, and materialistic approach to reality. In the search for an alternative, many are becoming open to the domain of mysticism. Although our society claims to live by reason, we search for something beyond the destructive logic of the nightly news. While we eschew any belief in magic, we secretly hope for some magical potion to dissolve the hard edges of our modern metropolis and allow us to create the future more humanely. The hard-nosed realist in us calls this magic nonsensical thinking indeed! Yet in this article we will entertain the possibility that the mystical view of reality can be the magic needed in our time.

What exactly is mysticism? The very word seems elusive. Webster's dictionary defines *mysticism* as: "the doctrine that it is possible to achieve communion with God through contemplation and love without the medium of human reason" or, "the doctrine asserting the possibility of attaining knowledge of spiritual truths through intuition." Another definition says that *mysticism* is "vague, obscure, or confused thinking or belief"! So mysticism is not reasonable, not rational, not clear. It is, after all, related to our word *mystify*, "to puzzle, perplex, bewilder deliberately."

Shifting from *mysticism* to *mystic*, we find that a mystic is "one who is initiated into the Mysteries, esoteric rites"; "obscure, occult"; "beyond human comprehension, mysterious, enigmatic", "filling one with wonder and awe"; "having magic power"; and finally, "intuitive comprehension of truths beyond human understanding."

What a suprise that *mystery* and *magic* came up so directly in the definition of *mystic*. *Mystery* comes from the root word *mystes* or one initiated into the esoteric rites. The Greek form, *mystos*, meant "keeping silence" and *mystes* "originally had the meaning to close one's eyes, to close one's mouth." *Mystery* is also traced back to the base *mu*, which is a sound made with closed lips, whence comes our word *mutter*.

The definition of magic that we are most interested in is "any mysterious, seemingly inexplicable or extraordinary power or influence, for example, the magic of love." If we trace back the word *magic*, the root of it is *magi*. And, of course, magi are "Persian priests who are reputed to have occult powers." What do these Persian priests do? They "work with derived rituals and symbols to concentrate the mind."

Magic is also associated with the root word *magh* meaning "to be able." So magic becomes important when we ask, "How are we able (magh) to get from where we are to where we want to be?" If, as the mystics say, we all yearn for and ultimately need reunion with God, that we all remember a oneness with God to which we want to return, how are we going to get there? We have to have some way of doing it. So magic can be looked at as a technique for remembering what Marilyn Ferguson calls, "the technologies of transformation." The magi work with ways to alter your consciousness, to shift your awareness and perspective. We all experience this spontaneously, but there are techniques whereby you try to alter your consciousness intentionally. This is one sense of how magic has been used throughout history.[1]

Mysticism is the alteration of your consciousness to such a point that you experience oneness with all life or union with God, however you choose to express this inexpressible state. Thus magic can be understood as a technique aimed at allowing a more mystical consciousness. When it happens, it is magical (mysterious, inexplicable, extraordinary) indeed!

The Church has usually denounced all forms of what it considered to be magic. My understanding is that magic was seen as associated with pagan or gnostic practices and was also condemned as an error of pride, an attempt to usurp by special practices what is given by divine grace. As we shall see, this denunciation is often well founded, for magic can easily become an ego trip. All spiritual traditions contain warnings against the seeking of special psychic powers or experiences or paying too much attention to them when they arise spontaneously. Nonetheless, certain practices are useful in promoting an expansion of consciousness and they need not be denounced merely because they involve "magic." Indeed, magic as the technique to be able (magh) to intentionally alter consciousness in no way contradicts magic as the mysterious, inexplicable, extraordinary power of what Christians call grace. Any spiritual technique is a preparation to receive what grace can give.

Furthermore, the root of the word *magic* is involved in the words "image," and "imagination." Magic shifts us into the realm of non-rational understanding and experience. This takes us into myth, symbolism, and art. One way out of the dilemma of trying to speak of something that cannot really be captured in words, is to play with some poetic images in an effort to get more clarity.

Before doing this, it may be helpful to clarify some general points about mysticism. First, as mentioned already, mysticism is transrational. Please note that we are not saying prerational or irrational but transrational. This prefix indicates that it includes, but also transcends, a purely rational understanding. One spiritual teacher, Da Free John, names his teaching the Way of Divine Ignorance. Our egos want knowledge and we hope that knowledge will give us certainty, but mysticism posits ignorance in the face of the overwhelming mystery of God. We cannot understand with the mind alone. Another mystic, Stephen Levine, says, "The mind creates the abyss, the heart crosses it."[2] And, "...understand that understanding is the ultimate seduction of the mind. Go to the truth beyond the mind. Love is the bridge."[3] Over and over again we get this notion of understanding with the heart.

Remember, one definition of mystery involved closing the eyes and mouth. Closing the mouth implies that true reality cannot be expressed in words. In contrast to the tomes we write to describe our everyday reality, Meister Eckhart says, "God is a Being beyond Being and a Nothingness beyond Being. The most beautiful thing that a person can say about God is for that person to remain silent from the wisdom of an inner wealth. So be silent, and quit flapping your gums about God."[4] We must be silent to hear the one who speaks with closed lips (note the root "mu") and makes no sound.

The second point is that the mystical experience is trans-egoic. In the mystical moment, boundaries dissolve, the feeling of separateness becomes blurred and oneness with God is attained. To anyone who has not experienced it, no words suffice. But to one who has experienced it, no words are necessary. In spiritual traditions, the ego is by definition a contraction from infinity. It is our feeling of being separate. When we transcend the sense of ego, we experience the oneness or wholeness and "the flow" (the Tao). But the ego shuts things down. We want solidity, we cannot tolerate that type of flux, we have to get our bearings. The function of ego prevents the experience of oneness and flow. The mystical experience is by definition a dissolving of the egoic boundaries that separate us, or rather give us the illusion of being separate, from life and from God. The ego prevents us from feeling the reality that the mystics proclaim, that is, that the basic energy of the universe is love. This sounds crazy to our everyday "normal" consciousness, yet all the great spiritual teachers proclaim that love is the ultimate truth of the cosmos. Love is the great magic and mystery.

Perhaps with this examination of the ego, the Church's admonitions against magic become clearer. Magic as a technique is, in a certain sense, neutral. It can be used for good or for bad, and therefore we get the notion of White Magic and Black Magic, or the Good Witch and the Bad Witch! It is tricky, because the ego will try to use magic to its own ends. As a Sufi mystic says, "The way is narrow and sharp as a razor's edge." In that sense we are always sinning. (To sin simply being to miss the mark.) However, we could perhaps also say that the "original sin" is simply the inevitable contraction of egoic existence. We are always missing the mark one way or another because the mind immediately comes in and says, "Aren't I wonderful because I'm having this wonderful experience?" or "I must be someone special to have this experience" or "Wow, this is wonderful; I want to have this forever." The ego is there, and we are off the mark to one side or the other. In the mystical moment we are expanded outside of ourselves. Then the ego/mind steps in, bringing us down from the experience of wholeness. This is why most mystical experiences are fleeting, until the full "death of the ego." It is easy to miss the mark, and difficult to dissolve those edges which we all have, so as to be able to experience love and flow more easily. But it can be done. Others have journeyed before us and left road marks to travel by. They even proclaim that the way is joyful!

Tied up with the ego is the mind. The Hindu image for the mind is the monkey, which does tricks of its own momentum. That is what we find when we try to meditate. We like to think that we are in charge of what we think. When we sit down to meditate and try to clear our mind and think nothing, we find out that we cannot control it. The mind has its own momentum. Then we start to develop awareness, to observe the mind without becoming attached to the contents of the mind, without identifying with it. As soon as we identify with the contents of the mind, we become that state. We have lost the feeling of spaciousness of being, because we have become anger or fear; we are contracted and worried. It is a process of loosening up, of observing the actions of the mind and the strategies of the ego, of being fully present in each moment but not defined by any particular moment's experience.

Developing awareness of ourselves and our consciousness can be done without any particular system of belief. Thus this practice can appeal to the traditionally religious person or to the so-called atheist. Da Free John points out that to ask the question, "Does God exist?" is already to be lost in the contraction of the ego. We obviously are a part of a greater whole that both includes and transcends us. To doubt God is therefore possible only when we are stuck in our own contraction and narcissistic attachment. God is Reality, the underlying matrix of Being. In a certain sense, the atheist may be more ahead of the game than people who are heavily laden with religious dogmas and beliefs. Mysticism in no way means we have to believe anything specific. The whole point is direct experience, finding out for ourselves. As Eckhart asks, "What good is it to me if Mary is full of grace if I am not also full of grace? What good is it to me for the Creator to give birth to his Son if I do not also give birth to him in my time and culture?"[5]

Conventional religion tends to approach people as empty vessels. Into them are poured dogma and the ethical structure of commandments, so that the child/person will be a well-behaved little ego. We simply add a little of this and a little of that. But Eckhart says, "God is not found in the soul by the addition of anything, but by a process of subtraction."[6] Subtract. Take the belief out—let it go.

Another quote from Eckhart is: "I pray God to rid me of God."[7] What a paradoxical statement! But indeed, if what the word *God* triggers in us is beliefs, past experiences, and conditionings, then we must let go of these God concepts by a process of subtraction in order to find reality as only God. An atheist could be ahead in this process of subtraction. An atheist has dropped a lot of dogma, but may also get stuck in a mood of doubt and rebellion. Da Free John points out that while the traditionally religious person can be stuck in a childish relationship to God, the atheist can be stuck in an adolescent relationship to God. The point, however, is to continue to grow into a mature relationship.

So we are back to the question: how grow into this maturity? What magic (technique/grace) shows us the path? This brings us to the mystical notion that God is within. To paraphrase Eckhart, "God is in all things and all things are in God." It is a two-way dynamic, and the highest reality is the transcendence of all duality. As the Sufi poet Kabir says, "It rises above both coming in and going out."[8] Nonetheless, the mystical understanding does emphasize the notion of God within to offset the exoteric notion of God only as Other. The mystic hears the voice that speaks with a closed mouth, whether it is the whisper of the mystic's own soul or the revelation of a flower.

We are in God, and God is within us. How wonderful! But the result of this is that we cannot know God unless we first know ourselves. Thus the mystical path is one of self-understanding. Everything that we have repressed, that we have not wanted to acknowledge as part of ourselves, has to come up. It is basic psychology. We grow up with many "shoulds," such as "I should be a loving person." Then we become angry at people and want to clobber them. But, "Oh no, I wouldn't want to do that, not me, I'm a nice person, I went to Sunday School, I wouldn't hurt a fly." So we push those feelings down. They are not acceptable to our sense of who we are. Each of us wants to be a nice person, a smart person, a "together" person.

Substitute whatever your particular list or agenda is. Whatever is not on the agenda has to be pushed down and denied. Anything we are denying becomes part of our bondage. It prevents us from knowing God more completely. Kabir's imagery on this point is powerful. He asks, ". . . but if deep within you is a loaded gun, how can you have God?" We have to let all the repressed feelings and qualities come up; we must own them as our own, while at the same time not identifying with them. It is an intense process.

It is easy to mess ourselves up. The whole history of Christian asceticism attests to this. We say, "The senses are false, my desires are bad." Then we want to rid ourselves of them. We have already drawn the line and the battle is on! "The body is bad; I'll fight the body; I'll deny the body." Instead of oneness there is antagonistic duality. The mystic's path is a paradoxical process. It is something you have to both do and not do. You have to ask the question and listen at the same time, using what Eckhart calls the "bridle of love." We certainly need the techniques of laughter, humor, and forgiveness!

The mystical perception of reality is that wholeness and love are already present. We contract, so we do not experience their reality, but we do not have to create something that does not exist. God is, but we are not usually able (*magh*) to experience God. Hence the need for the magic of mysticism, for both the proven techniques of spiritual practice to let go of ego and thereby return to awareness of ever-abiding love, and for the magic of grace. I will not explain any particular techniques in this article. They can be sought out in the wealth of information already available. Rather, I want to explore magic in terms of poetic imagery to see what we can learn about the most potent magic, the magic of love. The whole journey may possibly be just the magic of allowing oneself to fall in love with the Divine.

As mentioned earlier, magic involves imagery and imagination, so we turn to those realms. Poetry, art, symbolism, and mythology are elusive, they draw you on. Because you cannot pin them down, they lead you into new discoveries. What I propose to do is to play with the striking imagery of some fantastic poetry by Sufi mystic Kabir, and see if that can evoke a finer understanding of the mystical experience of love and oneness.

The poet writes of himself: "How lucky Kabir is that surrounded by all this joy he sings inside in his little boat."[10] Yes, he is a separate little point of consciousness in a sense, but he is floating on that ocean with no sense of separateness. In another poem, Kabir raises the question, "Because someone has made up the word 'wave', do I have to distinquish it from water?"[11] Our minds create distinctions, which can be useful, but we forget that they are mind-created and take them for basic reality. "I laugh at the fish in the water who says he is thirsty."[12] We swim in an ocean of love, but we think we are thirsty (unloved), so we quest. In our questing, we lose touch with the truth that "the universe is shot through in all parts by a single sort of love."[13]

The feeling tone of Kabir's poetry is intimate and passionate. He writes, "When the Guest is being searched for, it is the intensity of the longing that does all the work. Look at me and you will see a slave of that longing."[14] Kabir celebrates intensity and the yearning for union with the Divine. He often writes imagery that depicts the mystical longing for God, and identifies with the woman who longs for her lover and lives only for the moment of reunion. This intensity of longing for the Divine is what Kabir says does all the work. This state of being in love gradually allows one to let everything blocking the union fall away. One desires and yearns for the Beloved. "The arrogance of reason has already separated us from that love. With the word reason you already feel miles away."[15] Getting there requires passionate commitment, devotion, and surrender to love.

Spiritual truth at our level of apprehension is always paradoxical. Whatever you get attached to is what you've got to let go of. As T.S. Elliot said, it is a "condition of the utmost simplicity, costing not less than everything."[16] One of the paradoxes involves the notion of desire. The word *desire* can be used positively, as Kabir uses it, or negatively, as in desires which must be mastered. The distinction is between desires of the ego and deeper desires of the self, the longing that wells up to embrace and be embraced by God.

Stephen Levine, in his book *Who Dies?*, talks about negative desire as the mental agitation of wanting this or that. He comments that the clinging and desires of ego flip one out of any awareness of fullness of being, but then he goes on to say, "The difficulty with our desires is that they are desires of me and mine. They do not include the universe. They are desires for what we want and not for who we are."[17] Who we are in our natural state is oneness, happiness, and love.

I was delighted recently to discover how the great poet Dante, in his *Divine Comedy*, portrays the power of the magical state we call love. What leads Dante through the descent into hell and the struggle up Mount Purgatory? His love for Beatrice and the image of the Divine, which she is to him. How does this love affect him? Early in his life, he writes in *La Vita Nuova*, "Whenever and wherever she appeared, in anticipation of her marvelous greeting, I held no man my enemy, and the flame of charity burned brightly within me, a flame that consumed all past offenses; and during this time if anyone had asked me about anything, my answer, with face free of all pride, could only have been 'Love.'"[18] We may be embarrassed by such adoration, but through his devotion to Beatrice, Dante is able, at the end of his life, to write his masterpiece of divine-love poetry, *The Divine Comedy*. I wish I had the time and space to share more of the revelations to which love leads him. I urge you to read for yourself Dorothy Sayre's beautiful translation of this mystical allegory of the soul's journey home to God. Dante's confession of love reverberates through the centuries to us. May we each be so afflicted with love!

Eckhart, with a similar theme of being caught by love, plays with the image of the fish in the water. He says:

> God lies in wait for us with nothing so much as love. Now love is like a fishhook. The fisherman cannot catch a fish unless the fish first picks up the hook. If the fish swallows the hook, no matter how it may squirm and turn, the fisher is certain of the fish. Love is the same way. Whoever is captured by love takes up this hook in such a fashion that foot and hand, mouth and eyes, heart and all that is in that person must always belong to God. Therefore, look only for this fishhook, and you will be happily caught. The more you are caught, the more you will be liberated.[19]

May we all be happily caught. Yet we know that we are experts at evading the hook! In our egoic, reasonable, everyday existence, we are afraid to appear so foolish and naive. As Da Free John says,

> The fundamental embarrassment is the confession of God. It is to dwell in obvious ecstasy in the company of other beings, to be already Free, to be fundamentally Happy, to be Conscious in God, and even to be outwardly expressive in that state, to speak of God, to think of God, to act in God, to be Ecstatic. That is the taboo, not mere mortal

confessions of pleasure and suffering, which mean nothing. To require it of a man to talk of God makes him feel embarrassed. He becomes ashamed, because in order to talk about God, he must lose face. To be extraordinarily and unreasonably Happy and to live that way embarrasses him. To be full of love and only talk that way, so foolishly, so naively, is socially unacceptable. We are supposed to be cool and hip and straight, oriented toward our survival, worldly and wise. But to be simply alive in God and Happy, and to speak about it and act that way and think that way, is absolutely unwanted and not allowed. So we become seekers.[20]

The end of all our seeking can never be more than what is available to us any moment we let go of ourselves and feel it—the radiant reality of love and happiness. As Kabir exclaims, "The damage I have done to myself fades, a million suns come forward with light, when I sit firmly in that world."[21]

I could happily go on and on quoting a multitude of sources on the magic of falling in love with the Divine, but time and space prohibit. Please take a lifetime to continue to fill in your own favorites. Better yet, write your own declarations. I will close with one more excerpt from Kabir that beautifully summarizes how the magic of mysticism has nothing to do with belief, dogma, ethical systems, and prescribed actions, but only with love. Kabir asks each one of us,

> Suppose you scrub your ethical skin until it shines, but inside there is no music, then what? Mohammed's son pores over words, and points out this and that, but if his chest is not soaked dark with love, then what? The Yogi comes along in his famous orange. But if inside he is colorless, then what?
>
> Every instant that the sun is risen, if I stand in the temple, or on a balcony, in the hot fields, or in a walled garden, my own Lord is making love with me.[22]

It truly seems that the entire mystical journey is simply allowing ourselves to fall in love with God. The quest of our lives is fulfilled by responding and surrendering to God as lovers to our Beloved. Love is the way and the way's end. We must love not as an ethical should, but as an ecstatic reality. Love is the true magic and mystery. May we each fall unreasonably and foolishly in love with the Divine!

Endnotes

1. Note, for instance, the book by Gareth Knight, *The History of White Magic*. (New York: Samuel Weiser, Inc., 1979).

2. Stephen Levine, *Who Dies?* (Garden City, N.J.: Anchor Books, 1982), p. 21.

3. Ibid., p. XV.

4. Matthew Fox, *Meditations with Meister Eckhart* (Santa Fe: Bear & Co., Inc., 1982), p. 44.

5. Ibid., p. 81.

6. Ibid., p. 45.

7. Ibid., p. 50.

8. Kabir, *The Kabir Book*, versions by Robert Bly, (Boston: Beacon, 1971), p. 58.

9. Ibid., p. 2.

10. Ibid., p. 58.

11. Ibid., p. 29.

12. Ibid., p. 9.

13. Ibid., p. 29

14. Ibid., p. 57

15. Ibid., p. 25.

16. Quoted in *The Aquarian Conspiracy*, Marilyn Ferguson, (Los Angeles: J.P. Tarcher, Inc., 1980), p. 363.

17. Levine, *Who Dies?*, p. 46.

10. Dante Alighieri, *La Vita Nuova*, trans. Mark Musa, (New Brunswick, N.J.: Rutgers Univ. Press., 1957), p. 16.

19. Eckhart, *Meditations*, p. 60.

20. Da Free John, "The Taboo Against God-realization," *The Laughing Man Journal* 6, no. 1 (1985): 10.

21. Kabir, *Kabir Book*, p. 57.

22. Ibid., p. 55.

Spiritual Growth, Psychological Growth: An Analogy

by Dave Lothrop

In its attempts to describe human existence, contemporary Western pysychology has generally avoided significant interaction with the works of the world's great religions. English translations of Eastern and Western religious materials have long been available; the problem is obviously more one of preference than of accessibility. Arguments against the use of religious texts in psychological discourse continue to persuade some people. Certain psychological perspectives argue that religion and psychotherapy cannot talk to one another, because religions (especially Eastern religions) tend to bypass and devalue tragedy, guilt, and the reality of evil. In this way religion is seen merely as a preoccupation with otherworldly concerns: God, mysticism, or a so-called "supernatural" plane. As a result of this compartmentalization, most psychological traditions refrain from entertaining the possibility that areas of congruence might exist between what religious texts convey and what psychological theories teach about the process of human growth and the "ideal" person.

This paper is an attempt to show, through an analysis of representative religious texts and certain psychological theories, that there are marked similarities and areas of overlap in their respective descriptions of the ideal human being and the path or process of attaining this status. More precisely, an analysis of psychological sources (from which we derive words like *authentic, whole, fully functional, healthy,* etc.) and an analysis of religious language in classical spiritual texts (from which we inherit words like *saintly, holy, sage, righteous,* etc.) show relationships in what the respective disciplines affirm about human life. Both types of discourse describe human existence, the evolving "ideal" person, and the path to attaining this status.

This is not a commonly explored area of discourse, and one reason is that each discipline espouses a different methodology and language. Nevertheless, it is our purpose to transcend these differences and show that a legitimate area of interface exists. Our efforts, then, are to show that what religious texts convey and what psychological theories teach about the process of human growth and the "ideal" person are not diametrically opposed to one another but do in fact converge and interrelate in describing a common area of human experience. The use of the above terms suggests analogous but not identical ways of describing what the respective disciplines affirm about human life.

We will focus on the interrelationship of person and process, pointing out those characteristics and common themes, and suggesting similarities in the respective disciplines of the ideal human and in the process of growing towards that ideal. From this effort we hope to support the claim that psychological literature often shares common concerns with the writings of the world's great religions.

The material we will be drawing from consists of four psychological perspectives and four classic religious texts. The psychology of Carl Rogers and the humanistic-existential psychology of Rollo May, M. Scott Peck, and phenomenologist Medard Boss constitute our psychological sources. Judaism's *Pirke Abot* (or *Ethics of the Fathers*); the classic Christian text, chapter 13 of Paul's First Letter to the Corinthians; a central spiritual text of Buddhism, the *Dhammapada*; and a Chinese classic, the *Tao Te Ching*, constitute our religious sources.

We now turn to the task at hand, suggesting interface between the psychological and religious perspectives by first pointing out two of the many similarities or common themes characterizing the process leading to the embodiment of the human ideal.

With regard to the ideal person, the first similarity found within the psychological and religious literatures is that of genuine love. Many names are used to describe this most precious aspect of real human-ness; phenomenological *eros*, and unconditional positive regard, for example, are used by psychological theorists, while loving kindness and compassion (*karuna*) are used by religious traditions. All these names point to a similar area of human experience: genuine love — a love of self and others. Both traditions make use of the term *agape*, one of the Greek words for love, to describe this reality.

From the perspective of psychology, love is reflected in the gen-uine care and concern that the therapist bestows upon the patient. Existential psychology, which is primarily concerned with persons experiencing their whole existence as real and meaningful, refers to this love as either phenomenological *eros*, or *agape.*[1] Medard Boss, a German phenomenologist, defines phenomenological *eros* as a will-ingness on the part of one being to be completely present for itself and another being. Rollo May defines *agape* as:

> . . . a transcending of *eros* (the Greek word for physical love) in enduring tenderness, and a lasting concern for others, thereby giv-ing more meaning to *eros*.[2]

In this way, love is the extension of one's self for another.

For Carl Rogers, in his person-centered, direct approach to psy-chology, love is understood as "unconditional positive regard for ano-ther."[3] It involves a genuine outgoing care and concern for another. It requires the acceptance of another person beyond the perspective of label, symptom, or category. As Rogers says of therapy:

> If I can provide a certain type of relationship, the other person will discover in himself the capacity to use that relationship for growth, and change and personal development will occur.[4]

For Rogers, love — unconditional positive regard — is the therapist's non-valuating acceptance of the other; it is the integrity that a thera-pist brings to a relationship. In this context, love involves putting aside one's own selfish prejudices and observing the person as he or she is present.

The religious traditions view this love in a similar light. In the

Jewish tradition, love is rooted in the famous teaching of the Torah: ". . .you shall love your neighbor as yourself. . . ."[5] The favorite commentary to this verse from Leviticus is attributed to Rabbi Hillel. When a Roman asked him to summarize the whole Torah while standing on one foot, the gentle rabbi complied with the Roman's request and said, " 'you shall love your neighbor as yourself;' the rest is commentary." It is the same rabbi who states in *Ethics of the Fathers*, the Talmudic tractate of spiritual teachings from the "fathers" of post-biblical Judaism:

> Be of the disciples of Aaron, loving peace and pursuing peace, loving mankind and bringing them nearer to the Torah.[6]

Another demonstration of this non-binding love found within the *Pirke Abot* is the love of spiritual friendship essential in the development of ideal Jewish righteousness:

> Whenever love depends on some material cause and the material cause passes away, the love passes away too; but if it does not depend on some material cause, it will never pass away. This is the love of David and Jonathan.[7]

True love which does not depend on material gain or pleasure is undoubtedly at the heart of the Jewish ideal of the wise and holy person.[8]

In perhaps the most classic rendition of Christian spirituality, Paul's First Letter to the Corinthians, chapter 13, love defines the central Christian ethic.[9] In this passage, words without love backing them up are useless and noisy.[10] So, if we happen to be gifted with prophetic insight, and charismatic power to move masses as well as mountains, without love we are merely marveling at our own spiritual and political prowess.[11] In order to move into a right relationship with God, and likewise into more holy areas of living, it is important that every action be done with love. Otherwise, we tend to marvel at deeds as extensions of our own selfish needs, not the manifestations of God's love.

Without this love we have nothing. To see our work as God's work, as the work of God's love in the world and not the achievements of our own selfish needs, is to act in accordance with this love. As Jesus himself prays shortly before his arrest: "My Father, if it be possible, let this cup pass from me; nevertheless, not as I will, but as thou wilt."[12] God's will is God's love and apart from that there is nothing.

What is this love that Paul speaks of? It is the love of God poured out in Christ. Christians, then, are called to be other Christs. They are called to love as Jesus loved:

> This is my commandment, that you love one another as I have loved you.[13]

For Paul, like John, when we love others as Christ has loved us, we are identified with the only abiding reality. Everything else, even faith and hope, will pass away; love alone remains and lasts into eternity because it is a participation in the very nature of God. This is the essential Christian ethic and a model of the ideal Christian person.

For Buddhism, and for one of its central texts, the *Dhammapada*, love is compassion (*karuna*) extended to oneself and to others by following the eightfold path of virtue.[14] Discipline and practice are needed to cultivate a deeper appreciation of the eightfold path, but by far and away the most important receptive means of deepening one's love, one's compassion, is to approach life with an open and pure mind:

> What we are today comes from our thoughts of yesterday, and our present thoughts build our life of tomorrow: our life is the creation of our mind. If a man speaks or acts with an impure mind, suffering follows him as a wheel of a cart . . . If a man speaks or acts with a pure mind, joy follows him as his own shadow.[15]

Thus the quality and receptive nature of our minds, together with discipline and practice in the eightfold path, promote a sense of compassion and love in the ideal Buddhist monk.

Taoism, and its classic spiritual text, the *Tao Te Ching*, speaks less directly of love, but love is related to the Tao, which is based on various appropriate relationships of living. The ideal Taoist sage is knowledgeable of the distinction between appropriate relationships and inappropriate ones. Appropriate relationships are those thoughts, words, or deeds that are nonbinding and nonattached; inappropriate relationships are attachments of desire, possession, and the general way we act in an effort to achieve what we need and want in the world. True love is readibly translatable as manifesting appropriate relationships to the other and to the world. At its best, true love, in the Taoist sense, is nonbinding and nonattached. In this way, it is related to other descriptions of love we have encountered.

We find, therefore, that one characteristic of the ideal person expressed in both disciplines is genuine love. M. Scott Peck, a practicing psychiatrist who attempts to bridge the gap between psychology and religion, successfully integrates the two respective disciplines with his own definition of love. Love for Peck is "the will to extend oneself for the purposes of nurturing one's own or another's spiritual (or psychological) growth."[16] This love is not intentional love (*eros*).[17] Genuine love, because it is rooted in willing, can be a permanent characteristic of one's behavior towards another. The opposite of love is not hatred but laziness.[18] Falling in love, on the other hand, is a necessary counterpart to falling out of love. It must be transitory, and though useful in interactions, is not what is taught in the spiritual disciplines. Love or compassion, which is characteristic of the ideal person, always flows into action from the decision to love.

This ability to decide to love leads us into the second characteristic of the ideal person — the ability to decide, to choose, and to commit oneself to life. Growth towards psychological and spiritual health involves the utilization of our human power for choice in the making of our lives. From the existential psychological tradition, we choose out of freedom, from the vast array of possibilities that we wish to actualize and make ours.

It is the belief of existential psychology that even if we *cannot* rightfully control the fact that we exist (i.e. that we are born and that we will die), we *can* control how we wish to exist. We can choose to a large degree the way we want to live. The open possibilities (i.e. personal options and choices) are those numerous existing potentials which we have to fulfill and actualize through personal willingness. For instance, I might not be able to choose the fact that now I exist in this country. I can, however, choose to some degree in what way I wish to exist in this country. Thus, there is always a kind of interplay between the givens of life and what we are able to choose, create, and make of life. The "ideal" psychologically healthy person operates out of this type of an awareness. It is the task of the existential therapist to see to it that individuals are capable of deciding for themselves, capable of making those significant daily decisions required of healthy, growing people.

Carl Rogers, in a similar way, recognizes the power of choice as reflected in the person's own willing movement away from defensive maneuverings (i.e. avoidance of life's situations, not taking stands, and projections), and towards more caring ways of living. In Rogerian therapy, choice is viewed as a self-directed, teleological quality that characterizes the ideal, fully functioning person:

> The client moves towards being autonomous . . . he chooses the goals towards which he wants to move. Freedom to be oneself is a frighteningly responsible freedom and an individual moves toward it cautiously, fearing with almost no confidence at first.[19]

To be oneself is a natural process of self-direction for the ideal person, but it is one requiring courage to change and overcome the fear of freedom and responsiblity. The ability to reassume command of one's life by accepting the challenges of new experiences, even if it means changing previously established patterns of living, is the hopeful outcome of successful Rogerian therapy and a primary characteristic of the ideal, fully functioning person.

In the spiritual literature, the power of choice plays a crucial role in determining our response to the world, to ultimacy, and to ourselves. Both Buddhism and Taoism believe that we can freely choose the extent to which our relationships to the world are either appropriate or inappropriate, pure or impure. As we found with Buddhism, the mind is the creator of the world,[20] thus it is ultimately our responsibility and decision to establish whether we wish to operate from the pure or the impure mind in our worldly creations.

In the Western religious traditions, the power of choice plays a similar role. The *Ethics of the Fathers* points out that we choose our own spiritual destiny:

> All is foreseen, and free will is given, and the world is judged by goodness; and all is according to the amount of work.[21]

God ultimately foresees everything; yet such knowledge does not deprive human beings of their free will to choose the right or wrong path. The call of the *Ethic* acknowledges a tendency, an innate capacity within everyone for becoming righteous. In the final analysis, humans are free to choose their own spiritual destiny.

In First Corinthians 13, the essential Christian ethic reflects this element of choice. Here, the Christian is called to love as God loves.[22] This implies that our decision to love or not to love determines the type of response we make to this call. We are free to embark on a spiritual journey and heed the word of God, or ignore it.

While love is perhaps more explicitly stressed in the religious discussions of the ideal holy person, the power of human choice is more central to psychological discussions of the healthy person. Nonetheless, the overall "ideal" person necessarily reflects adequate capacities both to love and to choose. These two characteristics, used by both disciplines to describe their ideal person, together constitute an important interface between psychology and religion.

In examining descriptions of the *process* of personal growth, we find two outstanding similarities. First, the role of difficulty and suffering as characteristics of personal growth is stressed in both the psychological and religious perspectives. These perspectives claim that a fairly large degree of suffering exists, either in oneself or in the world. It is not only the ground of our anguish and illness, but that which prompts us to further growth. It is not to be avoided, but dealt with, as in Buddha's teaching to trace the root of unreasonable desire (called *tanha*, Buddhism's second noble truth) in every suffering, and Jesus' teaching to take up one's cross.

In the psychological literature, we find that difficulty and suffering (i.e., anxiety) often function as necessary counterparts to the process of actualizing one's own possibilities in life. Why do we experience anxiety that in turn inhibits our decision-making process? The reason it is tremendously difficult to make a decision is because we must select, from an incredibly vast array, those choices we wish to make real and actual in our living. The extent to which we can perform this task constructively, despite the tremendous suffering involved, is the extent of our personal growth. Suffering and difficulty result in illnesses and mental problems when we do not opt for authentic living, that is, when we refuse to make choices for ourselves.

From the perspective of existential psychology, we create conditions of personal suffering and "stuckness" when we surrender the freedom to choose our own possibilities. There are reasons we become stuck, but by far the most important reason is letting others (i.e. the

group, institutions, etc.) make decisions for us. Therefore, when adequate social or personal values no longer exist (as is generally thought
to be the case today), a sense of anxiety and meaninglessness prevails
because there are no values "out there" to which we can cling. As Rollo
May points out:

> The real threat to existence is not to be accepted, to be thrown out
> of the group, to be left solitary and alone. . .One's own meaning be-
> comes meaningless because it is borrowed from somebody else's
> meaning.[23]

To invest in the view and directions of others, never questioning
what takes place, blocks movement along the path of greater growth.
When this happens, suffering, mental anguish, and a general despair
over living permeate existence. While healthy individuals uphold some
of the values of others, they do so through their own decisions, not
through a blindness to any other option. Thus, the task of the existential therapist is to help clients transform suffering and conditions of
stuckness into a situation in which they can grow.

For Rogers, suffering arises when there is a discrepancy and incon-
gruity between one's concept of self and the total organism. Here the
needs of the total organism (i.e. the needs for love, survival, purpose,
belonging, etc.) are not consistent with the needs of the self-concept
(i.e. the needs for being accepted, for being what the self wants to be,
one's upheld values, etc.). When this happens, the self-concept or
personality "denies to awareness or distorts in awareness, significant experience. . .thus creating an incongruence between self and experience."[24]

As a result, the natural process of growth is blocked and suffering
occurs. Defensive behaviors are used to create and perpetuate this
inconsistency.

In both the existential and Rogerian perspectives, the individual
in this difficult state of affairs is said to be living a life of stuckness,
anxiety, and general despair, thereby stifling his or her personal growth.
Therapy is aimed at breaking through stagnant conditions of suffering,
thus releasing one's psychological process and making personal living
possible once more.

In the religious literature, suffering has long been seen as a neces-

sary characteristic of the spiritual path. In Judaism, spiritual growth
and holiness are hardly tasks free from suffering. The *Pirke Abot* reminds
us that, "According to the suffering, so is the reward."[25] In Christianity
it is clear that loving entails suffering. We see this in the example of
Jesus himself who had a cup of suffering to drink, and in the example
of Paul whose ministry of love led him to boast of nothing except the
cross of Christ.[26]

In the Buddhist and Taoist account, suffering plays a more crucial
role in the process of spiritual growth. For Buddhism, suffering is its
first Noble Truth. *Dukkha* is that unsatisfactory quality permeating all
existence. Further, Buddhism is quick to point out that it is difficult to
choose a life of virtue as opposed to a life of suffering and vice:

> It is easy to do what is wrong, to do what is bad for oneself; but
> very difficult to do what is right, to do what is good for oneself.[27]

We suffer in part because we choose to suffer, but more importantly
because we are too lazy and inattentive to notice how the source of our
suffering is the clinging in our own consciousness, rather than the projected object in the world. For example, if one is fuming with anger and
frustration at the slowness of a grocery check-out line, one need only
be reminded that it is unreasonable to assume that check-out lines
should conform to one's schedule.

One of Taoism's central teachings holds that both good and evil
arise together and are mutually interdependent:

> Under heaven all can see beauty as beauty only because there is
> ugliness. All can know good only because there is evil. Therefore hav-
> ing and not having arise together. Difficulty and ease complement
> each other.[28]

This particular awareness of the interdependence of good and evil,
right and wrong, objective and subjective, is what is known as the
yin/yang principle. Since opposites arise together, conditions of suffering exist side by side with joy. The Taoist makes it our task to recognize that suffering exists to the same extent as its counterpart. In other
words, one is lonely to the degree to which he or she has a capacity for
companionship. Suffering and joy arise together and are defined and

experienced in terms of the other. The Taoist sage is mindful of this teaching as a part of the process leading towards spiritual growth.

The awareness of suffering (*dukkha*, the cross) is a step towards holiness in the religious traditions. In psychological literature, there is a kind of suffering, (anxiety) which results from the confrontation with many possiblities and can lead to growth through the very act of deciding or choosing. From the perspective of spirituality, being stuck at the level of frustration and suffering blocks growth in holiness. Similarly, unresolved anxiety results in the creation of mental illness and generally inauthentic patterns of living.

Since the role of suffering is such a strong part of the process leading to personal growth, all traditions stress the necessity of cultivating a relationship with an experienced guide. This guide, whether he or she is called master, *roshi*, sage, therapist, abbot, *kalyanamitra* (spiritual friend), or spiritual director, is one who provides support as well as an objective backdrop against which one can better assess spiritual growth.

In the psychological traditions, both the existential psychologist and Carl Rogers place emphasis on establishing a genuine therapist-patient relationship. In the existential tradition, the therapist as a guide attempts to facilitate growth in the individual by helping him or her learn to transcend the difficulties of living and fulfill various potentialities. For Rollo May, the goal of therapy is "that the patient experiences his (or her) existence as real."[29] Carl Rogers believes that therapy involves a helping relationship, nondirective in nature, whereby the therapist tries to reopen channels of communication in an effort to get the patient to reassume responsibility for making his or her own life. The Rogerian guide, the therapist, has to be able to bring the patient to greater areas of growth through the congruence that is established in interpersonal relationships. Furthermore, Rogers says that this type of therapeutic relationship can be applied to other areas of life, for as he sees it, it is the basis of genuine interpersonal interactions and facilitates the greatest degree of personal growth.

From the religious perspective, there is the long-standing tradition of an experienced guide to facilitate the spiritual growth of the monks. The ultimate duty of the abbot is to guide the disciples to greater union with God, and to help them judge their spiritual progress with greater objectivity. To accomplish this he needs the sternness of a master and

the love of a father. We are reminded that the word *abbot* comes from
the Aramaic *abba* meaning "father."

In Judaism, a spiritual companion is necessary for movement
along the path of spiritual growth. *Sage* is the term in the *Ethics of the
Fathers* for a spiritual teacher. Jose ben Joezer of Zeredeh said,

> Let your house be a meeting place for the sages, and sit amid the
> dust of their feet, and drink in their words with thirst.[30]

In rabbinic literature, the relationship to the sage or spiritual teacher
equals, in some instances, the relationship to one's blood relative.
Thus, in the text cited here, one's house is as much a meeting place for
spiritual teachers as it is a dwelling place for family members.

The *roshi* or master is the experienced guide in Zen Buddhism.
One Zen student speaks of her *roshi* in these words:

> Without anything said or done, just the impact of meeting a per-
> sonality so developed can be enough to change another's whole way
> of life. But in the end it is not the extraordinariness of the teacher
> which perplexes, intrigues, and deepens the student, it is the teacher's
> utter ordinariness.[31]

This comment makes it clear that the most important teaching is
frequently nonverbal. Like all effective spiritual teachers and coun-
selors, the *roshi* acts as a facilitator to the student; he or she provides
an interpersonal atmosphere whereby the student is able to move to
higher levels of awareness.

The Taoist sage incorporates the Chinese tradition in which the
ideal teacher is the emperor. He leads and guides primarily through his
humility and nonaction:

> If the sage would guide the people, he must serve with humility.
> If he would lead them, he must follow behind. In this way when the
> sage rules, the people will not feel oppressed; when he stands before
> them, they will not be harmed. The whole world will support him
> and will not tire of him.[32]

In this way, the Taoist is supported by the world as he or she supports the world. He or she acts out of humility and is able to rule more

effectively. The Taoist sage shows further support through actions of love, care, and compassion:

> Therefore, the sage takes care of all men and abandons no one.
> He takes care of all things and abandons nothing.[33]

Through the manifestation of these qualities, the Taoist sage is able to extend his or her self to others to nurture their own spiritual growth.

Thus far we have considered two similarities between the psychological and religious conceptions of the ideal person: love, and capacity for choice. We have also noted two similarities in their respective understanding of the process — namely, the role of suffering and the importance of a spiritual guide. This limited probe into the available material suggests further work which can be done to support the overall claim that psychological literature interacts and converges with the writings of the great world religions.

The bulk of our energy has been used attending to those areas of interface (or common themes) between what religious texts convey and what certain psychological theories teach about the process of human growth and its ideal personal embodiment. However, there is one major difference that should be mentioned. We have found that it is the aim and the intent of psychotherapy to assist the individual in rediscovering or developing his or her own identity, thus enabling that person to resume functioning as a free and healthy individual. The restoration or development of selfhood, of identity, is perhaps the most challenging and realistic goal of therapy. For the most part, psychology has made significant strides in this area.

The religious traditions, on the other hand, attempt to get beyond selfhood and identity, seeing our attachments to ourselves (egos) as a major stumbling block in the experience of religious truth. While psychology attempts to secure identities, religious traditions (especially the Eastern traditions) strive to get rid of them; that is, the direction is to let go of those very self-defining identities that consistently prevent our experience of God. It is the belief of most spiritual traditions that our own preciously guarded sense of self must be relinquished and surrendered, if true religious transformation is to take place. Up to now, this is an area where psychology and religion have been at odds.

Gerald G. May, younger brother of existential psychologist Rollo May, is one of the first psychologists to suggest the possibility that traditional psychology must take heed of religious teachings and strive to get beyond the confining realms of selfhood, if complete and total psychological experience is to be possible. In his book, *Will and Spirit: A Contemplative Psychology*, Gerald May attempts to extend the borders of psychology even further into the deepest realm of the spiritual. His is a move towards a contemplative psychology where one needs to "begin a consideration of seeing psychological experiences with spiritual eyes."[34] Dr. May goes on to say that,

> The goal of contemplative psychology is not separate autonomy of the individual (i.e. preservation of self-identities), but realization of one's own essential rootedness in God or in related creation.[35]

The suggestion being made here is that there is still greater room for psychological exploration into the realm of the religious. Moreover, this implies that even for maximum psychological experience, the self identities and images must be cast aside. Finally, and relating to the interests of this paper, May is suggesting the possibility of locating more significant parallels, areas of greater interface between the two respective disciplines.

While we have neither the time nor the place to entertain such a venture, the recent works of Dr. May along with the efforts of this paper suggest paying greater attention to many other areas of convergence and interface between these two bodies of knowledge and experience that have existed far too long in aloof separation. Further study is almost limitless in its scope and possibility. Hopefully, the synthetic methodology suggested here can provide a paradigm for this subsequent research.

Endnotes

1. Medard Boss, *Psychoanalysis and Daseinanalysis*, trans. Ludwig B. Lefebre (New York: Basic Books, Inc., 1963), p.28.

2. Nathaniel Lawrence, gen. ed., *Readings in Existential Phenomenology* (Englewood Cliffs, NJ: Prentice-Hall, Inc., 1967), p.371.

3. Carl R. Rogers, *On Becoming a Person* (Boston: Houghton Mifflin Company, 1961), p. 63.

4. Ibid., p. 32.

5. Leviticus 19:18, Revised Standard Version.

6. H.E. Goldin, trans. and annotator, *Ethics of the Fathers* (New York: Hebrew Publishing Company, 1962), 1:12.

7. Ibid., 5:20.

8. Ibid., 5:20.

9. I Corinthians, chapter 13, Revised Standard Version.

10. Ibid., 13:1.

11. Ibid., 13:2.

12. Matthew 26:39, Revised Standard Version.

13. John 15:12, Revised Standard Version.

14. The *Dhammapada: The Path of Perfection*, trans. from the Pali and intro. by Juan Mascaro (Middlesex, England: Penguin Books Ltd., 1973), p. 27.

15. Ibid., 1:1.

16. M. Scott Peck, *The Road Less Traveled: A New Psychology of Love, Traditonal Values, and Spiritual Growth* (New York: Simon & Schuster, 1978), p. 81.

17. Ibid., p. 84.

18. Ibid.

19. Rogers, *On Becoming a Person*, p.147.

20. The *Dhammapada*, 1:1.

21. *Ethics of the Fathers.*, 3:19.

22. See note 13.

23. Lawrence, *Existential Phenomenology*, p.372.

24. Carl R. Rogers, *Formulation of the Person and the Social Context*, vol. 3 of *Psychology: A Study of a Science. Study I. Conceptual and Systematic*, ed. S. Koch (New York: McGraw-Hill Book Co., 1959), p. 204.

25. *Ethics of the Fathers*, 5:27.

26. Galatians 6:14, Revised Standard Version.

27. The *Dhammapada*, 12:163.

28. Lao Tzu, *Tao Te Ching*, trans. Gia-Fu Feng and Jane English (New York: Vintage Books, 1972), ch. 2.

29. Rollo May, gen. ed., *Existence: A New Dimension in Psychiatry and Psychology* (New York: Basic Books, Inc., 1958), p. 85.

30. *Ethics of the Fathers*, 1:4.

31. Shunryu Suzuki, *Zen Mind, Beginner's Mind* (New York: Weatherhill, Inc., 1976), p. 18.

32. Lao Tzu, *Tao Te Ching*, ch. 66.

33. Ibid., ch.27

34. Gerald G. May, M.D., *Will and Spirit: A Contemplative Psychology* (San Francisco: Harper & Row, 1982), p. 22.

35. Ibid., p.27.

Reincarnation as Method for the Divine Quest

by Barbara Clow

In his preceding essay, Dave Lothrop suggested that traditional psychology and religious wisdom teach us love and capacity for true choice, which can result in a significant awareness of selfhood. He offers the vision that traditional psychology may be moving even more into the religious arena, that psychologists can opt for being guides of the spiritual quest. Reincarnation therapy—reaccessing past-life memory into present awareness—is a new and rapidly growing field in psychology which utilizes the therapist as a guide for the spiritual quest of the client. In this examination of reincarnation in light of Judeo-Christian roots, three healers who utilize exploration of past lives as a technique to release the soul in the body will be described. Although reincarnation is a basic tenet of most Eastern religions, the Western tradition will be the focus of this study. The fearful avoidance by Western religions of considering the possibility of more than one lifetime, and what this implies about the soul in spiritual time, appears to be propelling Western theology into a dead end. It is one of many over-identifications with past heretical definitions which are no longer needed and are now functionally destructive. Only a belief in the eternal return to this planet in communion with God can offer the individual the necessary passionate love of earth which results in hope for the future. Defining our experience in any limited way, such as having only one life, will always end up in despair. Eternal love is *eros*, a compelling love for life.

The struggle with the implication of many lives — that each one of us is in the midst of a time continuum which ultimately makes sense over these many lives — involves asking questions which start with the existence of evil in this world. Often Westerners, if you ask them, will tell you that they don't want to hear about reincarnation, because they don't want to come back to this place ever again! What does that say about their feelings about Earth? Lurking behind this response is a confusion about the question of evil. Unless Western spiritual disciplines have something to offer people faced with evil in their lives, the disciplines are useless. When faced with acute tragedy in our lives such as death of a child, murder, rape, war, or genocide, experience gained over many lifetimes offers perspective. Christianity attempts to justify suffering by teaching that it results in the spiritual progress. But this form of ascetic mumbo-jumbo is insulting in the face of civilian war casualties, mass starvation, or the grinding poverty of blacks in the midst of North American affluence. Perspective over many lives offers wisdom and meaning in the face of blinding tragedy.

But would a composite of many lifetimes add up to a cosmic joke? A meaningless series of ugly experiences dotted with small pleasures? A deep exploration of our past from an evolutionary point of view answers that question, and will be addressed by this paper. It does not matter whether their inner contents are past lives or not, but almost all seekers find a rich memory bank which offers them a complex awareness about who they are now. The truth is, our individual struggles over time are intensely meaningful and integrated. My focus is evolutionary, because a search into the past with the belief that growth is occurring yields a new and exciting perspective about the present. It frees us from determinism, fatalistic thinking, and negativity. The question of evil and reincarnation will be examined in Hebrew roots, in Christian history, and lastly in the work of three reincarnation-based healers. The evolutionary examination digs into deeply buried archetypes and cultural paradigms. It is painful to look closely at our past, particularly into the history of our own religious tradition. It is just as hard to look closely into our own personal past over long spans of time, to examine and consider letting go of old habits and patterns, but this has become an acute necessity because of the dangers in our culture today. Often an individual will not undergo such a complete inner search unless pushed to it by psychological breakdown. The same goes for our culture. If we are to alter our present behavior, which is destructive of the life-support systems we depend on, we must dig into all the places where evil, ignorance, and truth lie. However, when we finally do shine a laser beam into our historical past or into our individual memory banks, we find we are actually making progress. We are not the same now as we were before, and we don't have to hold onto past mistakes and repeat them, but we will continue to do so until we have explored our past experiences.

In the Hebrew tradition, reincarnation is not mentioned in the Torah, otherwise known as the Pentateuch or the Five Books of Moses. However, we can at least examine Yahweh's attitudes towards life and death as expressed through Moses. The Torah describes a time of almost constant warfare, mass chaotic movement of peoples, and great insecurity, which came after a probable thousand years of peace before 1800 BCE in parts of Canaan and all of Egypt.[1] Egypt as described in the Books of Moses was in a state of decline after a 200-year occupation by the Hyksos, but this came after a long period of peace. Recent digs in Canaan[2] reveal a total absence of warfare in the ancient kingdom of Mari, before the Hebrew takeover. The latest findings from Ebla[3] are tending to show signs of warfare before 2000 BCE, but generally the civilized world was free of massive obsession with militarism. Suddenly around 1800 BCE, mass movements came from the North, including the Hittites and various Indo-European peoples such as the Thracians.[4] The Mediterranean became a hotbed of warfare, pillage, slavery, and destruction. People suffered terribly during this time, and this suffering permeates the Torah. With that mediating view of history in place, the Yahwist attitude towards life and death can be looked at. The formation of the Hebrew State in Canaan occured just after Moses battled with the Midianites. This was just before the death of Moses when Joshua took control. In Deuteronomy 7, Yahweh has already instructed Moses on what to do with the nations Yahweh has given over to him: He is to conquer them, destroy them, show them no mercy, and destroy their altars.[5] After Moses had conquered the Midianites, he slew all the males, even the young ones, and he killed all women except for the virgins. Death pervades the Torah and it is final. Given the varied teachings of the afterlife in Egypt and Mesopotamia, it seems odd that neither Moses nor Yahweh mentions a heaven or a return. The crisis atmosphere and the obsession with gaining an earthly kingdom explain the lack of discussion about the abode of the soul. However, when we read the Scriptures for wisdom applicable today, then we question Yahweh's avenging behavior.

The extreme nationalism of the Chosen People would have been watered down by any consideration of an afterlife or return. The state and priesthood are empowered by any source of total control over individual destiny. If one life is all there is, then material and state goals take precedence over the destiny of the soul. Moses, under the direction of God, frequently threatened his people with annihilation. Without going too deeply into this leadership method, we need to look at the results of these threats on the psyche of both Jews and Christians, since Christians have attached their Scriptures to the Hebrew Bible. It is important to reflect upon what one thinks about this revengeful-God archetype and investigate its culpability for the extreme violence of the modern world.

A critical time in the formation of the Yahwist paradigm occurred when Moses came down from the mountain and smashed the tablets of the Ten Commandments because he found his people worshipping the Golden Calf. We are told that Yahweh saw what they were doing before he came down, and Yahweh told Moses he planned to destroy the people. Moses persuaded Yahweh to hold his fire this time, and he came down the mountain a hero. Moses called those who were with him to support him, and the sons of Levi responded. Moses commanded them to kill all the other men. They killed them all, returned, and Moses said, "Today you have ordained yourselves for the service of the Lord, each one at the cost of his son and brother. . ."[6] Then Yahweh sent a plague upon his people anyway for their sins. Is there any escape from sin but death, which is the final end? It is impossible for us to actually enter into the mind of the ancient Hebrews, but it is not hard to locate this attitude in many people today. Those who spend their time awaiting the Rapture have this archetype buried deeply within. This punishing-fire God was absorbed without examination into Christianity, and sado-masochism is but one possible consequence in the modern mind. Yahweh's wrath leaves only the power of sin in an evil world.

The prophetic and wisdom traditions are more subtle. They are filled with the richness of spherical time sense, of the life of the individual in linear time as it relates to the timeless spiritual realm. Job is asked the ultimate question by the Lord: "Where were you when I laid the foundation of the earth?" (Job 38:4). A long section follows concerning the complexity of creation, asking if Job has entered into the fabric of Earth and time. The Lord says, "You know, for you were born then, and the number of your days is great!" (Job 38:21). People generally presume that there is no solution to Job's dilemma, Job being one who suffers even though he is a good man and obedient to the Lord. However, to one who holds belief in reincarnation, the answer seems clear. If we read Job 38:21 as a truthful declaration of God and not, as it is usually understood, as an ironical taunt, then Job is being told that he will live from the beginning to the end of the earth, and he will have lives where he will suffer even if he is a good man. In Proverbs 8:21-23 the point is further clarified: "The Lord created me at the beginning of his work, the first of his acts of old. Ages ago, I was set up, at the first, before the beginning of the earth." Few would deny that this sense of spherical time persists throughout the Hebrew Bible, but many would deny that individual humans share in it. Yet is that not the only way we can integrate spherical spiritual time with human linear experience?

Isaiah lived in a time when the worst historical fears were actualized, and he raises questions even harder to answer than those raised by Job. Isaiah defines the day of the Lord as the time when God terrifies the earth. Calling to mind Sodom and Gomorrah, Isaiah hints of a cataclysm to come that will send men to caves for shelter. He also speaks of a time coming when "the wolf shall dwell with the lamb, and the leopard lie down with the kid" (Isaiah 11:6). Some have suggested that he foretells the birth of Christ in Isaiah 7:14, yet what does the coming of peace after travail mean to any of us unless we share in the experience? Isaiah says, "Therefore the Lord awaits to be gracious to you; therefore he exalts himself to show mercy to you. For the Lord is a God of justice, blessed are those who wait for him" (Isaiah 30:18). More than all the other prophets, Isaiah is meaningless unless we are all part of the eternal return. The universal power of Isaiah in the psyche comes from his profound ability to express the immersion in historical drama that we all intuit. Yet, Isaiah and the other prophets rarely say what they mean. Instead, they use images of the eternal return such as the tree of life, the vines and the vineyard, and the fig tree. In their culture, images were more empowering than specifics.

In prophetic tradition, the experience of sharing in history from the beginning to the end of time was triggered by those images. Now we are more literal, and that may be why we require reimmersion into past lives to recapture the passionate connection with our past, our history. The eminent Jewish theologian Gershem Scholem discusses the Hebrew mystics' sense of the utter inadequacy of words to express their true feelings. He sees that the mystics or *Kabbalists* at that time reflect two unusual characteristics which are interrelated: ". . . the striking restraint observed by the Kabbalists in referring to the supreme experience; and secondly, their metaphysically positive attitude toward language as God's own instrument."[7] The vitality of the prophetic tradition lies in the fact that the reader participates in it in his or her own time, and Jews further emphasize the wisdom by learning to read their tradition in the original language. Later Jesus, as a Jew, was incarnated as the Messiah from the Christian perspective. When the Incarnation becomes timeless for Christians, they also participate in history.

Creation-centered theology demands a reintegration of Hebrew wisdom into the Christian paradigm by understanding the wisdom tradition from the Jewish perspective. This gets Christians beyond thinking that the Jews are the people who missed the Messiah. I also believe that it is as crucial for Jews to experience a radical examination of Yahweh as it is for Christians to truly understand the Messiah they think the Jews did not notice. This needs to happen if we are to move into a new age of spirituality that is freed from old archetypal patterns. Hebrew-wisdom teaching is rich in its awareness of spherical time. Christianity may hold the key to understanding how divine energies can exist in the human realm. If the negative shadows can be completely cleared by those who cling to them, then the full power of the new wisdom will be available to us all. Meister Eckhart said six hundred years ago that we have to let go of God to have God, and that letting go may be the coming wisdom of our age. We must not underestimate the power of the new images as they come in. Two thousand years ago, Ignatius of Antioch wrote about the Incarnation: "The age-old empire of evil was overthrown, for God was now appearing in human form to bring in a new order, even life without end. Now, that which had been perfected in the Divine Counsels began its work; and creation was thrown into a ferment over this plan for the utter destruction of death."[8] Christians are just as far from beginning to grasp what happened at the Incarnation as Jews probably are from being able to let go of God, of Yahweh. In the short run, feminists may be our saviors. Both the Hebrew and Christian definition of the deity is patriarchal, and as the patriarchal Christian definition of God is altered by also making God a mother and a child, so can God become peaceful.

As we look to reincarnation-based healing techniques for the quest which radically reconnects us with our history, the critical need for Judeo-Christian reappraisal at this time becomes more apparent. In the period from around 100 BCE to the birth of Christ, I sense that intense spiritual issues surfaced on this planet which are still being resolved today. This was also a time of intense spirituality within the Hebrew esoteric orders such as Kabbalism and Merkabah mysticism (chariot mysticism),[9] and that richness has flowered periodically in, for example, the Hasidic tradition. Christians need to see how much we need the Hebrew esoteric wisdom, because so much of our esoteric tradition was lost due to the Church's destruction of original source material. Even the works of such bridgers between Christianity and Judaism as Marcion were destroyed. Marcion was a Jewish theologian who believed Christ was the Messiah. Due to the need to define Christianity in the midst of a pagan Roman Empire alive with the movements of Mithra, Isis, and the Gnostics, much of the richness of the early Christian fabric was destroyed, and now functions as a shadow. Ramsey McMullen notes Christianity's extraordinary conversion success against all competing sects, and notes a similiar willingness to do battle against evil in early Judaism.[10] He studies early conversion stories and questions whether the early Christians even knew the *Credo*, just as I question the theological enlightenment of the band of wanderers who conquered Canaan sometime in the second millenium BCE. McMullen notes that what did hold the early Christians together was a readiness for battle against outside evil. The analogy to early Judaism is obvious. The same tendency showed up in early Islam. The time has come to question whether the central energy of our devotion can persist in the fight against the other/the shadow. Now that shadow is the bomb — and we all know it. We will see if the survival instinct is adequate.

The writings of esoteric Judaism around the time of the Incarnation provide the richest background source for a Christian theology of reincarnation. Since the Christian esoteric or magical tradition was almost obliterated by the defensive early Church, Jewish mysticism affords us our richest source of the secret teachings of Jesus. These

esoteric traditions have resurfaced periodically in Christian movements, especially during the Middle Ages, and in Jewish movements,
such as the Kabbalistic tradition; but the sources going back to the time
of Jesus are the most valuable to Christians, and many of the sources
are Hebrew. The Kabbala is the hidden wisdom behind the Hebrew
Bible, and reincarnation is a basic tenet of Kabbalism. The time from
100 BCE to the birth of Christ was a rich period of Hebrew mysticism,
with such great Kabbalists as Jehoshuah ben Pandira, Hillel, and Philo
Judaeus. There is every reason to look to these teachings in an effort
to know Jesus better, and from that perspective it is very hard not to see
that Jesus might well have believed in reincarnation himself. How else
can we understand what Jesus said about John the Baptist in Matthew
11:7-15? The Master says of John, ". . . he is Elijah who is to come. He
who has ears to hear let him hear."

The Talmud is replete with attempts to identify living persons with
someone important from the past. It is filled with folktales about
present-day obligations and responsibilities in peoples' present lives
coming from past-life karmic duties. The great Jewish historian, Flavius
Josephus, who is the only historian contemporaneous with Jesus who
mentions him, frequently notes that the Pharisees believed they would
return again.[11] The Zohar, attributed to Rabbi Simeon ben Jochai in the
first century, ends with "the Books of the Revolutions of the Souls."[12]
Put simply, reincarnation is a fact of first-century Judaism, and since
Christianity built upon a Hebrew foundation, Christians are free to
investigate Hebrew mysticism. When the church fathers created the
scriptural canon, they should have realized that Christians would be
forced to look elsewhere for the missing material. Any religion will dry
up eventually without an esoteric tradition for those who need that
level of intensity, and many Christians today are avidly studying the
Dead Sea Scrolls, the Essene Gospels, and the other major finds of the
last hundred years.

Many Christians today think that reincarnation is officially regarded
as heresy by the Catholic Church, and so the records of the early
Church must be carefully examined. Richard Henry Drummond notes
that reincarnation theology is an ". . . intelligible option for Christians
who are willing to explore the cosmic significance of the Christ event
in all of its past, present, and future aspects."[13] Drummond's sense of
Christ echoes the spiritual-period sense of the prophetic tradition. He

observes that the belief was definitely present in early Christian times and is especially clear in the letters of Jerome.[14] The primary link between the Hebrew Bible (referred to by Christians as "the Old Testament") and the Bible is reincarnational. Malachi closes the Hebrew Bible with, "Behold, I will send you Elijah the prophet before the great and terrible day of the Lord comes" (Malachi 4:5). Mark and Luke quote suggestions by contemporaries of Jesus that he might be a reincarnation of John the Baptist, Elijah, or one of the other prophets. It is very interesting that this same sense of great prophets exists in the New Age healing movement. Some refer to our present times as the "cosmic party," a regathering of great mystics and prophets during a time of crisis. It is difficult not to conclude that there was a basic understanding during the times of Jesus that reincarnation was a function of the soul through time on Earth, and we need to open ourselves to the possibility that this was also Jesus' awareness. It is in the fourth through the fifth centuries CE and in the era of the Inquisition that we must search for the modern belief that reincarnation is heretical.

By the sixth century, there is strong evidence of anti-reincarnationist sentiment in the Church on the part of the orthodox members, and this feeling can easily be attributed to the rise in priestly control. Imagine if the confessional had to be an exploration of each person's past-life karma in relation to present deeds, instead of a short confession of a puny sin and then a quick paying-up! During the sixth century CE, the contents of the Bible were defined and various other early Christian sources were examined. Actually, it is surprising that any references to reincarnation survived at all. However, as mentioned before, the Christian Bible contains references to past lives, and the early church fathers also frequently mentioned reincarnation. Justin Martyr (100-165 CE) spoke of the soul inhabiting more than one body; Origen (185-254 CE) taught reincarnation and was later accused of Gnostic tendencies; Augustine of Hippo (354-430 CE) held reincarnationist views but they were thoroughly intermingled with notions of predestination, which played a role in the later Christian confusion about reincarnation and astrology. In fact, predestination is a separate philosophical question, and that fatalistic point of view can apply to one life or many. Augustine's negativity had a powerful effect on the development of early Christianity, and he seems to be the early church father who most significantly attached predestination to reincarnation.[15] The Gnostics were labeled as heretics by the orthodox, but many serious Christians are examining their teachings today as a source of the secret teachings of Jesus. In my own work, I am in the midst of an attempt to discern what the Gnostics were addressing in their texts, but I would agree that these texts are a valuable source for the understanding of early Christianity.[16] At any rate, the early Church turned against reincarnation and Gnostic theologians during the early struggles for survival and definition. I believe that this was a valid decision at the time, but that the Church should not now resist an examination of these points of view which were eliminated. The Church has nothing to fear now but its own monumental defensiveness.

At Constantinople in 543 CE, the teachings of Origen were condemned, and those teachings included reincarnational theology. This council was followed by a second in 553 CE at Constantinople, where the anathemas against Origen were submitted by the Emperor Justinian rather than by a theologian or church father! This council reflects the imperialization of Christianity, and I question whether modern Christians might not have the option to reconsider the validity of many of the doctrinal decisions made during those times. The pre-existence of the soul was one of these anathemas, which are prohibited from consideration by Christians under pain of excommunication. But even the *Catholic Encyclopedia*, 1913 Edition,[17] remarks that no one from Rome was present at the Fifth Ecumenical Council, which was an extra-conciliary or unofficial session called by Justinian. There is a serious question about the prohibitions declared at that time, yet as far as I can determine they were the source for later campaigns against heresy which resulted in the Inquisition. The Pope at the time, Pope Vigilius, was in Constantinople during the period of the Council and refused to attend![18] This gave rise to the Eutychian Heresies, since the president of the council was Eutyches, Patriarch of Constantinople. Earlier, Pope Leo I said of Eutyches that he was betrayed by "want of learning rather than by subtlety of thought,"[19] and Pope Leo in fact had excommunicated Eutyches before this Fifth Ecumenical Council. A council met in 449 CE at Ephesus which Leo called the *Latrocinium*, "a gathering of robbers," and basically the Eastern Church prevailed during those times.[20] Theologians have a lot of work to do on these early councils now that questions concerning some of the anathemas are being raised again by serious Christians, and an Inquisition is no longer an option.

The result of the murky theological definitions was that reincarnation was dropped from consideration by orthodox Christianity.

Later, Church councils stated that souls go immediately to heaven, purgatory, or hell. These pronouncements conflict with reincarnational teachings about the place of the soul after death only insofar as that reincarnationists would deny such static states. Again, a solution emerges when we allow Christianity an esoteric tradition. Reincarnation, on the level we are considering in this article, is a doctrine of karmic responsibility and sin at the most complex philosophical level. There is no conflict about the status one may deserve after living a life of moral choices; the only question is whether each soul has many lifetimes, and thus experiences the means to attain the growth necessary to its essence. One can view tragic and limited lifetimes as a form of hell, lifetimes of struggle and progress as purgatory, and lifetimes lived in essence as heaven. The same states can be thought of in relation to the experiences after death. The real question is whether any religious establishment has the ability to judge our status, and the Church has consistently maintained that it cannot. I am not a theologian and have no interest in becoming one, but I think the most fruitful place for finding an esoteric reincarnational teaching in the Church exists in the doctrines of bodily resurrection at the end times. Why would we be taught that our physical bodies will resurrect at the Second Coming? The wisdom of the Church contains many rich teachings, and in the doctrine of bodily resurrection at the end times, I hear the echo of biblical passages of our existence from the beginning to the end of time. I know of no other way to share in that except by understanding reincarnation from the perspective of personal experience.

In the twelfth century, the Roman Church was faced with the most powerful explosion of reincarnational thought yet in the teachings of the Albigensians and the Cathars, which resulted in the Inquisitions. Those movements were, in my opinion, a radical resurgence of early mystical Christianity. Nevertheless, history had its way, and the Inquisitions murdered so many people that the "heresies" were stamped out. There is only one explanation for the violence of the Inquisitions: individuals who suppress their own inner knowing of evil will eventually turn on what they identify as evil outside themselves and attempt to destroy it.

The Cathars and Albigensians attempted to learn about the inner violence with which each one of us must eventually deal. They wanted to take personal control of their growth and salvation, and they could not be controlled by the orthodox. The relevant question for those of us in the Judeo-Christian tradition (and I consider myself a Christian) is, what will be the next phase of religion? Reincarnation theology has always centered upon radical individual growth and responsibility, and religious structures are only helpful if they assist the growth within the family and community. Matthew speaks of the New Age in terms of birth pangs (Matthew 24:7-8) and implies a world where individuals will take control of their own karma and growth. Religious orthodoxies which seek to control individuals who are birthing themselves will cease to exist. If our Judeo-Christian structures will allow themselves to evolve into structures which assist the growth of responsible people, then they will become the new Asclepium, the healing temples.

There are three individuals on this planet with whom I have been privileged to work during the last four years, who utilize past-life therapy as a healing tool to release the soul within the body, to find the essence of eros. There are many great healers working on the planet now; I just have happened to work with these three. Looking back over this article, I see a chronology of religious orthodoxies which have defined themselves from fear. But the great religious teachers, including Christ, have defined themselves out of trust and have burned with love and compassion. At this time, my own hope lies in the breakdown of religious structural formations until they learn how to be the channels for the great teachers. Ron Miller suggests that we have greater need of new consciousness than of new churches. Dave Lothrop discusses the ability to *decide* to love as a way to spiritual growth. I agree with him, but how? Within the New Age healing movement, we have found the key again. I am convinced the ancients also knew the answer periodically. Gerald Ringer is correct in arguing that we have to let the snake back into the garden; we have to reawaken the energy in the body, the eros, from its long sleep.

The only force powerful enough to awaken the life-force in the body, to create the tree of life in consciousness, is a complete letting go of fear. At this time, the soul force lies deeply buried in the right-brain memory bank, repressed by centuries of violence, milleniums of fear. It was only by breaking through the pain and ecstasy of those milleniums of repression that I myself could release my soul force in these times. It is impossible to say whether this present extreme need to break through historical repression is always needed, or is just a factor at this point.[21] Study of past initiatory cultures would indicate that this level of breakthrough is a part of true soul evolution. I do not really care; what really matters is that we need to feel free to do this now. We need this level of intense revisioning to free ourselves from what the Gnostics called the Archons, what the Christians called the Daimones; we need to pass through all those gates, those fears. We need to have the courage to read again the teachings of the fire God, Yahweh, and ask whether we want to define the formation of human structures according to his rules. We cannot estimate how much this coming from fear has paralyzed our culture.

At the last millenium, people were frozen by apocalyptical fear. In 980 CE farmers stopped planting the fields in Europe and developing their herds because the end was coming. When the end did not come, there was a generation of famine and disease, resulting in the beginnings of the "heretical" movements.[22] We must improve our sight at this time; we must begin the healing right now and break the paralysis. We will do so, because we also have the power of the movement of the New Age as a result of the equinoctial precession into Aquarius. Just like the last millenium, the older generation has lost hope. They have created massive arsenals of destruction, and now they live out their retirement as sun worshippers. They lie like lizards in the sun, like dinosaurs frozen in their time. If my description of the work of these new healers seems radical or bizarre, remember that they were all born after the bomb was released on this planet. Their consciousness is Promethean.

Gregory Paxson of Chicago, Chris Griscom of Galisteo, New Mexico, and Tom Cratslie of Boston all use reincarnational theology as a tool to cast out the demons and heal the sick. Years ago, before any of us ever knew anything about the coming new age, they let go of normal ways of making a living and searched for a way to develop the skills they sensed we would need at this time. Any one of them could have gone to medical school, but they sensed that our understanding of healing would have to change. It is radical to assert that modern healers are Christ-like, but they are doing as Christ told us to do. Jesus returns to his disciples after his Resurrection to give them instructions for all future Christians: "And, these signs will accompany those who believe:

in my name they will cast out demons; they will speak in new tongues; they will pick up serpents, and if they drink any deadly things, it will not hurt them; they will lay their hands on the sick, and they will recover" (Mark 16:17-18). Then the Master says, after being asked by his disciples who can be saved, "With men it is impossible, but not with God; for all things are possible with God" (Mark 10:26). It is time to ask how we would have responded if we had been present to hear Jesus, and for us instantly to perceive that if we comprehend the prophetic sense of our times — then we need to hear Christ.

It is time to stop waiting for somebody else to do it. How many artificial hearts will they make before we learn that we need to heal our own hearts? How many bombs will they make before we learn that we have to trust God instead of men? Paxson, Griscom, and Cratslie stopped waiting for everybody else to do the work, and learned to do it themselves by making themselves willing servants of the divine forces; by learning to channel healing powers.

Gregory Paxson's goal in therapy is to help the client attune with the Greater or Higher Self by accessing past-life memory under hypnosis. By going deep inside and living other lives experientially from birth to death, the essential organizing self, the soul, is accessed and the true purpose of a lifetime is ascertained. Greg always begins with a prayer to bring in higher guidance and energy — to let God come through; then he is ready to guide the regression. He was presented with a real test of the need for prayer when he was asked to regress four people on live television on the "Oprah Winfrey Show" in January 1986. He could not do it unless the audience prayed with him. It is not Greg's own power, and he knows it. I chose to work with Greg because he believes we cannot connect with the soul unless we find the soul in the body.[23] This teaching has powerful resonance with the Incarnation, a divine act in history which we are now ready to know ourselves. God is not in the sky, he/she is in ourselves. However, the body is filled with blocks coming from negative experiences, and the God force cannot resonate in us without clearing. Christ clearly wanted us to break our chains so that we could love others as we love ourselves.

People have found Christ's commandment about true love impossible to observe, and nowhere is it more obvious than within our own families. The early work in regression tends to gravitate around negative emotional responses coming from past lives. There we find out why we cannot get along with a brother, a child, a parent, or a spouse. Often we choose to learn to love by marrying a person who was once a parent who abused us, by giving birth to a person who once tortured us, or by having children who were once our parents. It sounds like a waste of time to explore past lives with the people closest to us, but the result is a new freedom to strongly love and enjoy others, and a profound birth of compassion. In the early stages of regression, usually a death experience is recalled, and most people find that their puny obsession with their own mortality is outgrown. Courage comes into the heart instead of fear, and reconnection with others results. Once the primary blocks are clear — inability to love those we have chosen to live with, fear of death and historical chaos, understanding about why we came this time — then a space is cleared inside to allow true spiritual power to flow in.

After breaking the primary chains, the next issue confronted is their purpose or gift, and whether they can deliver it to the culture they live in. Greg comments,

> Any one Being, through its various incarnations, lives far longer than any culture. Cultures, as expressions of collective consciousness focused on specific areas of human evolution, vary in the kinds of learning and capabilities they favor. Thus the conditions of any one culture may or may not be simpatico for one's essence, or for the expression of that essence one has chosen for this lifetime. The state of our own culture has a lot to do with the present importance of past-life regression; because regression offers a means of discovering essence and defining of genuine self notwithstanding the cacaphony of the moment, and because it allows for a step outside the moment into a personal experience of the larger order of creation.[24]

As experiences of past lives as healers, initiates, simple village people, or parents begin to reflood our consciousness, new powers come into this lifetime, and new abilities to deliver our gift to the culture manifest. Suddenly we are living from our own center instead of being pushed around by fears triggered by the culture around us.

Tom Cratslie did graduate work at the Harvard Divinity School, and left when he realized that their theological training could not empower him for his work. These days, Tom is an itinerant healer and a powerful breaker of chains. His *a priori* premise, the beginning to build upon, is that each soul begins a series of incarnations with a cosmic purpose encoded in its essence, and that purpose will drive the person from within until they find a way to fulfill it. The soul could attain perfection if it could deliver its cosmic purpose during any lifetime, but it rarely occurs. The soul has created an emotional block, usually a long time ago, which blocks the cosmic purpose. Tom identifies the block with the person, breaks the chains, and the soul is free to become its essence.

The session with Tom begins with a probing conversation about the main frustration in our lives that seems to get continually in the way of what we'd like to do the most. His assumption is that the basic problem manifests in each lifetime and the present place of blocking contains the original block. In conversation, the essence of the blocking energy is discussed until its energy is recreated. Then an access point exists to get at the original problem. Tom then changes his position from sitting on the chair in front of the client to sitting at their right side. He asks the client to "space out a bit" and re-experience any kind of present-day emotional struggle which precipitates the frustration, and he asks for the client to move deeply into the body where the feelings lie. The assumption here is that the body is the repository of the soul essence; most healers in new fields are working with this premise, and the implications for the Catholic doctrine of bodily resurrection at the end times are certainly interesting. The situation seems to be that each time the soul incarnates in a body, it recreates a body imprint of its essence within that person.

Next Tom asks the client to return to the situation of the original conflict. Most do it easily, which demonstrates the power of past-life memory in the body. Of course, it can never be proved that these memories are past lives; all that matters is that memories exist in the body which have powerful emotional conflicts attached to them which can be released. The client explores the primary blocking experience from beginning to end while Tom listens for the points where the soul gave up on bringing in its true purpose. Once the primary conflict has been fully recalled, Tom enters into a sharing experience with the soul in which he helps release the primary block and guide the soul to choose again — to be free. As he is working the person through a new series of choices, he moves his left hand up and down the upper spine, six inches off the body. As the client lets go of old choices and assumptions, Tom seems to be pulling out electromagnetic energy where the block is located, from the medulla oblongata (the repository of primary protective brain material where the brain stem joins the cerebrum) down the spine. My neck actually cracked in the session and I felt electricity in the spine. Like a hanging, the blocking goes into the neck; now I can move my head farther from side to side. The purpose which I have been blocking for thousands of years is now coming through, and I am watching it unfold.

An encounter with Chris Griscom of Galisteo, the therapist described by Shirley MacLaine in *Dancing in the Light*, is like meeting Jeremiah the prophet. Chris trained with native healers and medicine women in South American villages in the early seventies, and began healing the physical body to bring in the soul with acupuncture needles in the mid-seventies. Shirley MacLaine said that an ancient Chinese doctor is always present guiding Chris when she works.[25] I asked her once if she was guided, and she laughed. Chris found she could activate higher awareness centers in the body by using needles to channel energies into the points which activate those awarenesses. It is very powerful, because any change in the spiritual body is always more efficacious than one in the emotions or mind. The medieval mystics who had very powerful visions reported many physical symptoms. Chris is adept at aiding the body into adjustment with the reawakening of the spiritual forces. She has found a technique for reactivating the temple of the soul. She is a radical teacher who knows that we will find the way out of our impasse if we simply move our awareness continually to the highest and deepest possible levels. We will do it, because spiritual energy is the strongest and most alluring power, and it will prevail.

Chris, her own guides, and the guides of the client move through blocks in the body as quickly as possible. There is an urgency in her work, a sense that we must move as fast as possible to reactivate enough souls to love the planet. She has founded an institute in Galisteo where therapists she has trained are working. Often the other therapists move clients through past-life sessions, and Chris does the next level of sessions, which I will describe in a moment. Chris has some interesting comments on the relationships closest to us — our family — and reasons why we must explore them in depth. "When you realize that you chose them [your parents] in order to work through certain emotional problems yourself, you don't blame them anymore. When you learn not to blame your parents, you learn also not to blame anyone else. Family life is the most intense of environments. Each member of the family is keenly intuitive about the behavior of the other. We feel victimized by the family, because they start with us when we're infants. Sometimes we get stuck in the emotional pattern of victimization."[26] When one moves beyond blame and into acceptance, then one can change the dynamic, and free will emerges. We are ready then to love and live compassionate lives.

The spiritual force moves through Chris powerfully, and the only question one faces when encountering her is whether you want to close the window or not. I chose not to. We began a process of breaking through every barrier in my essence that still blocked me from being able to take in energy. I had few past-life sessions because I had done so much work before I came, so we moved into the next level of sessions. We moved into kundalini enlightenment work, which I found to be very similar to ancient initiation techniques which I had studied in extremely spiritual cultures such as Egypt before 1400 BCE. By placing needles in the key energy meridians, Chris calls the Higher Self to assist in bringing in the spiritual or God force, and she guides it through the kundalini system — the chakras and spinal connection. The spiritual force races through the body until each cell is charged with electromagnetic energy, and one is never the same again after this experience. To me it was like being an apostle and hearing the call from Christ: all confusion dissipated, the spiritual fire brought the body into line with the spirit, and I was free in a new way. Christ talked about leaving our families to do the work, and I found out what he meant. He meant that we cannot limit our work for others because of our personal situations. As a wife and mother, I found a new way to do everything I needed to do because of the new level of integration. Right after the sessions I found I was called from many places to do things which I might have found impossible to manage. Whenever it seemed like a child's needs or my husband's need for companionship were keeping me from the work, I simply expanded myself. Then I found myself entering into that time with a child, my husband, or a friend, in an entirely new way. I found new insights there that fed the work. All became a time continuum.

Finally, Chris does channeling work with the clients. This is a technique to help bring in the greatest essence possible. It is a method for knowing exactly what is called for in our own time—a creation of an oracle, in a sense. I am in the middle of that process and cannot say much about it now, but the work reminds me of Matthew Fox's teachings on the royal personhood. It is work to bring forth all inner gifts to find a way to give them all back to the cosmos from which we came.

These three healers are teaching the wisdom of Christ; they are healing people, breaking the chains, chasing out the demons so that their clients are free to give completely of themselves. We have created a potential global disaster caused by the accumulation of sick energy from people who refuse to say yes to life. The need for the types of therapies described is unusually high right now because children are born into sick families and a sick culture. We really seem to need to go back through the past and relearn a new way. Fortunately we have found a way and the number of individuals doing this work is great. The resulting health, givingness, and love of life is contagious, and in that sense we have nothing to worry about. The New Age is about each one of us being as Christ asked us to be—to love and heal our neighbor.

Endnotes

1. Werner Keller, *The Bible as History* (New York: William Morrow and Co., 1981), p. 64. In an interfaith context, note that it is preferable to use the terms "BCE" (Before the Common Era) and "CE" (the Common Era), instead of the Christian designations "BC" (Before Christ) and "AD" (Anno Domini, the Year of the Lord). The Christian usages reflect a confessional bias— i.e., that Jesus is the Lord—not shared by other faith communities.

2. Ibid., p. 64.

3. Giovanni Pettinato, *The Archives of Ebla: An Empire Inscribed in Clay* (New York: Doubleday, 1981).

4. R.F. Hodinnot, *The Thracians* (London: Thames and Hudson, 1981).

5. Alfred de Grazia, *God's Fire, Moses and the Management of the Exodus* (Princeton: Metron Publications, 1983). My point of view is influenced by de Grazia in general.

6. Exodus 33:29.

7. Gershom G. Scholem, *Major Trends in Jewish Mysticism* (New York: Schocken Books, 1961), p. 15.

8. Betty Radice, ed., and Maxwell Staniforth, trans., *Early Christian Writings* (England: Penguin Classics, 1968), p. 81.

9. Gershom G. Scholem, *Kabalah* (New York: New American Library, 1974).

10. Ramsey MacMullen, *Christianizing the Roman Empire: A. D. 100-400* (New Haven: Yale University Press, 1984), p. 110.

11. Flavius Josephus, *The Works of Josephus*, trans. William Whiston (Philadelphia: David KcKay, no pub. date), see "Wars of Jews."

12. Joseph Head and S. L. Cranston, *Reincarnation: The Phoenix Fire Mystery* (New York: Crown Books, 1977), p. 131.

13. Richard Henry Drummond, *Toward a New Age in Christian Theology* (New York: Orbis, Maryknoll), p. 35.

14. Ibid., p. 157.

15. Joseph Head and S. L. Cranston, "The Church Fathers," *Reincarnation*, pp. 148-50.

16. Barbara Clow, sequel to *Eye of the Centaur*, note 26, work in progress. I am in the middle of questioning whether Gnostic texts must be understood more literally than allegorically, essentially a literal interpretation being potentially heretical for Christians except that the ending of the actual living existence of archons, daimones, demons, etc., may be the meaning of the "new order" delineated by Christ. Early Christian sources on this issue are Marcion, Origen, and others and the results of this research will be published in the sequel in 1989.

17. Joseph Head and S. L. Cranston, *Reincarnation*, p.157.

18. Ibid, p. 157.

19. James Williams Wand, *The Four Great Heresies* (AMS reprint, London. Mowbray, 1955), p.11.

20. Ibid., pp. 112-13. I would like to comment that the more one investigates the Constantinople councils in the sixth century, the more disturbing the heavy doctrinal influence of these councils on early Christian thinking becomes. My feelings are that Christians are free to question seriously any anathemas coming from those councils, and that subsequent doctrinal decisions must be viewed as more enlightening. There has never been any encyclical on reincarnation.

21. Geddes MacGregor, *Reincarnation in Christianity* (Wheaton: Quest, 1978), pp. 36 and 54. The real value of historical analysis lies in the permission it offers one to view values and doctrines within their contextual-historical times. MacGregor says on p. 36, "In the first century, the *parousia* or Second Coming of Christ was expected imminently, and with it the rolling up of the present world 'like a scroll.' Then would come a new and better order under Christ's kingship. In

such a climate of expectancy Christians could have little interest in
speculations about the pre-existence of the soul, and still less in reincarnationism." And later on on page 54, he says , "Reincarnationism
did not seem to him [Origen] to fit the Christian philosophy of
history." The only way I have been able to understand the Parousia in
my own times is to escape being caught in linear time, in only one
lifetime.

22.   Delno C. West, and Sandra Zimdars-Swartz, *Joachim of Fiore: A Study
in Spiritual Perception and History* (Bloomington: Indiana University
Press, 1983), p. xi. The authors comment, " The importance of
Joachim of Fiore is that he considered inquiry into history as another
path to knowing God." This is exactly the passionate immersion into
history which is triggered by the full understanding of our eternal
return till the end of time.

23.   Geddes MacGregor, *Reincarnation in Christianity*, p. 53. The whole
question of how the soul exists in the body is possibly the most subtle
and empowering question for all beings. The exploration of this issue
is central to the growing doctrinal formulations coming from creation-
centered spirituality. Theologian Jean Danielou had some fascinating
reflections on this question in his book on Origen, (*Origene*, Paris: La
Table Ronde, 1948) as far as my presentation of reincarnation as a
method for spiritual quest. Danielou comments that human freedom
is central to Origen's system, and that Origen is weak on human
freedom when it come to his doctrines on successive incarnations.
This weakness, according to Danielou, exists in Origen's thinking
because souls are not conscious in the present incarnation of
preceeding incarnations. Thus, they are not free. The three healers
presented in this article would all agree, and they would point out that
they teach that true freedom results from recovering the memory of
those previous incarnations.

24.   Barbara Clow, *Eye of the Centaur: A Visionary Guide into Past Lives*
(Minneapolis: Llewellyn Publications, 1986). See introduction by
Gregory Paxson.

25.   Shirley MacLaine, *Dancing in the Light* (New York: Bantam Books,
1985), p. 325.

26.   Ibid., p. 320. Here MacLaine is quoting Chris Griscom.

Particle, Wave, and Paradox

by Jim Kenney

This essay is predicated upon the belief in a radically new understanding of an ancient idea. That idea is simply this: that all existence is interdependent, that nothing is a thing-in-itself, and that no human being is an island. This new approach to understanding is made possible by the tremendous advances achieved in twentieth-century theoretical physics, and by the discovery of a powerful convergence between the worldview of new physics and the worldview so long championed by the great religious traditions. The present discussion will attempt to consider that convergence with a particular view to the relationship between the new physical model of the universe and the paradigm set forth in the philosophical systems of Mahayana Buddhism. We will focus primarily on parallels between the two approaches to understanding the nature of existing things, persons, and events.

It has often been suggested of late that the new physics has brought at least one important domain of Western thought onto a course seemingly parallel to that of traditional Eastern philosophy. As a matter of fact, a number of the quantum age pioneers observed years ago the growing similarity of their own descriptions of the world to ancient Eastern accounts of the nature of the universe. Werner Heisenberg, one of the giants of modern physical thought, called attention to a fascinating epistemological aspect of the parallel:

This modern science, then, penetrates in our time into other parts of the world where cultural tradition has been entirely different from the European civilization. . . .For instance, the great scientific contribution in theoretical physics that has come from Japan since the last war may be an indication for a certain relationship between philosophical ideas in the tradition of the Far East and the philosophical substance of quantum theory.[1]

Niels Bohr, the avowed father of modern quantum physics, sounded a similar note when he observed:

For a parallel to the lessons of atomic theory. . .[we must turn] to those kinds of epistemological problems with which thinkers like the Buddha and Lao-tzu have been confronted, when trying to harmonize our position as spectators and actors in the great drama of existence.[2]

Epistemology, that branch of philosophy which concerns itself with knowledge and how it is acquired, bears sharply on the convergence between science and religion. Perhaps the clearest demonstration of this can be derived from our perception of the "things" which make up the world of experience.

Despite their initial conviction that the subatomic world would be found to consist of an interplay of real and definable things, the first quantum physicists soon realized that this was not the case.

The particles of the subatomic world are not only active in the sense of moving around very fast; they themselves are processes! . . .Physicists view the objects in this world—the particles—not statically, but dynamically, in terms of energy, activity, and process.[3]

Notwithstanding the attempts of a generation of scientists to clarify the subatomic picture, the persistent misunderstanding of the term "particle" and the intransigence of the notion that all things exist in, of, and by themselves, have obscured the modern theoretical account of particle phenomena from the general view. A model-change of the sort that is required, if popular thought is ever to assimilate the new physical view of phenomena, cannot be accomplished without a thorough reexamination of our basic conceptual stance. Modern physics has revealed that the subatomic world is not so much an arena of interacting entities as it is a web of interconnected processes.

It is clear that one of the most exacting demands modern science has placed on understanding is for a new account of the nature of a "thing." The transition required will not, however, be easily made, for there is no more basic or fixed conception in Western thought. We cannot simply discard the notion of "thingness," nor would we wish to. Nevertheless, we can perhaps arrive at a new vantage point from which to view the order of existence and the character of existing things. Here, Buddhism offers a raft which may aid our crossing.

In Buddhist philosophy, things are regarded as impermanent and constantly in flux. As a consequence of this incessant dance of existence (*anityata*), nothing is possessed of self-character or self-nature. That is to say, no existent entity has an unchanging essence. Rather, existence is shaped by interaction. The root of the Buddhist ontological perspective lies in this doctrine of "no-self" (*anatman*).

However, the Mahayana doctrine of *pratitya-samutpada* (interdependence) is the chief source of Buddhist illumination on the twin problems of selfhood and thingness. All entities exist in relation to other entities. Relationship necessarily involves change, and change in its turn implies process. Existence is flux, and all things have the character of verbs rather than of nouns. As D.T. Suzuki put it, "Buddhists have conceived an object as an event, and not as a thing or substance."[4]

One hardly need point out that a tremendous gulf separates the Buddhist conception of existence from the Newtonian assumptions which still dominate Western culture. The modern physical picture of subatomic reality, however, clearly echoes the Buddhist emphasis on change and relationship. Consider the following passages, representative of two very different schools of thought within modern physics: Quantum Field Theory and S-Matrix Theory. Note their striking similarity to one another and to the Buddhist notion of the character of existing things.

> Thus, the "object" is an abstraction of a relatively invariant form. That is to say, it is more like a pattern of movement than like a solid, separate thing that exists autonomously and permanently. . . . For, as has been seen, relativity theory is not compatible with . . . an analysis

of the world into separate components. Rather, it implies that such "objects" have to be understood as merging with each other...to make one indivisible whole.
— David Bohm[5]

The important new concept in the S-Matrix Theory is the shift of emphasis from objects to events; its basic concern is not with particles, but with their reactions. Such a shift is required both by quantum theory and by relativity theory. On the one hand, quantum theory has made it clear that a subatomic particle can only be understood as a manifestation of the interaction between various processes of measurement. It is not an isolated object but rather an occurrence, or event, which interconnects other events in a particular way... Relativity theory, on the other hand, has forced us to conceive of particles in space-time: as four-dimensional patterns, as processes rather than objects.
— Fritjof Capra[6]

As we can see, the cherished classical notions of "objects" and "objectivity" are abandoned by many modern physicists in favor of an approach strongly resembling that of the Mahayana tradition. A number of factors are of particular importance in this connection.

First, it should be noted that the Buddhist and the physicist seem to share a basic epistemological stance. Neither denies the *apparent* reality of things; but each calls attention to the fact that the usual static conceptual picture does not accurately recapitulate experience. In both views the emphasis is on the dynamic character of reality and the inherent limitation of concept formation and use. Second, this emphasis on the dynamic pattern seems — with respect to both the ancient and modern models — to give rise to a strong intuition of the holistic nature of experience. Finally, in both the Mahayana tradition and the development of the new physics, the concept of entity or thing is closely tied to the understanding of time, space, space-time and, as a consequence, process.

Particle, Wave and Paradox

Historically, the electron...was to behave like a particle, and then it was found that in many respects it behaves like a wave. So it

really behaves like neither. Now we have given up. We say: "It is
neither."
        — Richard Feynman[7]

> Such is neither that which is existence nor that which is non-
> existence, nor that which is not at once existence and non-existence;
> it is neither unity nor that which is plurality; neither that which is at
> once unity and plurality, nor that which is not at once unity and
> plurality.
>   — Ashvaghosha[8]

Perhaps the most striking image of the quantum age is that of the
elementary particle as a wave. One uses the word "image" in this connection only after some reflection. The particle-wave model does not
prompt easy imagistic synthesis. It seems simply impossible to visualize a four-dimensional "wavicle" and yet, as many physicists will
attest, access to understanding remains even in the absence of visu-
alibility. Clearly, this raises another difficult epistemological problem.
How can we begin to grasp what reason's eye cannot see? Yet it may
well be that the problem one faces in dealing with the paradoxical pronouncements of a new age lies in the model of the universe which one
brings to bear on the novel data.

One of the greatest of Albert Einstein's contributions to the new
physical paradigm lay in his demonstration that light exhibits the
seemingly contradictory properties of particles and waves. That is, in
certain experimental situations, light appears to be made up of particles — tiny packets, perhaps, of energy. In other situations, however,
light clearly demonstrates a wave character, manifesting itself as a
widespread traveling disturbance, similar to an ocean wave. It is difficult for a modern thinker to imagine the consternation to which Einstein's pronouncement gave rise in 1905, for a particle is clearly one
thing and a wave another, of a very different sort. How indeed, his col-
leagues asked, could light be both?

With the dawn of the quantum age (from the Latin for "quantity"
or "packet" — a reference to the early hope that nature would be found
to be made up of tiny, indivisible particles), the confusion redoubled.
The quandary in which Bohr, Heisenberg, Dirac, Pauli, Schrodinger
and the rest soon found themselves was daunting indeed. Heisenberg
later recalled:

I remember discussions with Bohr which went through many
hours till very late at night and ended almost in despair; and when at
the end of the discussion I went alone for a walk in the neighboring
park I repeated to myself again and again the question: Can nature
possibly be so absurd as it seemed to us in these atomic experiments?[9]

In short, it had turned out that the long sought-after elementary
particles, the so-called "fundamental building blocks of nature," behaved
as light behaved. They could not be understood as the Greek atomists,
Leucippus and Democritus, had predicated, in normative conceptual
terms. Electrons, for example, manifested themselves as waves, or
spread out patterns of disturbance; yet they were known to collide with
other particles, to give off energy in such collisions, and to exhibit,
from time to time, granular rather than continuous behavior. Similarly
the atom itself, once believed to be a strictly material particle, came to
be seen rather as a field of energy which displayed a *particular* (particle-
like) character. Moreover, it became apparent that rather than behav-
ing under invariant laws, elementary "particles" acted with significant
degrees of irregularity. Thus, initial attempts to determine how they
must necessarily exist were gradually reduced to efforts at predicting
how they might behave at a given moment.

The lasting influence on Western thought of the fundamental
structures of Aristotelian logic makes it extremely difficult for the
Westerner to come to terms with any "thing" which is now a wave, now
a particle. Our characteristic approach to understanding is mechanical,
essentialist (i.e., concerned with the essences of things and their definitions), and grounded in the certainty that words can adequately and
non-contradictorily describe anything which *is*.

Yet we are now asked to digest new information about our universe, information so challenging to habitual patterns of interpretation
that our first reaction is perhaps to dismiss the new data as irrelevant
esoterism. If, however, one persists in the endless effort to refine the
models which direct conscious response and channel thought, new
modes of understanding can always be achieved.

In the case of the particle-wave discussion, it is possible to discern
a unique conceptual and linguistic difficulty which draws the episte-
mological-ontological problem into sharp relief. The term "particle"
has been part of the language of physics for many centuries. The Greek

atomists conceived of a world made up of the "smallest units" of matter, hard-shelled and irreducible, each with its characteristic properties and potentials. In light of the traditional concern in Western philosophy, theology, and science for determining the essences of things, it is not surprising that the first glimpses of the subatomic world gave rise to a renewed confidence that the basic "building blocks" of nature would quickly be revealed and defined. The word "particle" came once more into play.

The operation of the thing-in-itself model, and the difficulties it presented to understanding, can easily be glimpsed in various accounts of the formative years of the quantum revolution. Niels Bohr, in a 1922 conversation with Heisenberg and others in Copenhagen, captured the frustrations and hopes of the young science when he wrote:

> It seems likely that the paradoxes of quantum theory, those incomprehensible features reflecting the stability of matter, will become sharper with every new experiment. If that happens, we can only hope that in due course new concepts will emerge which may somehow help us grasp these inexpressible processes in the atom.[10]

Bohr and Heisenberg could not have foreseen, in 1922, just how long the struggle of quantum physics to come to terms with paradoxicality would be. The new physics has, of course, become firmly established at the forefront of the sciences. Yet the "perversity of physics" has increased.

The particle-wave model remains the prototypical riddle of the quantum era. It is ironic indeed that atomism, reductionism, mechanism, and determinism should eventuate in a subatomic model which so sharply undercuts the premises on which these philosophical and scientific attitudes were based.

In the following pages, we will consider some of the most suggestive of the parallels which exist between the particle-wave model and the characteristic themes of Mahayana Buddhist thought. We shall see that a philosophical system which embraces paradox may have much to offer a culture upon which paradox has descended.

Complementarity:
The Unity of Opposites

The theory of complementarity was developed by Niels Bohr in an attempt to address the contradictory behavior of subatomic entities. He described his notion in the following way:

> However contrasting such phenomena may appear at first sight, it must be realized that they are complementary, in the sense that taken together they exhaust all information about the atomic object which can be expressed in common language without ambiguity.[11]

Bohr, when he was knighted by the Danish Crown, designed his own heraldic device (coat of arms). His shield bears one of the classic images of the Chinese philosophical tradition, the *t'ai chi*, or *yin-yang*. This now familiar symbol gives expression to an ancient concept in Eastern thought: that unity underlies all apparent duality and that the subtle interplay of contradictories animates all existence. The banner displayed over the shield bears the Latin legend *Contraria Sunt Complementa*, "Opposites are Complementary." Bohr's use of the *yin-yang* device, giving visual expression to one of the most significant achievements of his scientific career, demonstrates the very real affinity felt by many of the first quantum theoreticians for the worldview of the East.

Buddhist thought consistently emphasizes the limitations inherent in the objective, essentialist view undergirding most of Western thought. The Mahayana tradition's consequent teaching of non-duality offers a powerful aid to resolution of the paradox inherent in modern physical theory. The problem quantum physics confronts is one of knowledge rather than of the real structure of the universe. That is to say, the particle-wave paradox has its origin in the conceptual process and does not really impute a contradictory nature to the phenomena themselves. It is this fact that moved Bohr, and has since prompted a significant number of physical theorists to turn to the East in search of an epistemological model that can account for the role of paradox in the attempt to describe experience.

Mahayana Buddhism does indeed provide such a model, and we

shall see that it reflects the physicists' paradigm in a number of mean-ingful ways. The principle of complementarity — one of the most fun-damental precepts of the quantum endeavor — corresponds strikingly to the teaching of non-duality. Each of these two powerful concepts affords us a metaphorical insight into the other. Together they present a challenge and a unique opportunity to Western understanding.

In the *Vimalakirti Sutra* (one of the spiritual classics of the Mahayana tradition), we encounter the following verse statement of the Buddhist teaching on non-dual reality:

> All these things arise dependently, from causes, yet they are neither existent nor non-existent. Therein is neither ego, nor experi-ence, nor doer. Yet no action, good or evil, loses its effect.[12]

This brief stanza, part of a long hymn of praise to the Buddha, offers a beautiful and succinct expression of the Buddhist doctrine of non duality. The central motif is clearly provided by the dichotomy be-tween existence and non-existence of things. Both are directly denied, but the dialectic proceeds to another level, for the verse also gives assent to both concepts. Things exist, for they arise from causes; yet they do not exist, for there is "neither ego, nor experience, nor doer." There is no actor, yet "no action . . . loses its effects." Thus we find in these four lines a telling reminder of a vital, though often-overlooked, implication of Mahayana teaching. To say that the universe is non-dualistic is not simply to imply that it is monistic, but rather to affirm that all such distinctions belong to conceptualization and not to reality. The Buddhist philosopher does not argue that all things are one, but rather that all things are one *and* many, or that all things are neither one nor many. Thus, multiplicity and unity, existence and non-exis-tence, doer and deed — all such pairs of opposites — must be transcended if real understanding is to take place. Every dichotomy, and conse-quently every conceptual structure, obscures the true nature of existence.

Nevertheless, concept-formation is vital to the ascent to wisdom. Buddhism readily acknowledges that its own doctrines are possessed of only relative truth. Absolute or transcendent truth can never be con-fined by any propositional statement, for it is, in the Buddhist view, non-dualistic and therefore beyond the reach of concepts. Intuition or wisdom (*prajna*) alone can grasp the truth of the way of existence. Yet intuition must necessarily rely upon intellection. The dialectical process (the juxtaposition of opposites and the resultant discovery of their complementarity) is itself a function of the intellect. The discovery of the apparently contradictory nature of phenomena, and the consequent realization of the limits of conceptualization, are the accomplishments of reason. It is not the intention of Buddhism to abandon intellect. The "Middle Way" redeems intuition.

The empirical character of the Buddhist dialectic thus anticipates the radical direction of quantum thought. In both systems, the paradoxes of existence disclose themselves to persistent inquiry, suggesting the limitations of purely conceptual thought. The dialectic—the unity of opposites—is engaged in order to demonstrate this conceptual character and to present an image to the intuitive faculty. The mystic and the physicist stand on the same plateau of relative understanding: that of the juxtaposition of opposite but complementary concepts.

Words, Names, and Concepts

Although we must make use of language and concepts, we can refine our understanding and avoid many of the hazards of wordplay by developing an awareness of the dynamics of dualistic thought and of the epistemological influence of concept formation. The conceptual process is based upon abstraction from perception. "To abstract" means literally "to take away from," and a concept may be regarded as a sort of mental picture taken from the flow of undifferentiated reality. As a consequence, concepts have a static, independent character quite unlike that of conscious experience. Because concepts are relatively fixed, they make possible the development and use of language, which proceeds from the arbitrary assigning of words as names to familiar perceptual patterns. The value of the naming process is obvious; however, its limitations must not be overlooked.

Because reality is dynamic in nature, no array of static conceptual abstractions can adequately represent it. No word can reflect the multidimensionality of the simplest event. Yet we are thinking beings and, as such, we cannot easily abandon the formation of concepts or the use of language, nor would it be to our advantage to do so. It is nevertheless possible and certainly advantageous to make the fullest use of the conceptual process itself, in order to come to an understanding of the nature of that process and the limitations inherent in it. Heisenberg describes another early conversation with his friend and mentor, Niels Bohr, in which this epistemological issue is once again pointedly raised:

> I therefore asked him: "If the inner structure of the atom is as closed to descriptive accounts as you say, if we really lack a language for dealing with it, how can we ever hope to understand atoms?"
>
> Bohr hesitated for a moment and then said, "I think we may yet be able to do so. But in the process we may have to learn what the word 'understanding' really means.[13]

The implication here is obvious. Normative rational modeling of the universe may fall far short of its exhaustive aim. That is to say, events in the physical world may not be describable in a non-contradictory way, in the static-valued words and concepts characterizing purely intellectual discourse. The discernment of complementarity may then emerge as a necessary strategy for the intellectual comprehension of events at every level of experience. Bohr implies that in order to come to terms with the subatomic heart of the phenomenal world we may have to engage in a thorough reevaluation of understanding itself. In this effort, the legacy of Mahayana philosophy may yet figure prominently. Comprehension proceeds not from intellect alone but from the subtle interplay of intellect and intuition.

Uncertainty: Disclosure and Concealment

Another of the cornerstones of modern physical theory is Heisenberg's Uncertainty Principle, which asserts that:

> . . . it is impossible with any of the principles now known to science to determine the position and the velocity of an electron at the same time — to state confidently that an electron is "right here at this spot" and is moving at such and such a speed." For by the very act of observing its position, its velocity is changed.[14]

Obviously, the Uncertainty Principle dramatically underscores the radical departure from the deterministic view ("each and every thing is a thing in itself") which characterized Newtonian physics and the whole course of Western philosophy. Moreover, the principle offers a powerful adjunct to Bohr's Complementarity by providing a precise mathematical formalism and an implicit account of the way pairs of opposites function in the knowing process. Fritjof Capra makes the following observation:

> The fundamental importance of the uncertainty principle is that it expresses the limitations of our classical concepts in a precise mathematical form . . . .The subatomic world appears as a web of relations between the various parts of a unified whole. Our classical notions, derived from our ordinary macroscopic experience, are not fully adequate to describe this world. To begin with, the concept of a distinct physical entity, like a particle, is an idealization which has no fundamental significance. It can only be defined in terms of its connections to the whole, and these connections are of a statistical nature — probabilities rather than certainties. When we describe the properties of such an entity in terms of classical concepts — like position, energy, momentum, etc. — we find that there are pairs of concepts — which are interrelated and cannot be defined simultaneously in a precise way. The more we impose one concept on the physical "object," the more the other concept becomes uncertain, and the precise relation between the two is given by the uncertainty principle.[15]

In other words, as we focus more closely and sharply on one side of a conceptual pair, there is a corresponding loss of resolution in the other image. The more one can say about the "particular" character of a process, the less one knows about its wave form, its aspect as a system of tendencies and possibilities. As physicists have repeatedly pointed out, no refinement of present measuring techniques can eliminate the uncertainty. The observer cannot be separated from the observed system. He or she is part of that system.

> This is the primary significance of the Uncertainty Principle. At the sub-atomic level, we cannot observe something without changing it. There is no such thing as the independent observer who can stand on the sidelines watching nature run its course without influencing it.[16]

Thus the Uncertainty Principle would seem to have some bearing in questions about being, as well as questions about knowing. In other words, we cannot overlook the implicit suggestion that the observer's coming to know is somehow involved in the observed objects coming to be. Quantum theory clearly rejects the Cartesian division of the world into thinking subjects and material objects. Now when physics speaks about the world, it has reference to the world of experience. The observer cannot be separated from her or his observations or from the thing observed.

When, for example, we say that the electron must be regarded as a process connecting various stages of measurement, we mean that, owing to its dynamic character, the electron is effected by the act of observation. Furthermore, one can argue that were it not for the interference by the observing system, the observed particle would not have existed. That is, the experimental situation evokes either the particle character or the wave character of the electron process. What is gleaned from the experimental inquiry is not so much a picture of nature as it is a picture of nature responding to our questions.

Neither the particle model nor the wave model affords us a complete account of the atomic process. Each consists of the application of conceptual analysis to the indivisible fabric of events. The Complementarity Principle maintains the necessity of both points of view for a consistent theory of subatomic events. The Uncertainty Principle postulates the impossibility of precisely observing both aspects at the same time. Thus we are led to realize the ineffability of the fundamental structure of existence. The concepts "particle" and "wave"—like all pairs of opposites—have great value for understanding, but do not refer to independently existing elements of reality. In a larger sense, particle cannot exist apart from wave; yet an event cannot with precision be known and understood simultaneously as particle and wave. The knowing process dichotomizes reality. We sharpen our *analysis* only at the cost of an inevitable uncertainty about *totality*.

In the Chinese "Hua-yen" formulation of Mahayana Buddhism, uncertainty is seen as a necessary consequence of conceptual dichotomy. Reality is single. Thought, however, fragments the totality. Concepts, as their limitations imply, are superimposed on existence, with the result that no conceptual expression has the character of certainty. As the Chinese Buddhist scholar, G.C. Chang, observes:

> Totality is usually hidden from man, because he tends to see one
> thing at a time from one particular frame of reference. . . .Usually
> when we make an assertion of something, we reveal that aspect but
> conceal the others. . . In the vocabulary of Hua-yen this is called the
> obstruction of the concealment and the disclosure. . . .It is a great pity
> that the human mind can only function in a one-at-a-time, from-
> one-level pattern, thus deprived of the opportunity of seeing the in-
> finite versions of a given thing at once.[17]

The Uncertainty Principle gives a mathematical form to a dynamic
inherent in experience. The physicist empirically discovers at the
subatomic level what the mystic learns in a different order of experience. In both cases, encounter with apparent limits to the conceptual
grasp of reality gives rise to an epistemological account of phenomena.
That is, both the mystical and physical descriptions of reality emphasize the *experienced* thing rather than the thing itself. Nothing can be
described without concepts and every concept is dualistic.

The particle-wave paradox recalls the *koan*, the riddle which plays
such an important part in the teaching and practice of the Rinzai Zen
expression of Mahayana philosophy.

> In Zen, a *koan* is a formulation, in baffling language, pointing to
> ultimate truth. *Koans* cannot be solved by recourse to logical reason-
> ing, but only by awakening a deeper level of the mind beyond the in-
> tellect.[18]

The attempt to understand a subatomic event in terms of its par-
icle or wave aspect alone is like listening for the sound of one hand
clapping. Particle and wave — the localized, actualized event and the
spread-out disturbance in the medium of existence — are not competing realities, but rather reflections of two modes for experiencing
the totality of experience.

> Buddhas and living beings do not hinder one another.
> The mountain may be high and deep the water;
> In the midst of contraries, clear understanding wins the day
> (and yet) the partridge calls among a myriad of flowers!

Possibility and Actuality: The Flux of Existence

> In the world as unity of opposites, moving from the formed toward the forming, past and future, negating each other, join in the present; the present as unity of opposites has form and moves, forming itself from present to present. The world moves as one single present, from the formed to the forming. The form of the present, as the unity of opposites, is the style of the productivity of the world. This world is a world of *poesis.*
>
> — Kitaro Nishida[20]

Kitaro Nishida, perhaps the best-known Japanese philosopher of our era, captures in this brief passage the elusive spirit of the quantum approach to understanding. His use of the term "poesis" (from Greek meaning "creation" and figuratively, "poetry") — to convey the movement of the world "from the firmed to the forming" — offers an elegant image of the universal dynamic of possibility and actuality. The process of becoming, which animates the subatomic, the intergalactic, and the human realms alike, is akin to the poetic process. From the complex of tension and resolution, image and word, potency and act, the universe emerges as a poem.

That the metaphor is an apt one becomes clear when one considers the dialectical nature of poetic imagery and the paradoxicality inherent in intellection. Moreover, the poetry of modern physics, like that of Mahayana Buddhism, finds one of its most important motifs in elaboration of the interplay between possibility and actuality. Creation itself is, as Nishida suggests, the incessant movement from present to present, from being to becoming, from the reservoir of constantly changing potential to the panorama of the actual. The notion of existence as the dialectical synthesis of the possible and the actual — as becoming — now plays a major role in physical as well as mystical expression.

Existence and Non-existence

Elementary "particles," as we know, are not particles at all, insofar as they are neither hard-shelled, nor irreducible, nor inert. They behave, as Richard Feynman puts it, "in a funny way."[21] Now displaying the charateristics of granular corpuscular entities, now the properties of wave disturbances, "the beasts of the sub-nuclear zoo" defy straightforward description."[22] Nevertheless, theoretical physics, under the aegis of paradox, has considerably clarified both the wave and particle pictures of elementary interactions.

A great deal is known, for example, about such attributes of individual particles as mass, energy, charge, spin, lifespan, etc. Similarly, physicists are able to tell us quite a bit about the wave character of subatomic phenomena. A wave is a traveling disturbance in a medium. Water waves, sound waves, and radio waves all propagate according to the same characteristic patterns.

Unlike a particle, which has a strictly localized, discrete character, a wave is a spread-out rhythmic pattern of agitation. The water wave is a disturbance in the water medium, the sound wave a perturbation of the air mass. In the case of light waves and the waves associated with the other elementary particles, however, the nature of the medium and of the disturbance pattern remain somewhat mysterious. The famous Michelson-Morley experiment (first performed in 1881) sought unsuccessfully to detect the "ether" through which it was believed light waves must propagate. The resolution of the problem came, of course, in the form of an even more puzzling hypothesis, which stated that the waves detected at the subatomic level are probability waves, shifting patterns which determine the likelihood that a given particle will exist at a certain place-moment. Capra explains the significance of this new approach to the particle-wave mystery as follows:

> The introduction of probability waves, in a sense, resolves the paradox of particles being waves by putting it in a totally different context; but at the same time it leads to another pair of opposite concepts which is even more fundamental, that of existence and non-existence. This pair of opposites, too, is transcended by the atomic reality. We can never say that an atomic particle exists at a certain place, nor can we say that it does not exist. Being a probability pattern, the particle has tendencies to exist in various places and thus manifest a strange kind of physical reality between existence and non-existence. We cannot, therefore, describe the state of the particle in terms of fixed opposite concepts. The particle is not present at

a definite place, nor is it absent. It does not change its position, nor
does it remain at rest. What changes is the probability pattern, and
thus the tendencies of the particle to exist in certain places.[23]

Our understanding of the philosophical, theological, and scientific
problem of existence / non-existence is considerably hampered by the
inflexibility of our language usage and our general lack of attention to
the problem of reality. Western thought, with its characteristic concern
for essence, has traditionally dealt with the matter of existence by
means of a simple, yes-or-no judgment. Something either exists or it
does not; there are no degrees of existence. Here we see a reflection of
the Aristotelian principles of identity and contradiction. A proposition
is either true or false. Truth, like existence, does not admit to degrees.
Herein lies our most serious obstacle to understanding the utterances
of the mystic and declarations of the physicist. Each seems all too frequently to violate the principles most basic to Aristotelian two-value
(i.e., yes-or-no) logic.

The quantum theoretical juxtaposition of wave and particle concepts gives an enigmatic, constantly shifting visage to the subatomic
entity. "In the light of the quantum theory," writes Heisenberg,
"elementary particles are no longer real in the same sense as objects
of daily life, trees or stones."[24]

Neither existence nor non existence can be predicated on protons,
electrons, kaons, sigmas, pions, neutrinos, cascades, or even quarks.
The same paradoxical state of affairs holds for every other elementary
particle, known or unknown. The mystic and poet have long been sensitive to the delicate balance between existence and non-existence in
the unfolding of events. Now the physicist gives voice to the same fundamental insight:

> It is a primitive form of thought that things either exist or do not
> exist; and the concept of a category of things possessing existence
> results from forcing our knowledge into a corresponding frame of
> thought.[25]

To deny absolute existence or non-existence to "things" does not
deny their reality. On the contrary, it simply challenges traditional
categories of explanation. Elementary particles — and by extension, all

things—must be understood as *tendencies to exist* rather than static objects. As James Jeans, the great British physicist and philosopher, once observed, "It is as meaningless to discuss how much room an electron takes up as it is to discuss how much room a fear, an anxiety, or an uncertainty takes up."[26]

Traditionally, Mahayana philosophy has taken the position that the nature of existence is the most important for one who would cultivate what Buddha termed "a right view" of the universe. Since all existing things exist in constant flux and intimate interrelationship with all others, no thing can be possessed of its own essence or "self-existence" (*Sva-bhava*). To say that a thing must either exist or not exist obscures the event-character of that thing, and leaves no room for real understanding of process change or relationship.

Metaphorical Particles

If particles were indeed the sorts of "things" that classical physics, mainstream Western philosophy, and common sense would lead one to expect, science should theoretically be able to give an exact account of their past behavior and to predict precisely their future course. As we have noted, this is not the case. At the subatomic level, events unfold with a regularity tinged with strange randomness. Particles do not always behave as they *usually* behave. Herein lies the wave nature of these curious realities. In order to model particle interactions, physics must have recourse to the probability theory. A large number of interactions can be described with great precision. In the case of the individual event, however, physics can speak only uncertainly. The capriciousness of the behavior of single particles does not limit the accuracy of physical descriptions of large systems. Nevertheless, the fact that one can never precisely determine how a particle will behave in interaction gives quantum mechanics its markedly non-classical countenance.

In order to understand the subtle interplay of regularity and apparent randomness at the sub-atomic level, we may construct the following metaphor: "my anger" as the particle. When it is *actual*, "my anger" can be detected, traced, and observed much like the proton in the laboratory bubble chamber. When it is not actual, that is, when it is not observed by myself or by others, it can nonetheless be described in terms of its tendency to exist in certain possible situations. It is this constantly varying tendency to exist which constitutes the wave nature of "my anger." We can discern, in this simple example, the problem which would be occasioned by the attempt to assign "my anger" unequi-vocally to one of two categories: "exists" or "does not exist." To be sure, the common sense notion that when I am not angry, "my anger" does not exist, has some validity. However, such a formulation obscures the shifting pattern of possibilities giving rise to the actualization of "my anger." No description is complete that does not encompass the poten-tial as well as the actual, hence the necessary juxtaposition of "wave" and "particle" concepts.

The dynamic of potency and act, or wave and particle, provides a powerful but extraordinarily subtle paradigm for the understanding of all interactions, subatomic as well as human. The modern physical model of existence as a dialectical synthesis of "what might be" and "what is" thus provides a radical insight into the Mahayana teaching on the relationship of emptiness and form. We read, in the Buddhist clas-sic, *The Heart Sutra*:

> Form is emptiness and the very emptiness is form; emptiness does not differ from form; form does not differ from emptiness; whatever is form, that is emptiness.[27]

Emptiness (*shunyata*) is, in Mahayana thought, a concept cor-responding closely to that of interdependence (*pratitya-samutpada*). Things are empty (of self-nature) because they exist in relationship. The emptiness of an existing entity is like the emptiness of a mirror. Reflection of the dynamic and constantly changing universe con-stitutes the "essence" of any existent. Things are able to enter into rela-tionship precisely because they are empty of any essential, static self-nature. That which does not change cannot enter into relationship. Entities in relation to one another are not static. The forms of existence are momentary, instantaneous, lacking any duration in time; if any form were to endure, even for a second, it would have to cease its rela-tion to the rest of the universe. The Mahayana insists that this cannot take place. We should note again that the Buddhist tradition does not deny relative truth inherent in the conceptual picture of things which arise, endure for a time, and pass away. Without such a relative account of phenomena, no rational discourse would be possible. Nevertheless, we find upon closer examination a description of existence.

From the viewpoint of an event's actuality, no discussion of its process character — the continual flux of its possibility — can take place. The reverse is true as well. From the point of view of potentiality, no real understanding of momentary actuality can be achieved.

The Present as Unity of Opposites

To put it simply, we may say that the term "particle" properly refers to a subatomic event which takes place, while the term "wave" refers to a changing system of possible future events. When the physicist poses a wave question, he or she inquires into the likelihood that a particular particle might be observed at a certain time-place or with a certain energy, etc.

Let us consider another helpful metaphor. In this instance, let the particle be "my vote" in an upcoming election. On the prescribed day, at a particular space-time location, an observational situation is set up. This is my voting booth. Our interest is in the possibility that "my vote" will be recorded — that it will be observed to "exist" — by the experimental apparatus. We are also interested, we shall suppose, in the nature of "my vote" — say whether it will be "yes" or "no." This electoral metaphor actually corresponds closely to the quantum mechanical reality. The apparatus can detect the existence of the "particle" and note its "charge." Outside the context of the experimental situation, or the voting booth, however, it becomes quite meaningless to speak of the actual existence either of a subatomic particle or "my vote." Neither exists with certainty when it is not observed. Both must be understood in terms of tendencies to exist.

However, prior to experimental observation, the vote, like the electron, can be described in the formal mathematical language of waves. The wave description can offer considerable precision. That is, the shifting tendencies which may result in the observation of the particle or the vote can be modeled with accuracy. As physicist and pollster alike can attest, the science of wave-forms is highly sophisticated. We must, nevertheless, never lose sight of the fact that the object of scientific scrutiny is, in this case, not an object at all, but a steadily changing pattern of possibilities, a shifting tapestry of what might be and what might not be.

Thus, the pattern of probabilities which is associated with any "particular" phenomenon is represented by the wave. The wave-form itself is changing continuously, in a manner defined by the dynamic wave-function. This latter is a theoretical element which reflects the relation of possibility to probability. "A wave-function is a mathematical fiction that represents all the possibilities that can happen to an observed system when it interacts with an observing system."[28] Thus, the wave-model portrays submicroscopic entities as interacting systems of potential and likelihood, real and yet curiously unreal, the dance of the future in the present.

It is important to realize that the change in the pattern of possibility / probability is instantaneous. That is, it is not a succession of states with real duration in time, but a continuously evolving process. The physicist employs calculus (the mathematical method based upon the concept of instantaneous rates of change) to deal with the wave-function and the probability wave. He or she is thus able to "freeze" the process and determine values relating to a specified moment in time. Nevertheless, the flow of potential never ceases. Needless to say, the conceptual and linguistic problem is well nigh insurmountable. We must once again rely on intuition.

This notion of the instantaneous nature of changing wave-forms finds its parallel in the Mahayana doctrine of momentariness (*kshanika*) of objects, states, and events in the world. In early Buddhism, we find the first hints of later Mahayana *kshanavada* (theory of momentariness, instantaneity) in such statements as this: "There is no moment. . . no particle of time that the river stops flowing."[29] The Mahayana view pursued further implications of such dicta along lines set by the time analysis of Nagarjuna, the second-century metaphysician regarded by all schools of Mahayana as the greatest single thinker after the Buddha. His formulation constitutes a negative approach (through the denial of thesis *and* antithesis) to the dialectical synthesis of past and future in the present moment.

In Nagarjuna's view, the past, that which has taken place (*gata*), and the future, that which has not yet taken place (*agata*), meet as unity of opposites in the present moment (*gamyamana*). The present moment is durationless; a steady passing-away, it has no extension in temporal reality. Separated from the assembly of events in relationship, time has no meaning. This concept of the present as dialectical unity of past and future seems particularly relevant to the discussion of the wave-particle aspect of phenomena. As Nishida writes:

> When past and future, negating each other, join in the present, when therefore the present, as unity of opposites, encloses past and future, and when the present has "form," then I say: the world forms itself. This world proceeds, as one single present, from the formed to the forming, forming itself infinitely. We are forming, by consciously mirroring this world; we are forming the world by acts of expression. (Expression is acting through the mediation of the world.) This is our "life."[30]

The concepts of the formed and the forming, and their unity in the present moment, can produce a new insight into waves, particles, and their unity in the unobserved entity. Wave nature can perhaps be understood in terms of that which has not yet taken place (and which, indeed, may not). Particle nature, in that case, must be regarded in terms of that which has taken place. The observed entity can be viewed from either vantage point. That is, it can be seen as actualized event or as a system of possible and probable future events. Yet its reality can only be spoken of in dialectical fashion; the electron, the vote, the human person has, in the present moment — its space-time location — the character of particle and wave, *gata* and *agata*, being and becoming. This is the nature of impermanence, process, change, and growth. It is the movement from the forming to the formed, and from the formed to the forming.

We can perhaps conclude with the following summary observations:

1. Objects and persons are *events*. Physical science now resonates with the ancient power of this vital observation.

2. The dialectic, the epistemologically transcendent unity of opposites, is, for Mahayana Buddhism and modern physics as well, the highest expression of the nature of existence and existing things that ideation can produce.

3. The dialectic of possibilty and actuality lies at the center of the physical model of things-as-events, and of the Mahayana account of

phenomena as impermanent and without self.

4. The centrality of the concept of interdependence, in both Mahayana philosophy and modern physical theory, suggests a universe of relationship as well as that of actuality. We exist not only as actual "particles," but also as future-shaping "wave-forms."

5. The categories "existence" and "non-existence," as expressions of a rigid, two-value logic, are inadequate for the description of events and processes.

6. The present moment, as a synthesis of past and future, of possible and actual, has a unique dialectical character. The "now-here" is the locus of continuing creativity. It is the transrational unity of emptiness and form, and the only context of real movement . . . from the formed to the forming. It is in the present moment that "who I am" and "who I might be" meet.

The Mahayana Buddhist *Avatamsaka Sutra* is widely regarded as one of the most sublime spiritual works of any tradition. It is also one of the most profound philosophical treatises ever penned. Its greatest exponent in Chinese Buddhism was a monk by the name Fa-tsang. Once he was summoned to the court by the Empress. She had heard his sermons and, indeed, had studied at his side for some years. Still, she failed to grasp the ineffable essence of the *Sutra's* message. She pleaded with Fa-tsang for some further explanation or illumination.

Fa-tsang proceeded quickly to construct one of the grandest spectacles that the court had ever witnessed. Emptying the largest hall in the palace, he directed servants to position within it ten thousand mirrors. (Ten thousand is the number most often associated with infinity in Chinese thought.) The mirrors were positioned cleverly, in such a fashion that each reflected every other, and that each was reflected in every other. In the center of the hall, he placed a single candle and an image of the Buddha, both, of course, displayed in every one of the ten thousand mirrors. When the Empress entered, legend has it, she immediately attained complete enlightenment.

It is not, perhaps, too far-fetched to suggest that our own culture stands on the threshold of the Empress' hall of mirrors. Every particle, every wave, every human life reflects every other and is simultaneously reflected in every other . . . and at the center of all, a single candle and an image of the Awakened One.

Endnotes

1. Werner Heisenberg, *Physics and Philosophy* (New York: Harper and Row, 1958), p. 202.

2. Niels Bohr, *Atomic Physics and Human Knowledge* (New York: John Wiley and Sons, 1958), p. 45.

3. Heisenberg, *Physics*, p. 45.

4. D.T. Suzuki, *The Essence of Buddhism* (Kyoto: Nokozan, 1968), p. 55.

5. David Bohm, "Quantum Theory as an Indication of a New Order in Physics," Part A, *Foundations of Physics*, vol. 1, no. 4, 1971.

6. Fritjof Capra, *The Tao of Physics* (Berkeley: Shambhala Press, 1976), p. 264.

7. Richard Feynman, *Lectures on Physics* (Reading, Ma.: Addison-Wesley Publ. Co., 1963), pp. 37-41.

8. Ashvaghosha, *The Awakening of Faith*, trans. Timothy Richard (New Hyde Park: n.p., 1960), n.p.

9. Heisenberg, quoted in Capra, *Tao of Physics*, p. 37.

10. Bohr, in Heisenberg, *Physics*, p. 41.

11. In Ruth Moore, *Niels Bohr* (New York: Knopf, 1966), p. 159.

12. Robt. A.F. Thurman, trans., *The Holy Teaching of Vimalakirti* (University Park: Penn State Univ. Press, 1976), p. 13.

13. Heisenberg, *Physics*, p. 41.

14. Lincoln Barnett, *The Universe and Dr. Einstein* (New York: Bantam, 1948), p. 34.

15. Capra, *Tao of Physics*, pp. 159-160.

16. Gary Zukav , *The Dancing Wu Li Masters* (New York: William Morow and Co., 1979), p. 134.

17. Garma C. Chang, *The Buddhist Teaching of Totality* (University Park: Penn State Univ. Press, 1973), p. 126.

18. Philip Kapleau, *The Three Pillars of Zen* (Boston: Beacon Press, 1965), pp. 336-337.

19. Traditional. In Lu K'uan Yu, *Ch'an and Zen Teaching* (second series) (Berkeley: Shambhala, 1971), p. 138.

20. Kitaro Nishida, *Intelligibility and the Philosophy of Nothingness* (Westport: Greenwood Press, 1973), p. 186.

21. Feynman, *Lectures on Physics*, pp. 6-10.

22. Douglas Hofstadter, *Godel, Escher, Bach: An Eternal Golden Braid* (New York: Basic Books, 1979), p. 146.

23. Capra, *Tao of Physics*, pp. 153-4.

24. Werner Heisenberger, *On Modern Physics* (New York: Clarkson Potter, 1969), p. 13.

25. Arthur Eddington, *The Philosophy of Physical Science* (Ann Arbor: Univ. of Michigan Press, 1958), p. 155.

26. James Jeans, in Barnett, *Universe and Dr. Einstein*, p. 28.

27. Edward Conze, trans., *The Heart Sutra, Buddhist Wisdom Books* (New York: Harper and Row, 1972), p. 81.

28. Zukav, *Dancing Wu Li Masters*, p. 97.

29. R. Morris and E. Hardy, eds., *Anguttara-Nikava* (London: Pali Text Society, 1885-1900), pp. 4 and 137.

30. Nishida, *Intelligibility*, p. 191.

Modern Cosmology and the Yoga Tradition

by Beatrice B. Briggs

The phrase "fireball and the lotus" suggests to me the merging of contemporary Western and ancient Eastern spirituality. More particularly, this image refers to the creation myth, which comes out of modern science and the teaching of the yoga tradition. The dynamic interaction between the fireball of the West and the lotus of the East is reshaping the lives of religious seekers in North America. This essay will explore the ways in which this interaction transforms human self-understanding, and helps us find our place in the cosmos. The intention is not to blur the very real and valuable distinctions between Western science and yoga. Rather, it is to examine how the two traditions are connected in those who become engaged in their power. The preceding essay, "Particle, Wave, and Paradox," by Jim Kenney, performs a similar service by showing how the new physics and Buddhism mutually illuminate one another.

This exploration will begin by taking a closer look at the seed images from which this paper draws its title. The term "fireball" is a standard description given by modern science to the origins of the universe. Fifteen billion years ago, we are told, a stupendous event occurred from which everything else in the cosmos emerged. In the beginning there was tremendous heat, great light, and great activity of elementary particles: electrons, positrons, photons, and neutrinos. As the temperature cooled, nuclear material was formed, followed a few hundred thousand years later by atoms of hydrogen and helium. Later came supernovae, galaxies, stars, our solar system, and all the life forms on planet Earth. Contemporary science teaches us that humanity descends directly from this fireball at the beginning of time. In us, the great cosmic fire still rages.

In Indian iconography, the lotus symbolizes the flowering of spiritual life. This image affirms the vegetative power of the Earth, the fertility of the goddess, and the sinuous beauty of the natural world. The lotus is pictured as having a thousand petals, suggesting manifold aspects of creation. Rooted in the mud of earthly existence, this blossom floats serenely on primordial waters, fully open to divine bliss. In the mystical physiology of yoga, energy rises up the spine to the top of the head where, in an enlightened being, it breaks through to the transcendent plane. This breakthrough point is imaged as a lotus.

Both the fireball and the lotus brim with numinous power. Like all effective images, they lead us beyond the threshold of our normal awareness and engage us in a larger, more mysterious world. The fireball connects humanity to a vast, space-filled reality, teeming with the vibratory power of heat and light. The lotus places us in a more intimate terrestrial environment, enriched by the fecundity of earth and water. When the two images interact in our consciousness, they ground us more deeply in both the physics and biology of our existence. Together they place us squarely on the Earth and in the cosmos. They root us in our origins and remind us of our potential. They transform our understanding of who we are and what we can be.

The central message of the fireball myth, and by extension the central discovery of modern science, is that matter is not dead. Ours is a universe of fire-created butterflies, and all of creation is involved in this work. Subatomic particles teem with unpredictable vitality. Molecules are soaked with information. Chemical elements are dynamically attracted to one another, forming compounds of amazing complexity. Plant technologies exhibit great sophistication. Every fin and claw and snout in the animal world is matter that has learned to function effectively in its environment. The continent's land masses move constantly. The mountains and valleys and deserts that our forbears considered "timeless" are now known to have had a beginning, and to still be in flux. Water, so essential to our survival, did not always exist on this planet. It was created out of the molten core of the Earth. Out of the water came the amphibious and reptilian ancestors of humanity.

Even this thumbnail sketch of the evolutionary story suggests that not only is matter alive, but it is dreaming. Matter probes around in the dark to discover new forms of self-expression. The physical manifestation is always shaped by dream, by psychic activity. The imagination of the trilobite insisted on the condor's great wing span. The interaction of the psychic and the physical dimensions of matter is profoundly creative. Humans are accustomed to admiring the creativity of Picasso and Mozart, but we fail to appreciate the artistry of matter itself, just as we often underrate our own personal creative capacity. We simply do not notice that creativity is built into our bones. Nor do we acknowledge that human beauty is largely due to the creative efforts of our nonhuman ancestors, dating back to the time of the primeval fireball.

Yoga is a spiritual tradition which also has a long evolutionary history. From the time of its origins in India 5,000 years ago, yoga has undergone several metamorphoses, incorporating the ascetic and ecstatic techniques of Vedic times, the sacrificial symbolism of the Brahmans, the mystical physiology of the Upanishads, the goddess imagery of tantrism and the devotional fervor of bhakti. With the perspective of modern science, we can begin to appreciate the ongoing metamorphosis of yoga as an aspect of this planet's vitality.

In other words, yoga, like all vital spiritual traditions, is alive and changing only because the Earth—and Earthlings—are alive and changing. The planet sustains human life not only physically, but also spiritually and intellectually. If the planet were to lose its inner dynamism, then our religious imaginations and our capacities to express ourselves symbolically would also collapse. To put it more explicitly, if the waters dry up or become too polluted, the lotus will no longer bloom. On the other hand, because yoga is still a living system, it shapes those whom it touches. But the interaction goes both ways: Yoga is also challenged by its environment, which now includes the world of Western science.

The term "yoga" is usually understood by Westerners to mean physical postures, ranging from simple to pretzel-like. This is not a wrong understanding, merely a limited one. As mentioned above, yoga is protean: It assumes many forms, of which hatha yoga, which emphasizes the physical postures, is the most well known in the West. Among the many other dimensions of yoga are those which focus on intellectual comprehension (jnana yoga), devotion to a personal god (bhakti yoga), recitation of sacred sounds (mantra yoga), raising the energy of consciousness (kundalini yoga), or action in the world (karma yoga). None of these are discrete entities, entirely separable from each other. They are all aspects of a rich spiritual tradition that sees many ways for humanity to unite with the divine.

The concept of union is important in Indian religious thought. Most English-language books about yoga mention that the word "yoga" is derived from the Sanskrit root *yuj*, which means to join together or to harness. Our word "yoke" is cognate with *yuj* and "yoga." The first step in yoga is to yoke the various parts of the individual into a coherent whole. Harmonious relationships between head and feet, arms and legs, and chest and spine must be established so that intelligence can flow throughout the body. The masculine and the feminine parts of the psyche must be integrated. The senses and the mind must be channeled. Only by freeing the body, mind, and spirit does union with God occur. This is a difficult and strenuous task, but it is within reach of anyone who is willing to be disciplined and to practice.

For Westerners, in fact, it may be more helpful to translate "yoga" as "discipline," rather than as "union." "Discipline" underscores the process by which, if all goes well, "union" is attained. All yogic teachings emphasize systematic, daily practice. But behind mere discipline lies the urge to grow, to change, to find God. And behind this urge lies love, the binding and abiding force in the universe.

Yoga is a way of life. Union with the divine is not something one just thinks about, it is something one experiences, moment to moment, on the physical plane. Many Westerners who are attracted to yoga because they want "to be more spiritual," often drop out once they discover how much hard, physical work is involved. On the other hand, a system that requires one to "get out of one's head," and to delve deeper into the inner mysteries of the body, has much to recommend it to those who are truly committed to change.

Radical transformation of the human is another way of stating the goal of yoga. The Sanskrit term for this experience is *moksa*, or liberation. Bold Western spiritual voyagers may embrace this aim, but their understanding of what is meant by *moksa* is necessarily very different from an Indian's. According to the Indian perspective, the purpose of all religious practice is to liberate one's self from *samsara*, that is, from the endless cycle of death and rebirth which characterizes earthly existence. Belief in multiple incarnations is as axiomatic in India as it is culturally alien in the West. While some Westerners are immediately comfortable with the notion of rebirth, others are either mystified or outright hostile to the whole idea. (Barbara Clow's essay on "Reincarnation as a Method for the Divine Quest," found elsewhere in this book, explains the sources of Western resistance to these teachings.) However, rebirth (and "redeath") can be understood by Westerners in ways that, while they are not incompatible with Indian views on the subject, reflect more accurately the concerns of the Western time and place in history.

The liberation (*moksa*) that we seek is from our patterns of behavior that are destroying Earth's capacity to support life. We seek freedom from our enchantment with technology, from our addiction to consumerism, from our dependence on militaristic solutions to personal, political, and economic problems. We recognize that unless we reinvent ourselves, both as individuals and as a species, we are doomed and so are future generations. We need to find a way of being human that does not require us to kill the very planet that gives us life. The magnitude of this challenge calls for radical solutions.

The yoga tradition provides a means for reinventing the human, for historically it has aimed at nothing less than complete transformation. The remainder of this paper will focus on ways in which ancient techniques of yoga can be used to accomplish this goal. Hatha is selected both because it is the kind of yoga with which I am the most familiar, and because it is widely taught in the West. The term "hatha" is somewhat misleading, however, for it suggests that the practice of physical postures is separable from other aspects of yoga, which is not the case. Therefore I will continue to use the more inclusive term, "yoga," for the system which utilizes the human body to experience the source of spiritual power and revelation.

It seems ironic that Westerners, and especially Western Christians, should have to journey to the East to find a religious tradition which truly honors the incarnation. While there is a repressive, anti-body element in India, as indeed there is in most cultures in which the priestly caste is male-dominated, the physical dimension of the spiritual quest has been better understood in India than in the West. Not all kinds of yoga include the practice of physical postures, but those that do remind us that matter is sacred and that the divine is as much within us as outside of us.

In the next several paragraphs, I will outline a few of the ways in which yoga, practiced in the context of Western science, can assist in reinventing the human. Yoga fosters three kinds of experiences which facilitate evolution: Differentiation of the polarities out of which life springs; awareness of the inner dimension of the creative process; and the interconnectedness of body, mind, and spirit. These three experiences are present in every aspect of yoga from the moment one's practice begins. The longer one practices, the more obvious and yet the more mysterious they become.

Central to the experience of differentiation is the ability to pay attention to significant details. For students of yoga, the breath is often the first aspect of our psycho-physical state to become differentiated. We begin to notice that when we are afraid, we hold our breath, witholding the life force rather than letting it flow through us. We learn to use the breath as a means of directing awareness to parts of our bodies that are stiff, painful, or inert. Breathing, once done "automatically" or without awareness, becomes a conscious activity, a way of venturing from known to unknown, a way of releasing the body from the bondage of the mind.

Heightened sensitivity brings the yoga student into direct contact with their own particularity. We learn which hip joint is more flexible, which foot has the higher instep, which lung inflates faster. We begin to notice how the alignment of the limbs affects the "happiness" of the spine. We start to differentiate between bones and muscles, muscles and tendons, skin and flesh. Awareness of these physical and physiological details leads to greater sensitivity to other environmental conditions. The effects on the body of food, drink, air, temperature, sound, smell, and color all become more noticeable. Some things feel more "right," more life-enhancing, more energizing, or more relaxing than others. These discoveries often bring about changes in habits, the first reliable sign that transformation has begun.

By closely observing their experiences with postures, students can gain useful information about their personal patterns. After all, the way one "does" the postures is no different from the way one "does" one's life. People who try to force their bodies into positions for which they are not ready behave with similar greed and aggression outside of yoga class. People who are lazy or "spaced out" or afraid when practicing will manifest those same tendencies in other situations. Similarly, those who are calm, optimistic, relaxed, and attentive in class are able to infuse the rest of their lives with those qualities.

Learning to watch oneself doing the postures is a form of meditation. Westerners often mistakenly view meditation as a passive withdrawal from "real life," when in fact it requires a heightened attention to emergent reality. Meditators become self-conscious observers of the universal creative dynamic. The more closely we watch, the more we discover about the currents of life in our own bodies. We learn where these currents are blocked and where they flow freely. We begin to recognize that the power in our bodies comes to us directly from the fireball at the beginning of time. And we realize that our spirituality flowers most fully when we are in contact with this fiery power, which connects us to the source of all life.

To meditate, one must achieve mental and physical stillness. The yoga student soon discovers that in order to still the mind, the body must also become quiet. The simplest yoga posture becomes a direct experience of the interconnectedness of body, mind, and spirit. If the ankle wobbles, then the mind is unsteady. If the arm is lifeless, then the spirit is limp. If the eyes are hard, then the brain is frozen. If the pelvis is dead, then the spirit cannot be completely alive. If the imagination cannot visualize an action, then the body will not be able to perform it. Learning to hold a posture means integrating all the parts of one's being into a vibrant whole.

Wholeness requires the ability to move freely between the polarities of life. Most people are either overly attached to one polarity, or never venture beyond the familiarity, safety, and boredom of the "middle way." Being overly identified with an extreme position is to be a fanatic.

Clinging to the middle is to be stuck. Yoga invites extremists to be more balanced, and middle-of-the-roaders to be more courageous. To practice yoga is to commit oneself to changing in a bold, but balanced way.

Moving freely between polarities requires interaction with life's paradoxes. For instance, the value of achieving mental and physical stillness was mentioned above. But stillness without vitality is death, so yoga practitioners must be equally committed to bringing life into all of their limbs, while becoming perfectly still. Another polarity that can be explored through yoga is that of determination and surrender. Wisdom seekers must be steadfast in their intention to be transformed, yet they must let go of egoistic attachment to results. Yoga also teaches the polar relatedness of inner and outer. The examined life, as understood in India, is one of deep interiority. Westerners often mistake this exploration of inner space as rejection of the outer world, when in fact yoga places as much emphasis on skillful action as it does on non-participation. The challenge is to hold the paradox.

Sometimes Western students worry that in practicing yoga they are being selfish, narcissistic, and vain, placing their personal well-being over that of other suffering souls in the world. This attitude is an unfortunate by-product of a culture which has taught us to think of ourselves as essentially separate from each other and the rest of creation. The Indian spiritual tradition has long expressed a more holistic view of the universe, seeing all creatures as inextricably bound together by the intrinsic universal order, which includes the activities of all creatures.

Western science has now begun to articulate a similar understanding, using language and data that we may find more culturally accessible. For instance, science tells us that our bodies are made of the same chemical elements that form the Earth itself. Each individual life is an expression of the Earth's creativity, a manifestation of the power of matter to organize in complex and beautiful ways. Because we are so intimately connected to the Earth, we are as damaged by the effects of twentieth-century living as is the rest of the planet. Automobile emissions destroy our lungs, just as they do the breathing capacity of trees along the highway. Poisoned waters leech into our food supply as quickly as they defile the habitat of marine life. Unnecessary surgery leaves as deep a scar on the human psyche as strip mining does on an Appalachian hillside.

When we begin to heal our bodies through yoga practice, we are, in effect, committing ourselves to the healing of the planet. When we treat our bodies with reverence and respect, we begin to feel the sacredness of the Earth. When we soften the carapace of our own body armor, then we take a meaningful step toward world disarmament. When we pay attention to the organs and muscles that we have systematically discriminated against, we combat prejudice on a fundamental level. Making these connections does not, of course, absolve us from the responsibility of working for peace and justice outside of ourselves. But to ignore the inner dimension of global issues is to cripple one's effectiveness as an agent of change.

To make the above assertions less theoretical, imagine the following scene: A diligent yoga student is standing in class, feet wide spread, arms outstretched, but shoulders bunched up around his ears. The teacher gently places her hands on the student's shoulders and, in an instant, the shoulders are released, the neck is freed, the spine lengthens, the arms extend further, the breath softens, and the student is, for the moment, more at peace with the world. These kinds of experiences occur repeatedly under the tutelage of a skilled teacher. They demonstrate, in a way that words cannot embody, the truth that everything is connected to everything else, and that the tiniest change is felt throughout the system. Yoga students feel in their bodies what religious leaders, ecologists, social activists, and now even physicists have said: What you do makes a difference. Local actions have global consequences. Energy patterns can be altered with the mind. "As ye sow, so shall ye reap."

The challenge for today's yoga students is to appropriate this tradition in a way that honors both its unique cultural heritage and the highest insights of our own place and time. We must learn all we can about the historical roots of yoga, and about the language, mythology, and customs of India, for this will enrich our understanding, broaden our sympathies, and deepen our practice. But we must not fall into the trap of slavishly imitating cultural expressions which are not truly our own. Our task is to be more creative.

We live in a time in which humans have split the atom and traveled in outer space. We have touched moonrocks and discovered the DNA molecule. We have measured the background radiation which flooded the universe at the moment of creation, 20 billion years ago.

Where did we come from? Why are we here? What is our relationship to the mysterious shaping power of the universe? Our most profound insights into these great questions, which have always perplexed humanity, are coming to us through Western science. These insights, incorporated into the yoga tradition, enable us to enter into a transformed mode of being.

Thus when we practice breathing exercises, we must do so meticulously, following the traditional instructions but also holding in our consciousness the knowledge that when we breathe, we inhale atmosphere that was created by a star exploding to form our solar system. The air that supports life on this Earth did not just "happen" — it emerged out of the primeval fireball. Through it, we are linked directly to the time of our origin, to the great mystery of our beginning. Each inhalation also links us physically to every other inhabitant of the planet, both past and present. The air that we breathe has been recycling since before the first fish experimented with breathing on land instead of in water. At any given moment, our bodies contain molecules of water vapor that Plato, Shakespeare, or Rachel Carson once breathed. After twenty minutes in the same room, people are literally trading breath. The intimacy of our interconnectedness through the life-giving aspect of breath, called "prana" in the yoga tradition, is truly astonishing.

Yoga also provides us with daily opportunities to enter into conscious communion with other species which share the planet. The lion, the eagle, the crow, the fish , the snake, the peacock, the dog, the tortoise, and the scorpion are but a few of the postures named after other Earth dwellers. Assuming these positions helps us to recognize these animals as manifestations of the divine, and remember our indebtedness to them for the part they have played in the ongoing evolutionary drama. Our own form as a creature with head, spine, and four limbs was invented by the four-limbed vertebrates who came before us. To hold a posture is to praise their imaginations. As we struggle to master these positions, we understand in a new way the uniqueness and preciousness of each life-form. We realize how impoverished our experience would be if these creatures had never existed, and what a loss their extinction would represent.

In fact, every yoga position invites us to become aware of the cosmic, geologic, and biological beauty which preceded human creation. As we strive to achieve perfect alignment, full extension, fluid movement, flexibility, strength, and prayerful attitude, as the yoga tradition advocates, we embody the living memory of the cosmic process. The ability to reflect consciously on this inheritance is the distinctive gift of the human. Recognizing the ongoing activity of the fireball in our postures transforms them from exercise into prayer.

Twentieth-century Western yoga might be called "fireball yoga," since it is the scientific story of creation that provides the context in which we practice. This "fireball yoga" must be informed by the heart of bhakti, the intellect of jnana, the sexual power of tantra, and the physical groundedness of hatha. But it must also include the wisdom of the astronomer , the paleontologist, the geologist, the botanist, the zoologist, and the physicist, who collectively have given us a new image of the divine: The picture of a beautiful, blue-green planet, fragile yet resilient, the only place in the known universe where life expresses itself in such an abundance of forms.

Using the techniques of concentration and meditation taught by the Indian masters, we internalize this vision until we feel our essential oneness with it. Then we know that we are Earthlings, that we are none other than the living Earth itself. We know that the planet, the galaxies, and the supernovae have given us birth. And we know that our lives, in turn, are to be surrendered to the stars, to the Earth and to the future generations. At this moment, the lotus pollinates the fireball, the fireball ignites the lotus, and love, the mysterious, creative power of the universe, explodes anew.

The New Natural Selection

by Brian Swimme

In her article, Bea Briggs sets sail on a profound journey: the reinvention of the yoga tradition within the context of contemporary science. Guided by her insights, we begin to see our spiritual practice as rooted in the dynamics of the fifteen-billion-year cosmic process, and we catch a glimmer of a great hidden truth: our spiritual development is biologically essential for the evolutionary flowering of the living Earth.

We are living out a myth that has many similarities with that of Oedipus. We can see that we live in a sickened state of life. The realm deepens in its pathology each day, and yet we do not quite know what to do. We thrash about, but it seems only to make matters worse. Evils proliferate, needless suffering is on the increase, worse scenarios threaten beyond the horizon, and we ourselves agonize in the central role of the drama. It is not one thing that is wrong; it is everything. It is not a single situation that depresses us; it is the wide choice of disasters, cruelties, and poisons, the whole selfish disregard for all that is good. We stagger into the future tragically aware of our responsibility in all this as Americans, as Westerners, even as humans, but we remain profoundly ignorant of what we might do to bring health to the whole.

The central crime is precisely our failure to evolve into a larger role as Earthlings. We have performed mightily in our role as Americans, and we have succeeded in our role as scientific Westerners. Even as humans — in the role of subduing, conquering, and controlling the environment — we have accomplished wonders. But we have failed as yet to evolve into our role as human Earthlings, and this failure lies behind our present pathological impasse. Our deep-seated arrogance toward the nonhuman components of the Earth community has crippled evolutionary advance. The nuclear impasse stems from our delusion that territorial and ideological disputes qualify as issues for which the four-billion-year process of life can be sacrificed. The commercial/industrial impasse results from our delusion that consumer demands are reason enough to ruin any habitat, any community of life, even the very conditions from which life emerges and evolves on this planet. The sickness of the present situation will continue to escalate with evermore cruelty and suffering until we learn the fuller dimensions of our role within evolution's unfoldment. Oedipus could not move toward health until he discovered that he had unknowingly been violating his mother. We are only now realizing that we have been violating Mother Earth for centuries. The task of furthering evolution is the task of becoming full Earthlings. It is, as Thomas Berry has suggested, the challenge of living within a new story — a story of cosmic and terrestrial dimensions.[1]

We must concern ourselves, then, with discovering this macrophase role of the human. We must learn to conceive of ourselves and our genetic powers within the total life-process of this planet. Previous conceptions of the human have failed to reach this larger, planetary dimension. Former conceptions might well have been adequate for certain earlier historical periods, each with its own specific needs, but those situations have now disappeared. Even the ancient threat of survival in the midst of a violent natural world no longer applies. We must ask the basic questions all over again: What is the nature of humans and their powers of mind? What is the purpose and place of these creatures in the larger dynamic of evolutionary unfolding within the integral Earth process?

I am proposing that the present evolutionary impasse will be broken only when humans go beyond their arrogance towards the nonhuman components of the Earth, and further activate the deeper planetary dimensions of being. When we learn to live with cosmic dynamics brought into the conscious mode, the genuine ripening of the Earth will occur. In particular, I would like to discuss what it might mean to bring the dynamics of natural selection into the conscious mode of being — what it might mean for the dynamics that have been operative in the Earth process for billions of years to advance suddenly into a modality of consciousness through the human component of the planet.

Natural Selection

The principles of natural selection are exhibited by whole systems of life, whether we are considering a forest, a seashore community, or a major bioregion. Natural selection is a holistic concept pointing to the dynamics of interaction among the beings of the community. An organism that finds itself in the midst of an ecological community must learn to mesh with the existing order of relationships, so that it may live and continue its genetic line within this context of life. If the new organism cannot fit into the existing order, it either leaves or dies. As Gregory Bateson has emphasized, it is a question of fitness.[2] The survival of the fittest refers to those organisms that can fit into the existing coherence of interacting life systems within the community. Fitness cannot be reduced to strength alone. Strength is but one aspect of many that are involved when an organism confronts a community. Natural selection is a holistic phenomenon that amounts to a test for each new organism or species, and determines if it is able to fit into the existing patterns of life within the community.

It is when we move beyond the biological realm and attempt to include cultural activities in our discussion of natural selection principles that our difficulties begin. What can the principles of natural selection indicate about art, politics, mathematics, music, technology, or law? Our cultural disposition is to regard each of these activities as largely disconnected from the dynamics of the natural world. Of all our cultural activities, mathematics resists inclusion in the natural world more so than any other. Our 2500 years of Western intellectual, philosophical development has assumed in large part that the human mind is ontologically distinct from the natural world. This claim has been championed especially on the basis of our abstract system of mathematics. We have assumed for millenia that mathematical truths have a certainty that places them outside time, in a transcendent and eternal realm.

To see the place of mathematical activity within evolutionary dynamics, we begin by identifying the principles of natural selection with the proof procedures of logic. Just as natural selection tests a new organism before allowing it to enter the community of life, so do proof procedures test new mathematical propositions before allowing them to enter the body of mathematical knowledge. If logic can show the proposition to be true, the proposition is allowed into mathematical knowledge. If the logical procedures can show that the proposition is false, it is rejected from the body of mathematical knowledge. Logic decides which novel mathematical ideas shall be accepted and which shall be rejected, in a manner similar to the way natural selection principles decide which novel organisms shall be accepted into the community of life and which shall be rejected. The logical procedures represent a form of natural selection brought into the conscious phase.

Throughout the centuries of Western intellectual development, at least as far back as Plato, the proof procedures of mathematics have been regarded as transcendent. They were altogether separate from the conditions characterizing the natural world. Mathematical knowledge then was certain and eternal, and the proof procedure provided a method for being absolutely sure of this. We saw ourselves as arriving at ideas and knowledge that were separated by a chasm from the activities, generation, and transience of the natural world, and this primary assumption about the human mind deepened our Western alienation from nature.

Twentieth-century mathematics, however, has discovered that these proof procedures are developmental. The most abstract creations of the human mind can now be understood as sharing in the fundamental dynamics of the evolutionary unfoldment. An ancient tradition in the West has been called into question in our century, for now an understanding of mathematics has come to mean an understanding of its development. This interpretation is possible only through the work done in the foundations of mathematics, culminating in the stirring results of Kurt Goedel. The notion of a transcendent logic that can be employed for arriving at eternal, certain truths outside of time, has been shown to be false. Our ancient assumption that human knowledge is ontologically distinct from the developing universe has been undermined; in this development, within our most theoretical enterprise, we find hope that the alienation that has split human from non-human for so many centuries is finally ending.

An evolutionary understanding of mathematical logic begins with the observation that bodies of mathematical knowledge exist prior to the logic. Arithmetic and geometry and their truths emerge in human experience before any attempts are made to articulate a logic. Logic is understood simply as a later explication of a fundamental coherence, tying any body of mathematical knowledge into a fundamental unity. Humans examining the knowledge extract those forms of interconnectivity that hold the body together. That coherence characterizes any established body of knowledge can be recognized by inspection. This articulation of the patterns of coherence and interconnectivity is logic. Since each age develops and extends the knowledge it has received from its ancestors, its logic develops as well. Logic, understood in this manner, is a characteristic of the body of knowledge in a particular historical period; it is the pattern of coherency of the whole. To say that we have proven a mathematical result through logic is to say that this new mathematical proposition can be shown to fit into the patterns of coherency of the existing body of knowledge. To say that a mathematical proposition has been shown through logic to be false is to say that it violates the coherence of the knowledge. Thus logic is a holistic phenomenon of a system that tests for fitness of novel mathematical ideas, just as natural selection is a holistic phenomenon that tests for the fitness of novel organisms or species. Further, logic develops as the body of mathematics develops, just as selection principles within the natural world develop as the ecosystem evolves.

For our purposes, the most important similarity between mathematical logic and natural selection is the concern of each for the vitality of the whole. Established mathematical knowledge is a precious and highly complex reality. Logical proof procedures are created to protect this vitality from the crippling that would ensue should fundamental contradictions be allowed into the body of mathematics. These contradictions could entangle themselves so deeply in the organism that their final extirpation would be nearly impossible. Just so, the principles of selection in the natural world ensure that the most vital, most interesting, most capable organisms — those that are able to fill out all the various niches available in an ecosystem — will be the ones contributing to the future of the species of the whole community. An ecosystem is as fragile as foam on a seawave, and should genetic mediocrity be allowed to dominate the future generations of the community, the whole system risks a much more probable collapse. Both logic and natural selection work to promote the vigor and vitality of the whole systems in which they operate.

By analogy, we can see how the selection dynamics of evolution operate within all cultural activities. The literary critic serves as an agent of selection dynamics in literature and the arts. The body of classical works is protected from the enervation that would follow should all cultural novelties whatsoever be included. Through a test with the works of excellence, both the diversity of achievement and the intensity of activity are evoked, and through this the vitality of the enterprise is protected and enhanced. In law, perhaps the clearest example of the conscious phase of selection dynamics can be seen. The work of lawyers and courts is fundamentally one of testing particular patterns of behavior against the established patterns of the norm. Those patterns that do not fit the accepted coherence of the norm are known to be debilitating, and are to be extirpated for the sake of the whole society's vitality. In this and in similar extensions, we see how humans have been operating within a pattern fundamentally congruous with the dynamics of evolution's unfolding.

Qualitative Advance

Within any stable biological or cultural regime, the dynamic interaction between novel creations and selection principles proceeds with a smooth, overall growth in complexity and vitality. But moments occur when the regime breaks down. The stability of the system is ruined. It is, as Erich Jantsch calls it, an introduction of a disequilibrium that throws the previously functioning stable regime toward chaos.[3] In such a situation, the principles of natural selection cannot maintain the previous system's stability, for the novel organism or the novel conception is so powerful or alien that it overrides all the tests for fitness that are put to it. The system enters a time of breakdown and chaos as this new organism unfolds its novel powers and enters the community.

From a biological perspective, presently the most important example of a disequilibrium that destroyed a previously harmonious community is the arrival of *Homo sapiens* into the Earth community. Considered from the four-billion-years of life's development, the scientific/technological human has been on the Earth one instant and yet in that instant everything has changed on the planet. From a shy creature that had to make its way into the existing patterns of feeding, mating, eating, preying, hiding, and nurturing that were established within the community of beings, the human has erupted during the last two centuries into the dominant organism of the planet. Rather than having to adjust and fit into the interactive patterns of the rest of the Earth community, the human has come to dominate the Earth process, which involves every other life-system. Indeed, changes wrought by the scientific/technological phase of *Homo sapiens* now accomplish—or destroy—in a week what required millions of years of fashioning by the prehuman Earth community.

Thus we lay down hundreds of thousands of miles of asphalt; we let loose millions upon millions of steel machines that crisscross the land and crowd the skies; we infiltrate the atmosphere with chemical creations never experienced before in the Earth community; and we spew millions of tons of materials noxious to all forms of life through our waterways and soil communities. Suddenly, this shy creature is creating the total environment into which all other life-systems must either fit or perish. Once we were frightened creatures attempting to learn the patterns of the Earth community so that we might fit in and survive. Now we are the dominant factor in this world. Every other species must approach us with even more fright and terror than we first approached them. Our cultural novelties overwhelm the entire system of natural selection devised to protect the health of evolution's development.

Fundamental to any qualitative emergence within a biological or cultural system is the total breakdown of the existing principles of natural selection. Even in the 1700s, the principles of the Earth community that had been developing over the previous millions of years functioned throughout major portions of the Earth. The 700 million humans alive at that time certainly created some sad situations, for instance in the forest destructions of Europe and China, or in the disastrous agricultural regimes of the Middle East and elsewhere. But the presence of the human was the presence of one rather strange organism among others. The interactions between the human and natural worlds were not substantially different from what they had been for the previous 8,000 years, and not enormously different from what they had been for the previous two million years.

With the emergence of the power of scientific/technological knowledge and development, the fundamental principles of natural selection failed to assure the vitality and health of the whole Earth community. The Earth's organisms cannot effectively interact with bulldozers. The Earth's community cannot select against agricultural machines that, for instance, destroy four billion tons of topsoil on the North American continent each year. It took thousands of years to fashion the topsoil, and it disappears forever in a season. The principles of selection are impotent in the face of the noxious chemicals rained upon the land. A glut of oil invades a seashore community and a billion interactions and selections and novel emergences vanish. Ancient achievements are nothing when confronted with machines designed to gut a forest. We have broken the very principles of natural selection constructed to safeguard the vitality of the planet's life.

I would like to compare this biological scenario with a situation from the history of mathematics. The introduction of calculus in the seventeenth century was a disequilibrium event that has no rival in mathematical history. Through the creations of Isaac Newton, Gottfried Leibnitz, and Pierre Fermat, mathematics as a whole was profoundly transformed over the course of two centuries. Indeed, all of science was transformed. Yet, from the beginning, these novel mathematical ideas *could not be proven*. This strange fact did not go unnoticed at the time. Bishop Berkeley, for one, made a career of ridiculing the attempts of both Newton and Leibnitz to prove their calculus. A strange situation. Tremendous new mathematical ideas and yet no one could prove they were actually mathematical knowledge. We see here a novelty that overwhelmed the principle of selection that was supposed to test these novelties. No one could prove these mathematical assertions and no one could answer Berkeley's criticisms. Mathematicians were ready to agree that the ideas of calculus had not in fact been proven, but they were prepared to accept them as mathematical knowledge nonetheless.

As these new ideas of calculus entered Europe, a creative blossoming of science and mathematics followed. No branch of the sciences remained the same. Humans had gotten hold of something new, strange, powerful, and fertile, and for the rest of that century and throughout the eighteenth as well, they extended and deepened these new ideas. It is doubtful if there has ever been a more significant period of mathematical activity in the history of scientific thought. European science was buzzing with these transformed modes of thought that soon permeated areas of culture much removed from the strictly scientific. And though many mathematicians continued to try to prove these results within the logic then available, they repeatedly failed. The principles of natural selection that had served for so long were suddenly unable to test effectively against the novel conceptions which followed calculus.

This rapid creative outburst of mathematical development did not come without a price. From the beginning, discrepancies had appeared within the great new body of work. Contradictions and ambiguities could be found in many areas of development. Most disheartening were situations in which the greatest minds of the eighteenth century produced proofs for opposite results. Were these indications of deep, structural contradictions in calculus and its development? Sensitive minds began demanding a process that would enable mathematicians to decide what was to be accepted and what was to be rejected. It was a demand that the vitality of the whole enterprise of modern mathematics be protected. It was, in essence, a demand for a new set of selection principles that could be used to test the many extravagant creations, the many bizarre novelties.

Beginning in the early nineteenth century with the work of Augustin-Louis Cauchy, and proceeding throughout the century with the work of people such as Karl Weierstrauss, the principles of selection to be used in the great body of mathematical analysis were constructed. These logical principles were extracted from the existing body of mathematical knowledge, and represented fundamental patterns of intelligibility of the whole achievement. After all, calculus and its developments had already been in existence for over a century. That was adequate time for humans to observe the form and structure of these new conceptions. Calculus had grown organically into its own special, interconnected shapes; the fundamental and essential structure could be extracted and codified in the processes of the limit of uniform convergence, and in the definitions of integral, derivative, and continuous function. The health and vitality of the mathematical enterprise as a whole were the aims of this endeavor, and mathematicians proceeded with vigor to construct these principles of natural selection. They wanted to be able to recognize and pluck out powerful vital ideas while rejecting sickly and unimportant ones. Their success in establishing these principles endowed nineteenth-century mathematics with unparalleled depth, nuance, confidence, and imaginative freedom. The whole of mathematical sciences had never been so vibrant, its overall health never so apparent.

The Task of the Earth Community

If we return now to the consideration of the planet and the violent disequilibrium of the scientific/technological human, we can see that the basic task before the Earth community today is the creation of a new set of natural selection principles out of the ruined conditions we find ourselves in. The emergence of our powerful and talented species has overwhelmed the Earth and destroyed the very principles which the Earth community created for its vitality through millions of previous years of evolution. But just as the emergence of calculus led to a wild proliferation of mathematical ideas, and then to the recognition that the mathematicians must create a new set of selection principles, so too do we awaken to our fundamental task within the impasse of our situation. The Earth community has been watching the human being over these last two centuries and has been able to determine the kinds of powers and extravagances and constructions that are possible for this new member of the family of life. It is now time to create the norms of an "Earth Justice," so that the vitality and continuing evolutionary unfolding of the entire planet will be protected.

The creation of these selection principles depends upon one central act. The human must activate its terrestrial and cosmic dimensions of life. Previous to our era, humans considered themselves as beings within the small context of the tribe; or within the boundaries of a religious or cultural group; or as members of a scientific/technological nation-state. A few even regarded themselves as members of what was considered the ultimate universal context—humanity. All of these self-definitions are true, but a further dimension has emerged during these last two centuries. The full context of the human must include the cosmic and terrestrial dimension of life and being. Humans are, as Teilhard celebrated, the conscious mode of coevolution.

In the past we created principles of natural selection, for instance in our law codes, that reflected the boundaries of our limited self-conceptions. We understood justice in terms of those principles that protected human from human. We protected the state and the religious institution. We protected our businesses with our selection principles. In all of these contexts, we have established codes and norms that test patterns of behavior as well as conceptions that might weaken the whole person, the whole state, the whole corporation. But our task at present is much vaster. We are called to create selection principles that will enable the evolutionary processes of unfoldment to deepen throughout the Earth process. At present we are called upon to evoke those macrophase dimensions of the human person that will allow the dynamics of evolutionary process to blossom into its conscious mode within the Earth community. That is the task of justice today: we are called upon to represent Earth as its conscious mode of life and being.

Oedipus, too, needed to bring a larger awareness into his realm. So long as he continued to live within his limited framework, he only worsened the sickness of his world. Our situation over the whole planet is the same today. So long as the evolutionary process exists in its present crippled state, the pathology and fundamentally rancid nature of the whole planet will continue. Only when the deeper dynamics of evolution break through and assume their destined role in a conscious mode, will we move through this impasse and into the more harmonious beauty possible within our planetary system of living and nonliving beings.

Guidelines for Articulation of a Macrophase Justice

Principles of natural selection exist in any ecologically interconnected community of beings. These principles are profoundly embedded in the functioning systems of this planet. We speak only from an examination of Earth's history when we speak of the natural and spontaneous emergence of ordered and harmonious wholes throughout life's development. The coherence of the living world is taken as a fact, just as the coherence of established bodies of knowledge is taken as a fact. It is not something that is proved. But it is most definitely something that can be observed through billions of developments in the history of the planet.

To attempt to discover those principles of natural selection against which we must test all future technological, commercial, industrial, political, and economic decisions and inventions, we turn not to a priori assumptions about the nature of life, but rather to the whole display of life's dynamic development. It is through its history that we encounter the actuality of life's emergence into our world. In the last two centuries of scientific/technological development, we have come to understand the nature and development of life in ways that are stupendous to contemplate. From this great body of knowledge we extract those central dynamics. The process of evolution teaches us how we must proceed in order to bring the inner dynamics of unfoldment into a greater conscious expression for the vitality, vigor, and splendor of this planet, with all its systems of life and being.

I have indicated that our past selection principles are inadequate for the task before us at this time. Thus, though some principles have been used to test commercial and technological processes, these were microphase concerns focusing on the individual person, business, or state. Beyond these, there was the simple and dominant test of profits. In the main, if a device, process, program, or policy would eventuate in greater profits, it would find its way into the planetary system. Our failure to develop the planetary dimensions of the human person is clearly indicated in our insensitive complacency before such obviously inadequate selection principles for the vitality of the earth. The evolutionary development of our integral community demands a greater justice for its living and nonliving components than the criterion of profits.

I present, then, three principles that characterize the dynamics of the life process on this planet. It is upon these that we will create our macrophase principles of natural selection.

Depth of Being

Scientific investigation has revealed that every individual organism, every mineral, and every ecological community possesses within itself a significant story in relation to the whole emergence of life on Earth. Each existent being or community of beings can be considered a voice that speaks from 20 billion years of cosmic development. We are only just now understanding how to listen to the voice that speaks in these systems of life and being. Only in the last few decades have we been able to listen to the story of the universe's origin that is contained in the radiant energy bathing the Earth. Each wave of photons brings even more information from the earliest moments of the universe. Then, too, it is only in the past few years that we have been able to listen to the story contained in the continents of their journey through the transformations of the Earth. And only now are we able to hear the story of the prokaryotes, and their symbiotic fashioning to create eukaryotic cells some one-and-a-half billion years ago. Only in the last few years have we realized that all cellular nuclei, even of our own skin, must be considered fossils from the ancient origins of the symmetry breaks in the heart of the primordial fireball. In these and many other examples, we are beginning to appreciate the way in which every existent being is the whole universe's story told from a particular viewpoint and history. We must, therefore, insist that all future inventions and policies recognize and respect this great truth, this great mystery of history's presence within each being. A voice that is lost means knowledge and information lost for all time: a story that will never be recaptured. We must move into the future with a deep reverence for all beings and the story that each is able to tell.

Now that we have come to understand that the remaining primitive peoples of the Earth must be cherished as a precious source of story and wisdom, we must extend this stance to include all living and non-living systems of being. We must insist on this reverential stance toward every species of plant and animal, and every major geological formation. The Himalayas and the Philippines and Southern California are permeated with the history of this planet's journey; should they be demolished or blacktopped, a billion-fold voice of our past and its meaning and wonder is silenced forever. We must understand that every living being, every community, and every underwater formation rests quietly with a great realm of intelligent history folded into its being. If we are yet unable to read these stories, we must not deny the possibility that a future generation might learn to listen and learn from them.

Creative Power

The one stubborn fact of our cosmic creative unfolding is the dependence of each being's emergence on the totality of evolution's previous achievement. Only because the stars created the chemicals that form the bodies of every form of life could the Earth emerge with all its splendor. Only because prokaryotes created the oxygen of the early Earth system could the higher animals emerge. Only because the microorganism created the basic set of genes could their later, complex combinations allow the higher animals, and eventually consciousness, to emerge into the planetary system. We are certain of one thing: The future unfolding of evolutionary development depends on precisely those beings — and their inherent creative powers — that presently inhabit the Earth system.

If we remove any species from the Earth system, we are in that act forever limiting the possibilities of the future. Remove all the species and there is no future. Remove a significant portion of them and the future possibilities are profoundly diminished. Our ignorance of the dynamics of this mystery is overwhelming. We do not know in either a general or a specific sense anything about the interactions and processes that will enable the future to unfold. All we know for certain is that all future, all possibilities, all unrevealed beauty, is presently contained in those beings that exist in Earth's system. No species and no individual can be considered redundant or unnecessary for the ongoing unfolding. We live in a vast multiform event that has required all 20 billion years of the universe's creativity. We must begin now with a profound reverence for the inherent power of self-emergence that each being possesses. It is out of, because of, and through precisely these powers of creativity that all future destinies of the Earth will be fashioned. We are evolutionary dynamics brought into the conscious phase when we act with an awareness that these creative powers need to be evoked, defended, and nurtured with the fear and trembling that reflects our awareness of all futures of our present actions.

Intimacy of Community

Though untold millions of species have vanished from the Earth system, the present community is more complex, diversified, and intimately involved as a single community than any previous Earth. The overall effect of this stupendous story of life's emergence in this Earth system is a story of a continued growth in the great complexity, diversity, and community of being. The vitality of this complex whole must take precedence over all else. Though our human processes might involve destruction, it must be a destruction that promises to nurture those conditions enabling an even more diversified emergence of life. All aims, policies, and values must begin with this affirmation of the total community of beings on this planet. The integral community — complex, splendid, vastly differentiated — is *the* principal accomplishment of the long history of the Earth process. *Our* principle accomplishment of the long history of the Earth process. Our principles of natural selection must work to enhance this fundamental achievement, to aid in the development of a richer and more intimately interrelated Earth community.

We, like Oedipus, must admit that we are blind, even though we think we have eyes. We have attempted to see this planet through the eyes of the industrial exploitation of both capitalism and socialism, but that was not seeing at all. The eyes we must use to see the Earth are provided by centuries of work in mathematics, physics, chemistry, biology, astronomy, paleontology, and anthropology. Though some of the ideas of Adam Smith and Karl Marx will continue in a transformed manner into the new era of the Earth, their overall theories as well as their extensions in present economies of the Earth must be considered barbaric and irrational, completely ignorant of the context of life on this planet. The medieval doctors thought in their ignorance that they could bleed their patients to health. The industrial nation-states thought in their ignorance that they could bleed the planet and arrive at wealth. Both must be regarded, in light of present scientific understanding of the Earth process, as superstitious groping toward the evolutionary truth of our bodies and our planet.

The continued evolutionary unfolding into the unknown, unimaginable, and unspoken splendor begins when we leave the dead-end of human arrogance and disregard for the integral dynamics enfolding this planet into a single process. We must activate the deeper dimensions of the human person so that our legitimate demands for justice will enter their macrophase role as planetary selection principles. Only then will we restore health, vitality, and vigor to the whole Earth community, for only in that way will we be entering into our destined role as the planetary process brought into a conscious phase of unfolding.

Endnotes

1. Thomas Berry, "The New Story," *Teilhard Studies*, Number 1 (London: Teilhard Centre for the Future of Man, Winter, 1978).

2. Gregory Bateson, *Mind and Nature* (New York: Bantam, 1979).

3. Erich Jantsch, *Self-Organizing Universe* (New York: Pergamon, 1981).

About the Authors

STEVEN KOZAN BECK graduated from Lake Forest High School in Lake Forest, Illinois and attended Iowa State University in Ames, Iowa where he majored in architecture. In 1968 he transferred to the University of Washington in Seattle to search for mountains and a Zen teacher. Steve met Roshi Jiyu-Kennett during his third year of college, while attending a San Francisco march and rally calling for an end to the Vietnam War. He was ordained as a novice in July, 1970 in Oakland, and then returned to Seattle to finish his last year at the University. He received his bachelor of arts in environmental design from the University of Washington, and then went to Shasta Abbey in Mt. Shasta, California to continue seminary training under Roshi Kennett. He was certified as a Zen Buddhist priest and later as a teacher of Buddhism. In 1979 Steve became the resident priest and prior of the Berkeley Buddhist priory in Oakland, California, a Zen center affiliated with Shasta Abbey. After three years there, Steve left for Sonora, in the foothills of the Sierra Nevada Mountains of California, where he now lives and works with the Sonora Buddhist Meditation Group. Steve has been involved with the work of Common Ground for several years; he has given lectures at Common Ground and directed one of the Common Ground weekend retreats.

BEATRICE BRIGGS is co-director of The Yoga Circle in Chicago, where she teaches several classes a week. She holds master's degrees in religion from Mundelein College and the University of Chicago, where she is currently working on her doctorate in the history of religions. She began studying yoga in 1973 at the local YMCA. Since then, she has been to India to study with B.K.S. Iyengar. She studies regularly in the United States with Ramanand Patel and other teachers in the Iyengar tradition. Before becoming a teacher and writer, Bea had a career as a marketing and public relations executive. The mother of two daughters, she lives in Chicago except when she escapes to her mountain retreat in Montana. Bea worked with both Ron Miller and Jim Kenney in Matthew Fox's Institute of Creation-Centered Spirituality when it was housed at Mundelein College in Chicago. She became aware of Common Ground and its work at the same time, and began networking between that organization and The Yoga Circle.

BARBARA CLOW is author of *Stained Glass: A Basic Manual* (Atlantic Little Brown, 1976), *Eye of the Centaur: A Visionary Guide into Past Lives* (Llewellyn, 1986), and *Chiron: Rainbow Bridge Between the Inner and Outer Planets* (Llewellyn, 1987). She holds a master's degree from Mundelein College, and studied religion and history of religion extensively at Seattle University from 1964-66. She began research into astrological techniques for counseling in 1967, began practicing as a counselor in 1974, and studied at the Jung Institute in Evanston in 1981. Her astrological work began to focus on healing techniques in 1982 as a result of her work with past-life regression under hypnosis, combined with her graduate studies with Matthew Fox during 1982-83. Her book on the newly discovered planet, Chiron, is an astrological study on techniques to train astrologers to be healers, initiators, and fine-tuners of consciousness potential. She assumed the position of editorial director at Bear & Company in 1983, is currently working on a series of articles, and is doing the research for her next book, *Heart of the Christos: A Visionary Guide Through the Age of Pisces*. She and her husband Gerry are raising four children — Tom, Matthew, Christopher, and Elizabeth. They first encountered Ron Miller at a presentation from Common Ground in their parish church in Evanston, Illinois in 1981.

SISTER MADELEINE SOPHIE COONEY is a religious of the Sacred Heart who lives in San Francisco, where she is engaged in research, writing, lecturing, and editing *RSCJ: A Journal of Reflection*. She holds a doctorate in English literature from Leland Stanford University. Her 42 years of college teaching (1940-1982) were spent in six colleges of her congregation, including Seishin Gakuin Daigaku in Tokyo. From 1970 to 1982 she was chairperson of humanities at Barat College in Lake Forest, Illinois. During that period she was also closely associated with Common Ground, serving on the board and teaching numerous workshops, especially in the area of relationship between literature and spirituality. She led a Common Ground study tour of Israel with Yechiel Eckstein, a tour to Greece with Ron Miller and Dan Cole, chairperson of the Religion Department at Lake Forest College, and one to Hawaii with Jim Kenney.

YECHIEL ECKSTEIN received his bachelor's in psychology from Yeshiva University in New York, where he was ordained a rabbi. He earned a master's degree from Yeshiva in Jewish philosophy, and continued his education at Columbia University and Union Theological Seminary, where he received a second master's in philosophy of religion. Yechiel is the founder and president of the Holyland Fellowship of Christians and Jews, a national organization based in Chicago. The Fellowship seeks to foster greater cooperation and understanding between Christians and Jews, and a broad base of moral and humanitarian support for Israel. He is the former national co-director of interreligious affairs for the Anti-Defamation League of B'nai Brith, and the author of *What Christians Should Know About Jews and Judaism* (Word Books, 1984). He has served as board member and resource person for Common Ground, and led a Common Ground tour to Israel with Sister Madeleine Sophie Cooney. He lives in Skokie with his wife Bonnie and their three daughters, Tamar, Talya, and Jael.

MIKE FOSTER, a native of Middlebury, Vermont, has the distinction of being the youngest contributor to this volume. In addition to being a business major, he completed an Independent Scholar program under the direction of Ron Miller on the subject of the dynamic interplay of psychology and religion in the writings of Alan Watts. He graduated from Lake Forest College in 1986, receiving the first-place award in the Independent Scholar program. A young man of diverse talents, Mike also designed sets for college theatre productions, coordinated weekly meditations for the Interfaith Center, played keyboards for a school band, and served as one of four student members of the College Council. After graduation, he received a summer fellowship for intensive Chinese language study at Beloit College in Beloit, Wisconsin, through the Program for Inter-Institutional Collaboration in Area Studies (PICAS) at the University of Michigan in Ann Arbor. Mike then spent a year in Evanston, Illinois, where he studied Chinese and continued research in Eastern thought. After another summer of intensive Chinese — this time in his native Middlebury, Vermont — he moved to Madison to begin a graduate program in Asian studies at the University of Wisconsin.

MARC GELLMAN, a native of Milwaukee and graduate of the University of Wisconsin at Madison, was ordained a rabbi at Hebrew Union College in Cincinatti. He served as Hillel rabbi at Northwestern University while pursuing a doctorate in philosophy. Marc met Ron Miller and Jim Kenney when all three were graduate students. They developed the idea for an interfaith organization, and Common Ground was legally incorporated on May 7, 1975. Marc was a key resource person, as well as board member, in the early years of Common Ground. He then went east to serve as a pulpit rabbi in New Jersey, and is currently with Temple Beth Torah in Dix Hills, New York, where Marc lives with his wife Betty and their children, Mara and Max. He is a contributing editor of *Moment Magazine* and has served on the faculty of Hebrew Union College's Jewish Institute of Religion. He has two forthcoming books which will be published by Harper and Row: *A Tent of Dolphins*, a book of midrashim for children and adults, and *The Jewish Thing to Do*, a book of modern Jewish ethics.

MICHAEL HUGO is originally from a rural community near Pittsburgh, Pennsylvania. His undergraduate schooling was at Duquesne University in Pittsburgh, where he studied sociology and theology. Michael's aspiration for the Catholic priesthood in a contemplative religious community took root in his undergraduate years, and was deepened after a visit to the Thomas Merton Center in Quebec. He then heard about Shantivanam, a community described in his article. After his residence there, the lure of lay priesthood assumed ascendency over the appeal of traditional religious life. Loyola University of Chicago's Institute of Pastoral Studies became the training ground for this newly found vocation, and in 1978 he received his master's degree in pastoral studies. Michael served as youth minister at St. Mary's Church in Lake Forest from 1978-1982. During this time he became acquainted with Ron Miller and the work of Common Ground. Michael then went on to pursue a degree in social work at the University of Chicago, and currently is a psychiatric social worker for Lutheran Social Services in Chicago. He married Adrienne Maisel in 1982 and they now have two children: Joshua Paul and Maria Colleen. They share a home in which both Michael's Catholic Christian tradition and Adrienne's Jewish heritage are celebrated.

STEPHEN INFANTINO, a native of Chicago, entered St. Mary of the Lake Seminary after high school. He went on to earn his licentiate in theology at the Gregorian University in Rome, where he was ordained a Roman Catholic priest during the Second Vatican Council. He received his doctorate in classical languages, literature, and philosophy from the University of Chicago. In 1974 he entered the Episcopal Church, and in 1976 he was licensed as an Episcopal priest. He currently serves as a part-time assistant at St. Lawrence Episcopal Church in Libertyville, Illinois, where he resides with his wife, Cindy Percak Infantino. Steve has a full-time professional career as professor of philosophy at the College of Lake County in Grayslake, Illinois. He and Cindy are engaged in research on American spiritual communities. They recently pilgrimaged around the country and produced a series of video documentaries on communities in the United States that are connected with world religions. Steve and Cindy have been connected with Common Ground for several years, and have participated in Common Ground study tours led by Jim Kenney to Hawaii and Japan.

CHARLOTTE KAMIN originally trained as a teacher and psychologist. She worked in those fields at the secondary school level in Illinois, California, and Maryland, before settling in the Highland Park, Illinois area twenty-seven years ago. There she raised a family of five children, who are now grown and living far afield. She returned to Northwestern University in 1975 for graduate work in the history and literature of religions, becoming acquainted with Ron Miller and Jim Kenney as she earned a master's, and went on to doctoral studies, specializing in Judaism and Christianity. She taught in the religion department at Barat College in Lake Forest for three years and currently works with Common Ground as a lecturer and resource person. Charlotte has visited Israel on numerous occasions since 1958 for periods of two weeks to six months, and has traveled widely in Europe, South America, and the United States. Her special interests and lecture topics include: Christian-Jewish history, Bible, women in religion, Zionism, moral conflict and decision making, and Judaism and Islam. Charlotte has a particular interest in interreligious dialogue and study, and the transformation of religious ideals into human relationships and everyday living — looking for "connections" and the "sparks of holiness" in creation.

JIM KENNEY hails from the mountains of Colorado. While attending Regis Jesuit High School in Denver, Jim had Ron Miller as a Greek teacher and speech coach. Moving on to Dartmouth College in 1965, Jim completed his undergraduate studies as a psychology major. His Dartmouth career gave him the further opportunity of spending his junior year abroad in the Soviet Union, where he both gained proficiency in the Russian language and met his first wife. Jim spent several years in Silver Plume, Colorado, while he was teaching Russian language and Western culture at Denver's Country Day School and developing his talents as silversmith and banjo player. During this period, Jim became enamored with the religions and philosophies of the Far East. In 1974 he enrolled at Northwestern University in a doctoral program in comparative religions. His principal focus was in the area of Japanese Buddhism, which he studied under the tutelage of Dr. Isshi Yamada. His doctoral dissertation, entitled "The Eye of the Triangle," was a comparative study of Buddhist philosophy, Christianity, and modern physics. This work received second place in the 1980 decennial Bross competition, an award for outstanding works comparing Christianity and other disciplines, presented by Lake Forest College. Jim taught for several years at Barat College, where he was chairperson of the Department of Religions. He collaborated with Ron Miller in the founding of Common Ground, and currently serves with him as co-director. He teaches several workshops at Common Ground, and has also served on the faculty of the religion department at Lake Forest College. In 1984 he married Cetta Armato; they now live in Lake Forest with Olya, Katya, Brian, and Mary Jo.

DAVID LOTHROP has long been interested in the relationship between the spiritual and psychological aspects of human existence. He came to Lake Forest College from Massachusetts and focused his undergraduate program on an interdisciplinary study of philosophy, psychology, and world religions. He was accepted in the college's Independent Scholar program, where he worked under the direction of Ron Miller and produced a senior thesis entitled "Wholeness and Holiness: Psychological and Spiritual Approaches to Personal Growth." Dave also served as student coordinator of Lake Forest College's Interfaith Center and became involved with programs offered at Common Ground. After his graduation from Lake Forest College in 1983, Dave was accepted in a master's program in psychology and phenomenology at Duquesne University in Pittsburgh, Pennsylvania. He completed the master's program and was accepted for doctoral studies in psychology, working as an intern in the student counseling center, and gaining experience in psychotherapy. Before commencing his dissertation, Dave opted to move to Maine and spend some time attending to personal psychological and spiritual growth. He currently resides in his Maine retreat.

JANE LUKEHART describes herself as "a resistant, fearful lover of the Divine Person, who continues to woo her ardently." She reports that writing this article was one round in an ongoing affair of embracing God more fully. Jane is a member of the Free Daist Communion, associated with the living adept, Heart Master Da Love-Ananda (formerly, Da Free John). She is also a wife, mother, astrologer, lecturer, and workshop facilitator. Jane is a Phi Beta Kappa graduate of Iowa State University, but calls herself a "much happier graduate" of Matthew Fox's Institute of Creation-Centered Spirituality (subsequently renamed The Institute in Culture and Creation Spirituality) when it was housed at Mundelein College in Chicago. It was there that Jane met Ron Miller and Jim Kenney, and became involved with the work of Common Ground. Jane has since conducted workshops and given numerous presentations at Common Ground, where her expertise and her personable and open manner of communication are greatly cherished.

THOMAS MICHEL is a native of St. Louis, Missouri. He received a master's in theology from Kenrick Theological Seminary, and subsequently joined the Society of Jesus. He did his doctoral work in Arabic/Islamic Studies at the University of Chicago. It was at this time that he met Ron Miller and Jim Kenney, and became acquainted with the work of Common Ground. The article published here was originally delivered as a Common Ground special-forum presentation. Tom studied at the Middle East Centre for Arabic Studies in Lebanon in 1971-72, and at the American University in Cairo in 1973-74. He returned to Cairo in 1976 with an ARCE grant and Fulbright Fellowship for research at the Arab League Library. He has taught at the Institut Filsalat Teologi at Yogyakarta, Indonesia, since 1978. After 1981, while retaining his academic position in Indonesia, he also served as attache for Asia at the Vatican Secretariat for non-Christians. Since 1983, he has been counselor for Islamic Affairs for the Society of Jesus in Rome. In addition to his regular circuit between Yogyakarta and Rome, he has delivered papers at aca-

demic conferences in Indonesia, the Philippines, Malaysia, Taiwan, India,
Lebanon, Pakistan, Tunisia, Jordan, Thailand, Austria, and the U.S.A.

RON MILLER is a native of St. Louis, Missouri, where he was edu-
cated by the Jesuits and entered the novitiate of the Society of Jesus
after high school. He completed graduate degrees in philosophy and
theology, studying at St. Louis University and the University of Frei-
burg im Breisgau, West Germany. He received his doctorate in comparative religions at Northwestern University, focusing on Jewish-Christian
dialogue. Ron's career took a significant turn in the mid-seventies when
he left the Jesuits, founded Common Ground, and began teaching on
the religion faculty at Lake Forest College, as well as coordinating the
campus Interfaith Center. He is now dean of students at Lake Forest
College. Common Ground and Lake Forest College continue to occupy
his professional life, though he also serves as adjunct faculty at Loyola
University's Institute of Pastoral Studies, at Holy Names College in
Oakland, and at Matthew Fox's Institute in Culture and Creation Spirituality. Ron wrote an article on Franz Rosenzweig for *Western Spirituality*, a book edited by Matthew Fox. He has also published translations
of sermons by Meister Eckhart and letters by Hildegard of Bingen. Ron
lives in Lake Forest with his wife Sherry, and their children, Meredith,
Jim, and Carrie.

GERALD RINGER received his doctorate in the humanities at Florida
State University. His dissertation, which bore the title, "The Bomb as
a Living Symbol: An Interpretation," set the course for a career in research, meditation, teaching, and writing. A former Marine Corps jet
pilot, he resigned his commission when he realized he could never
obey the order to drop a bomb on a city. He served as associate editor
for the international quarterly, *Our Generation Against Nuclear War*. He
has worked as college professor, airline pilot, and social worker. Jerry
became acquainted with Ron Miller, Jim Kenney, and the work of Common Ground, while living and working in Chicago's North Shore area.
Currently he resides with his wife Carla in the Perris Valley of California, an area he describes as "an embracing desert-place suited for expressing the Satori through which our culture is now passing."

MARK SMITH led a workshop for Common Ground in 1980. He and his wife Elizabeth have been extensively involved in biblical studies and languages, and are actively concerned with Jewish-Christian dialogue. Mark's doctorate from Yale University is in Hebrew scriptures and northwest Semitic languages and literature. Elizabeth is a doctoral candidate in Syro-Palestinian archeology at the University of Chicago. Mark was assistant professor in Old Testament at the Saint Paul Seminary of St. Paul, Minnesota from fall of 1984 to spring of 1986. He is currently assistant professor of northwest Semitic languages and literature at Yale University. Among his recent publications are "The 'Son of Man' in Ugaritic," in the *Catholic Biblical Quarterly*, and "The Magic of Kothar wa-Hasis, the Ugaritic Craftsman God" in *Revue Biblique*. In their spare time, Mark and Elizabeth manage to function as the proud parents of their young son, Benjamin.

BRIAN SWIMME is a popular physicist and associate director of The Institute in Culture and Creation Spirituality, Holy Names College, Oakland, California. His first book, *Manifesto for a Global Civilization*, was coauthored with Matthew Fox in 1980. He wrote *The New Natural Selection* during a year of study with Thomas Berry, director of The Riverdale Center for Integral Earth Studies. His 1985 book, *The Universe is a Green Dragon*, has been widely used in classes and workshops, with Common Ground being no exception. Brian was already known to Common Ground members through a weekend program he had conducted with Langdon Gilkey, Ron Miller, and Jim Kenney. Brian writes of himself: "My life as a scientist was probably determined by my birthplace, Seattle. The Pacific Northwest is nearly always overcast. When the clouds do break, we run from the strange sun, not coming out until evening, when we are completely flabbergasted by the beauty of the night sky. If as a child you see the stars once a year, you never really get over their magnificence. I set off to graduate school in pursuit of this cosmic beauty; I ended up with a Ph.D. instead — a real letdown, of course, but one that convinced me the universe has a sense of humor."

SUGGESTIONS FOR FURTHER READING

Aho, James A. *Religious Mythology and the Art of War: Comparative Religious Symbolisms of Military Violence*. Westport, CT: Greenwood Press, 1981.

(Swami) Ajaya. *Psychotherapy East and West*. Honesdale, PA: Himalayan Publishers, 1983.

Argüelles, José. *Transformative Vision*. Berkeley: Shambala, 1975.

Attenborough, David. *The Living Planet*. Boston: Little Brown and Co., 1984.

Barnet, Lincoln. *The Universe and Dr. Einstein*. New York: Bantam, 1948.

Bateson, Gregory. *Mind and Nature*. New York: Bantam, 1979.

Berry, Thomas. "The New Story." *Teilhard Studies* (Winter 1978).

Bialik, Hayim Nahman. *Halacha and Aggada*. Translated by Siegal.

Bohr, Niels. *Atomic Physics and Human Knowledge*. New York: John Wiley and Sons, 1958.

Bonino, José Miguez. *Doing Theology in a Revolutionary Situation*. Philadelphia: Fortress Press, 1975.

Boss, Medard. *Psychoanalysis and Daseinanalysis*. Translated by Ludwig B. Lefebre. New York: Basic Books, Inc., 1963.

Capra, Fritjof. *The Tao of Physics*. Berkeley: Shambhala Press, 1976.

Cloud, Preston. *Cosmos, Earth, and Man*. New Haven: Yale University Press, 1986.

Cobb, John B., Jr. *Beyond Dialogue — Towards a Mutual Transformation of Christianity and Buddhism*. Philadelphia: Fortress Press, 1982.

Cook, Francis K.. *Hua Yen Buddhism*. University Park: Pennsylvania State University Press, 1981.

Dayl, Har. *The Bodhisattva Doctrine in Buddhist Sanskrit Literature*. Delhi, India: Indological Publishers, 1932.

de Grazia, Alfred. *God's Fire, Moses, and the Management of the Exodus*. Princeton: Metron Publications, 1983.

Eckstein, Yechiel. *What Christians Should Know About Jews and Judaism*. Waco, TX: Word Books, Inc., 1984.

Eliade, Mircea. *The Sacred and the Profane*. New York: Harcourt, Brace, and Jovanovich, 1959.

Flusser, David. *Jesus*. New York: Herder and Herder, 1969.

Fox, Matthew. *Original Blessing, A Primer in Creation Spirituality*. Santa Fe, NM: Bear & Company, 1983.

Fox, Matthew. *WHEE, We, wee All the Way Home*. Santa Fe, NM: Bear & Company, 1982.

Garaudy, Roger and Quentin Lauer, S.J. *A Christian Communist Dialogue*. Garden City, NY: Doubleday and Company, Inc., 1968.

Goldin, H.E. *Ethics of the Fathers*. New York: Hebrew Publishing Company, 1962.

Graves, Robert. *The White Goddess: A Historical Grammar of Poetic Myth*. New York: Creative Age Press, 1948.

Head, Joseph, and S.L. Cranston. *Reincarnation: The Phoenix Fire Mystery*. New York: Crown Books, 1977.

Heisenberg, Werner. *Physics and Philosophy*. New York: Harper and Row, 1958.

Howe, Quincy. *Reincarnation for the Christian*. Philadelphia: Westminster Press, 1974.

Hume, Robert. *The Thirteen Principal Upanishads*. Delhi: Oxford University Press, 1983.

Jantsch, Erich. *Self-Organizing Universe*. New York: Pergamon, 1981.

Jones, Franklin (Da Free John). *The Knee of Listening*. Clearlake, CA: The Dawn Horse Press, 1973.

Jung, Carl G. *Answer to Job*. Princeton, NJ: Princeton University Press, 1969 (1958).

Jung, Carl G. *The Collected Works of C.G. Jung*. Edited by Herbert Read, Michael Fordham, and Gerhard Adker. Translated by R.F.C. Hall. New York: Pantheon Books, 1959.

Kapleau, Phillip. *The Three Pillars of Zen*. Boston: Beacon Press, 1965.

Keller, Werner. *The Bible as History*. New York: William Morrow and Company, 1981.

Kung, Hans. *On Being Christian*. Translated by Edward Quinn. New York: Wallaby Pocketbooks, 1978.

Lao Tzu. *Tao Te Ching*. Translated by Fu-Feng and Jane Gia. New York: Vintage, 1972.

Lawrence, Nathaniel, gen. ed. *Readings in Existential Phenomenology*. Englewood Cliffs, NJ: Prentice-Hall, Inc., 1967.

Levine, Stephen. *A Gradual Awakening*. Garden City, NY: Anchor Press/Doubleday, 1979.

MacGregor, Geddes. *Reincarnation for the Christian*. Wheaton, IL: Quest, 1978.

MacLaine, Shirley. *Dancing in the Light*. New York: Bantam Books, 1985.

Mascaro, Juan, trans. *Dhammapada: The Path of Perfection*. Middlesex, England: Penguin Books, Ltd., 1973.

May, Gerald, M.D. *Will and Spirit: A Contemplative Psychology*. San Francisco: Harper and Row, 1982.

May, Rollo, gen. ed. *Existence: A New Dimension in Psychiatry and Psychology* New York: Basic Books, Inc., 1958.

Merton, Thomas. *Contemplation in a World of Action*. New York: Double Day, 1971.

Merton, Thomas. *The Seven Storey Mountain*. New York: Harcourt, Brace, and Company, 1948.

Merton, Thomas. *The Way of Chuang Tzu*. New York: New Directions Publishing Corporation, 1965.

Montefiore, Claude. *The Synoptic*. Riverside, NJ: Macmillan and Company, Ltd., 1910.

Moore, George Foote. *Judaism in the First Centuries of the Christian Era*. New York: Schocken Books, 1971.

Mott, Michael. *The Seven Mountains of Thomas Merton*. Boston: Houghton Mifflin Company, 1984.

Nishida, Kitaro. *Intelligibility and the Philosophy of Nothingness*. Westport, CT: Greenwood Press, 1973.

Pawlikowski, John T. *Christ in the Light of the Christian-Jewish Dialogue* New York: Paulist Press, 1982.

Ranya, Swami Hariharananda. *Yoga Philosophy of Patanjali*. Albany, NY: State University of New York Press, 1983.

Rogers, Carl R. *On Becoming a Person*. Boston: Houghton Mifflin Company, 1961.

Sagan, Carl. *Cosmos*. New York: Ballantine Books, 1980.

Scholem, Gershom. *Major Trends in Jewish Mysticism*. New York: Schocken Books, 1961.

Simon, Merril. *Jerry Falwell and the Jews*. Middle Village, NY: Jonathan David Publishing, Inc., 1984.

Spangler, David. *Emergence, The Rebirth of the Sacred*. New York: Delta Merloyd Lawrence Book, Dell Publishing, 1984.

Stuart, David. *Alan Watts*. New York: Stein and Day, 1976.

Suzuki, D.T. *The Essence of Buddhism*. Kyoto: Nokozan, 1968.

Suzuki, Shunruyu. *Zen Mind, Beginner's Mind*. New York: Weatherhill, Inc., 1976.

Taimni, I.K., trans. *The Science of Yoga*. Wheaton, IL: Theosophical Publishing House, 1961.

Urbach, Ephraim. *The Sages: Their Concepts and Beliefs*. Translated by Israel Abrahams. Jerusalem: Magnes Press, 1979.

Vermes, Geza. *Jesus the Jew*. Philadelphia: Fortress Press, 1981.

Watts, Alan Wilson. *The Book on the Taboo Against Knowing Who You Are*. New York: Vintage Books, 1966.

Watts, Alan Wilson. *Psychotherapy East and West*. New York: Vintage Books, 1962.

Watts, Alan Wilson. *The Wisdom of Insecurity*. New York: Pantheon Books, 1951.

Weaver, Warren. "The Religion of a Scientist." *Religions of America*. Edited by Leo Roster. New York: Simon and Schuster, 1957.

Whitehead, Alfred North. *Process and Reality: An Essay in Cosmology*. Scranton, PA: Harper Torchbook, The Academy Library, Harper and Brothers, 1929.

Worthington, Vivian. *A History of Yoga*. London: Routledge and Kegan Pub., 1982.